WITHDRAWN
FROM
UNIVERSITY OF PLYMOUTH
LIBRARY SER

Innocence, Knowledge and the Construction of Childhood

Innocence, Knowledge and the Construction of Childhood provides a critical examination of the way we regulate children's access to certain knowledge and explores how this regulation contributes to the construction of childhood, to children's vulnerability and to the constitution of the 'good' future citizen in developed countries.

Through this controversial analysis, Kerry H. Robinson critically engages with the relationships between childhood, sexuality, innocence, moral panic, censorship and notions of citizenship. This book highlights how the strict regulation of children's knowledge, often in the name of protection or in the child's best interest, can ironically, increase children's prejudice around difference, increase their vulnerability to exploitation and abuse, and undermine their abilities to become competent adolescents and adults. Within her work Robinson draws upon empirical research to:

- provide an overview of the regulation and governance of children's access to 'difficult knowledge', particularly knowledge of sexuality;
- explore and develop Foucault's work on the relationship between childhood and sexuality;
- identify the impact of these discourses on adults' understanding of childhood, and the tension that exists between their own perceptions of sexual knowledge, and the perceptions of children;
- reconceptualize children's education around sexuality.

Innocence, Knowledge and the Construction of Childhood is essential reading for both undergraduate and postgraduate students undertaking courses in education, particularly with a focus on early childhood or primary teaching, as well as in other disciplines such as sociology, gender and sexuality studies, and cultural studies.

Kerry H. Robinson is an Associate Professor in the School of Social Sciences and Psychology, and a member of the Diversities, Ethics and Education Research Group at the University of Western Sydney, Australia.

90 0929416 7

Innocence, Knowledge and the Construction of Childhood

The contradictory nature of sexuality and censorship in children's contemporary lives

Kerry H. Robinson

University of Plymouth
Charles Seale Hayne Library
Subject to status this item may be renewed
via your Primo account

http:/primo.plymouth.ac.uk
Tel: (01752) 588588

Routledge
Taylor & Francis Group

LONDON AND NEW YORK

PLYMOUTH UNIVERSITY
9 u09294167

First published 2013
by Routledge
2 Park Square, Milton Park, Abingdon, Oxon OX14 4RN

Simultaneously published in the USA and Canada
by Routledge
711 Third Avenue, New York, NY 10017

Routledge is an imprint of the Taylor & Francis Group, an informa business

© 2013 Kerry H. Robinson

The right of Kerry H. Robinson to be identified as author of this work
has been asserted by her in accordance with sections 77 and 78 of the
Copyright, Designs and Patents Act 1988.

All rights reserved. No part of this book may be reprinted or
reproduced or utilised in any form or by any electronic, mechanical, or
other means, now known or hereafter invented, including photocopying
and recording, or in any information storage or retrieval system, without
permission in writing from the publishers.

Trademark notice: Product or corporate names may be trademarks or
registered trademarks, and are used only for identification and
explanation without intent to infringe.

British Library Cataloguing in Publication Data
A catalogue record for this book is available from the British Library

Library of Congress Cataloging in Publication Data
Robinson, Kerry H.
  Innocence, knowledge, and the construction of childhood : the
  contradictory nature of sexuality and censorship in children's
  contemporary lives/Kerry Robinson. — 1st ed.
     p. cm.
  Includes bibliographical references and index.
  1. Sex instruction—Australia. 2. Early childhood education—Social
  aspects—Australia. 3. Multicultural education—Australia. I. Title.
  HQ56.R63 2013
  613.9071—dc23   2012021449

ISBN: 978-0-415-60967-8 (hbk)
ISBN: 978-0-415-60763-6 (pbk)
ISBN: 978-0-203-11753-8 (ebk)

Typeset in Galliard
by Book Now Ltd, London

MIX
Paper from
responsible sources
FSC
www.fsc.org   FSC® C004839

Printed and bound in Great Britain by
TJ International Ltd, Padstow, Cornwall

For CD and Coco

Contents

Figures

Foreword

This very important book opens up the paradoxical space in between our desire to maintain the innocence of childhood and the vital importance of giving children knowledge about sexuality.

It is in the nature of any paradox that we don't know how to make our way into it and we don't know how to resolve it – they appear to be intractable. This particular paradox may generate in us a sense of moral panic, or, perhaps less dramatically, avoidance and denial. We are so deeply immersed in contradictory discourses about children and sexuality and the associated anxieties that some readers may not even have been able to get past the front cover. Even reaching out to pick up this book may have seemed dangerous, revealing the potential reader, in that act, as willing to countenance the deeply forbidden – and as willing to think about that which has become unthinkable. Other readers, who have got this far, may nevertheless still be worrying about what dangerous knowledge this book is inviting them into.

Dear reader, this book will provoke you, it will sometimes even shock you, but it will also certainly open up new ways of thinking. Those of you who read this book will discover that what is dangerous, more than anything else, is the withholding of knowledge from children – the deliberate construction not of innocence but of ignorance.

In a very carefully argued and considered manner, Kerry H. Robinson lets you see how it came about that protection of children became the dominant motif in our dealings with children, to children's detriment. She will show you how the fears on which protectionism is based have been constructed out of phantasms like 'stranger danger', despite the fact that almost 90 per cent of sexual assaults on children come from people they know, most often members of their own family circle. Constructing the danger as coming from the unknown Other, the stranger, saves those who are closest to the children from thinking about what dangers they themselves, or their loved ones, might be exposing children to. It is a comfortable arrangement at a terrible cost: a kind of blindness and ignorance among adults and a profound lack of agency on the part of the children.

What Robinson makes absolutely clear throughout this book is that it is important to educate children, to give them both knowledge of sexuality and the critical literacy skills with which they can evaluate the normative and taken-for-granted knowledges through which their lives are being constructed, both by themselves and others.

The fear that knowledge about sex will lead to an increase in sexual promiscuity is not borne out by the research. Quite the reverse – it seems that knowledge opens up greater agency, and a capacity to choose not to be coerced into engaging in undesired sexual activity. Indeed, where school children are taught in an open and positive way about sex, there is more likely to be a delay in sexual activity. That which is taboo or secret has an added excitement attached to it just by virtue of its unspeakability. And where no options other than the normative appear to be available, it is difficult for anyone to resist taking up undesired activities. Learning how discourses work on us and through us, and learning counter-discourses through critical literacy is fundamental to personal agency.

But here we find ourselves caught in a quandary. Robinson's research shows that for many adults, speaking openly and frankly about sex is not an easy task. The paradoxical nature of the space marked by children and sexuality is such that responsible adults may find themselves afraid to be the one who speaks openly, even when they have a very strong belief that they should do so. This fear arises out of our own immersion in normative discourses, but also perhaps because 'knowledge about sex' is taken, in children, to be a tell-tale sign that the child is being sexually abused. Thus telling one's children about sex in an honest and open way may give them knowledge enabling them to make informed and safe choices, but it may also lead to charges of sexual abuse.

Children and sexuality is thus an impossibly complex and difficult space that we must urgently and responsibly open up, at every level of society, for some serious re-thinking. Current sex education curricula are not adequate to the challenge that Robinson's book so deftly sets out – and it seems adults are neither confident nor competent to enter this complex and fraught space without the advantage of an education programme that grants them critical literacy skills too.

How then are we to open up the serious re-thinking that is so evidently required?

First, we need to understand how is it that we have allowed ourselves to talk ourselves into a paradox where, in the name of protection, we fail to arm children with the knowledge they need to protect themselves. How have we bought so deeply into the model of the child as innocent – that is, asexual – when there is so much evidence in front of our eyes that maintaining this image is not about protecting the child at all, but rather about building a prudish society full of people with a false and misleading – even dangerous – sense of self-righteousness? Robinson helps us understand how we got ourselves into this mess, and lays out a knowledge base with which to begin to think against the grain of normative taken-for-granted clichés and platitudes.

One of the most interesting aspects of Robinson's book is that it enables us to listen to children reflecting on the contradictions that we find between those powerful normative discourses (through which they construct their own identities and projected futures) and their first hand experiences of people who do not fit these normative models. Robinson invites us to listen carefully to the children, not dismissing them as cute and innocent, but learning to respect and admire them as they search for insights into the way the social world works, even while they find themselves trapped in normative versions of identity, gender and human relationships.

What becomes clear is that, if taught to these children, an ethics of commitment to openness to the Other and valuing of difference would enable them make their way through these thorny contradictions. The dominant images and storylines that children encounter in the media and at school are saturated with clichéd, binary thought, where difference is not a positive value, and openness to the Other, in their difference, is not encouraged. They deserve better than this.

Constructing difference as a positive value – not something merely to be tolerated – opens up the space of ethics for children and adults alike. Robinson carefully maps out this space of ethics, offering us a way out of the quagmire of contradiction and fear that lies at the heart of our current constructions of childhood.

Ethics is not just for adults, it is also for children. As Robinson points out, the possibility of ethical practice involves informed reflection, and a willingness to confront dilemmas and make informed choices based on sound knowledge. What we have instead – and what we need to unseat – is the substitution of surveillance for ethical thought and practice that currently pervades neoliberal societies.

At the same time as government has stepped up strategies of surveillance over children (and the adults who share their lives) so much of the violence that is perpetrated against children – including sexual violence – has been normalized. That is, it is no longer visible as something we should be concerned about. Sexual harassment in schools is violent and shocking if we pay attention to it, instead of turning a blind eye to it as current systems of thought and practice enable us to do. The need for ethical sex education for children of all ages is made starkly evident in this book, particularly in the face of the current pervasive reliance on surveillance, and government through fear of risk. What we need is the education of responsible citizens capable of engaging in responsible decision-making that takes into account the effects of those decisions on the well-being of both self and Other.

The courage to open up the conversation about children and sexuality is vital. This book is an excellent place to begin – to find the courage, the knowledge, and the know-how to de-mythologize children's innocence, to see it rather as an undesirable, imposed ignorance. Robinson provides an important and timely knowledge base with which adults – both parents and teachers – can work toward giving children the skills of critical literacy and a positive appreciation of difference. Children are entitled to the critical literacy skills that would enable them to make informed decisions, and to resist normative pressures where these are unethical and where they undermine the valuing of difference. Ethical practice is not the mindless following of rules, or even obedience to authority, but the continual evaluation of each decision that is made, recognizing that each decision makes a difference.

We are each responsible for the differences we make in the world – none of our actions is without effect on others. We must constantly ask what those effects are. When we support the normative order and uphold the innocence and ignorance of children, we must ask what effects do we have on children's lives? And what effect might we have if we behaved differently?

Robinson will help you to answer these questions.

Bronwyn Davies
University of Melbourne

Acknowledgements

I would like to thank all those friends, colleagues, and acquaintances who have supported me through the writing of this book – I could not have done it without your collective encouragement. In particular, I would like to thank Elicia O'Reilly for her sharp editorial work and her critical eye in the last couple of months of bringing the book together – your calm and methodical processes were very much appreciated once I got over and understood all the colour-coding! I would also like to thank Peter Bansel for his critical reading of chapters and structuring advice which really helped me to move forward at those critical times. In addition, thank you Peter, David John, Kellie Burns and Kate Hansen for the many dinners, fine wine, laughter and overall caring that has also kept me moving forward. I would like to acknowledge my appreciation to Georgia Ovendon for her thorough research assistance and to Rowena Braddock for her research assistance in the earlier periods of developing this book. My appreciation also goes to my colleagues with whom I have conducted various research projects over the past decade that have influenced my thinking – Cristyn Davies, Criss Jones Díaz and Anthony Semann. Bronwyn Davies needs special mention and acknowledgment for her continued support of my work and for writing the foreword to the book. Bronwyn continues to be an inspiration in and out of the academy. A thank you to my University of Western Sydney colleagues, particularly in the Diversities, Ethics and Education Research Group – Moira Carmody, Peter Bansel, Nida Denson, Nutan Muckle, Georgia Ovendon – for their continued support and sharp wits. Additionally, I would like to thank UWS for supporting components of the research on children and sexuality informing this book through a UWS Research Grant. A special thank you is also given to Anthony Browell for permission to use his photograph *The Kiss*. I would also like to acknowledge the copyright permission from Corbis Images for use of the images *Children Bride Groom Wedding* and *Children Kissing in Paris*, and to Getty Images for the use of the image *Boy and Girl Dressed up as Bride and Groom, Outdoors on Steps*. My thanks must also be given to the many children, educators and parents who have offered their time and perspectives which have been foundational to my thinking – the inclusion of their voices grounds many of these ideas. Finally, but certainly not least, my great appreciation goes to Cristyn Davies, for her continued support and encouragement, critical editorial advice, exceptional thinking, care and patience daily.

Chapter 1

The contradictory nature of children's contemporary lives

Writing this book and overview of the research

My interest in writing this book has developed over many years and has arisen from my professional experiences in several different and complementary contexts. It is based largely on a body of research I have undertaken over the past 15 years or so that has focused on children and sexuality issues. This body of work has involved multiple projects conducted either individually or collaboratively with colleagues, and has examined the various discourses, practices and policies associated with childhood, childhood and sexuality, childhood innocence, the sexualization of childhood, children's access to sexual knowledge, and children's early education around diversity and difference more generally. Each of these research projects was conducted in Australia, in regional, rural and metropolitan contexts, and included numerous interviews, focus groups and surveys with early childhood educators, parents, youth and children from a broad range of cultural, linguistic and socio-economic class backgrounds. The research projects can be grouped around three main foci. The first was an examination of early childhood educators' perspectives, pedagogical practices, workplace policies and curricula which regulate children's access to knowledge associated with diversity and difference, including a focus on sexuality and the inclusion of same-sex families. This research was conducted with my colleague Criss Jones Díaz (Robinson and Jones Díaz 2000, 2006). The second area of research involved a New South Wales state-wide survey of early childhood educators' perspectives, pedagogical practices, workplace policies and curricula specifically focusing on children and sexuality issues that I conducted with a colleague, Anthony Semann. The third research focus explored the socio-cultural construction of childhood and its intersection with sexuality through identifying the historical, socio-cultural and political discourses that operate in relation to children and sexuality, and children's access to sexual knowledge and sexuality education, as well as exploring children's perspectives and knowledge of sexuality and relationships. This research was conducted with my colleague, Cristyn Davies (Robinson and Davies 2008b; Davies and Robinson 2010).

Currently, as I write this book, I am leading a research team (including Moira Carmody from the University of Western Sydney, Australia, and Sue Dyson from the Australian Research Centre of Sex, Health and Society at La Trobe University, Australia) on an Australian Research Council Discovery Grant project which explores building ethical relationships in young children's lives. This project is being conducted in two Australian states, New South Wales and Victoria, and involves interviewing primary school teachers, parents of primary school children (5–11-year-olds), and the parents' primary-aged children. The first year of this three-year project was completed at the end of 2011. Many of the issues around childhood, sexuality and sexual knowledge that I have explored with young children in early childhood education in the past are taken up with teachers, parents and children in primary schooling contexts in this larger study. Additional foci in this study include examining sex education curricula in primary schools in New South Wales and Victoria, and investigating parents', children's and teachers' perceptions of ethical and respectful behaviours; how each group practices ethical behaviours; and what strategies parents and teachers use to build children's understandings of ethical behaviours and encourage children's engagement in ethical practices with others. Although the project is not yet complete, the research to date has reconfirmed the findings of my earlier research upon which this book is primarily based.

This book also touches on issues that have been the central focus of my earlier research around sexual harassment in schooling (Robinson 2000, 2005d, 2012a). In this empirical research, I investigated students' and teachers' experiences and perspectives of sexual harassment occurring in schooling contexts. What was eye-opening in this research was just how normalized sexual harassment was in young people's everyday lives, and how integral such practices were to many male students' and teachers' identities, especially to their performance of hegemonic masculinity. For many female teachers (and some male teachers who did not fit dominant representations of masculinity), sexual harassment from male students and peers was also a common experience. What was particularly significant in these cases was how sexual harassment is used as a technology of power to discipline subjects into conforming to hegemonic discourses of gender and sexuality, as well as to institutional practices of power. This research, which was conducted in the late 1980s and during the 1990s, pre-empts many of the concerns that were recently raised in the UK report titled *The Sexualization of Young People (Review)* by Linda Papadopoulos (2011). The practices identified in this report are not new. Young children learn to engage in hegemonic practices very early in life, but much of this behaviour is so normalized in the construction of hetero-gendered relationships that it is rendered invisible through the discourse of childhood innocence, often being referred to euphemistically as 'child's play' or 'children being children'.

In addition to this body of research, the development of the ideas and arguments I outline has also been informed by my experience over many years in the area of child protection. As an academic I have taught child protection issues at university to teacher trainees, and I have also been invited to conduct workshops for early childhood educators working in the field. My expertise in this area was primarily informed by my experience as a community crisis worker, working with homeless young women in a refuge for more than five years. As a crisis worker, I undertook training in the area of sexual assault and child sexual abuse, run by the Adelaide Rape Crisis Centre in South Australia. Many of the young women who stayed in the refuge had been sexually abused as children, and the consequences of this abuse had played out in their lives in highly destructive ways. It was during this time that I became acutely aware of the *vulnerabilities* of young women to sexual abuse, especially in their family homes, and the contradictions inherent in 'stranger danger' campaigns. These campaigns take the focus off the fact that in a large proportion of sexual abuse cases, the perpetrator is someone the child knows – often a family member. Many of these young women continued to experience exploitation as gendered and sexual subjects throughout their early adult lives. What was equally concerning was their lack of knowledge about their bodies, of sexuality, and their lack of skills and confidence around negotiating intimate relationships in their lives. I also became critically aware of how these young women were often viewed by the community at large. They carried a stigma that stemmed from a perceived *loss of innocence*, which was often exploited again by others. These young women continued to experience the impact of prevailing discourses of childhood innocence. What I found particularly telling was that many of the young women declared that more knowledge of sexual matters at a younger age, and more options to talk openly about these issues as children and young people, would have made a considerable difference to their early lives.

Theoretical frameworks relevant to this book

My discussions around childhood, childhood and sexuality, and knowledge are framed within a post-developmentalist perspective, and are informed by feminist poststructuralism, queer and postcolonial theories. Through feminist poststructuralism, we are reminded that knowledge is constituted through discourse, is only ever partial, and is political – shifting and changing according to relations of power (Robinson and Jones Díaz 2006). Michel Foucault's notion of discourse is foundational to this perspective. Foucault (1974, 1978, 1980) argued that meaning is not a given, but is socially constructed across different institutional sites and practices. What becomes important to understanding knowledge are the multiple positions and viewpoints from which subjects speak, and the power relations these positions allow and presume. There are multiple discourses or 'truths' that construct the objects of which they speak, vying for a position of power in the production of meaning. Poststructuralism is concerned with language, signs, images, codes and signifying systems, which organize the psyche, society and everyday social life, and are linked to broader social, political and economic institutions that make up the social body (Robinson and Jones Díaz 2006; Foucault 1980; Sawicki 1991). Viewing childhood within this framework – as discursively constructed – allows for critical multiple readings of what it means to be a child, and opens up different and new understandings of the historically-shifting socio-cultural, political and economic functions that childhood performs in society.

The construction of subjectivity, or of the self, is constituted in the discourses made available to the subject and is always a relational process, involving the negotiation of power (Ball 1990; Burr 1995; Foucault 1974; Robinson and Jones Díaz 2006). Subjectivity is complex, shifting and contradictory, and in this process of negotiation, individuals assess – often unconsciously – the investments of being located in one discourse rather than the others that are available to them (Hollway 1984). Central to the subject within a feminist poststructuralist perspective, regardless of whether the subject is a child, adolescent or adult, is agency: that is, the ability to act with intent and awareness. The child, like the adult, is instrumental in the construction of their own subjectivity and that of others around them, rather than being a passive and powerless victim of socialization as is often assumed (Davies 1994). Stuart Hall (2004: 127) points out that 'we are subject to discourse, not simply subjects through discourse, with the ability to turn around, contemplate, and rework our subjectivity at will'. Children are capable of critical reflection around the choices that they take up; I have seen them work through this process based on the knowledge they hold and the way that they view the world. In debates around the 'disappearance of childhood' (Postman 1982), anxieties arise when the production of subjectivity brings attention to its own construction – in this case, the production of gender and sexual subjectivities. The fluid, unstable and changing nature of subjectivity is brought to the fore, highlighting its inherent openness to new possibilities and definitions (Butler 1990).

Postcolonial theory is also useful in appreciating the ways in which understandings of childhood have been colonized through Western hegemonic modernist discourses. It provides important insights into the socio-cultural construction of discourses of childhood and the adult/child dualism that underpins Western relationships between adults and children. Additionally, it provides a critical framework for demonstrating how the life experiences, voices and knowledge associated with non-heterosexual subjects – constituted as the *Other* in the heterosexual/homosexual binary – have been disqualified and subjugated through colonizing practices. The term Other relates to groups that have been marginalized, silenced, denigrated or violated; defined in opposition to, and seen as other than, the privileged and powerful groups that are identified as representing the idealized, mythical norm in society

(Robinson and Jones Díaz 2006). Hegemonic discourses of the child and childhood innocence have been mobilized to support the othering process experienced by non-heterosexual subjects. Power – and how it is used to define and control the lives and silence the voices of the Other – is central to postcolonial perspectives.

Queer theory, stemming from poststructuralist theoretical frameworks, is important in reinforcing understandings of childhood as fluid and unstable, and in reminding us of the socially-constructed nature of the relationship between childhood and sexuality – and equally, between adults and the child (Robinson 2005c; Bruhm and Hurley 2004). Queer theory views all aspects of subjectivity as performance and challenges normalizing practices, especially in terms of sexuality and heteronormative constructions of gender. Within this perspective, the dualistic relationships of male/female and heterosexual/homosexual are destabilized through acknowledging a plurality of sexualities and a multiplicity of genders. This perspective is important for understanding the fluidity of gender and the ways in which young children – as epitomized in the performances of gender represented in 'princess boys' – can take up non-conforming performances of gender which most often lead to parental, community and societal concerns and fears (Kilodavis 2010). The concept of queer encompasses those who feel marginalized by hegemonic discourses of heterosexuality (Morris 2000), and queer perspectives operate to question the privilege afforded to heterosexuality as the 'natural' and 'normal' sexuality by which all other sexualities are othered and subjugated. These theories inform my discussion of contemporary childhood.

The rest of this introductory chapter provides an overview of the critical issues relevant to the discussions throughout the book.

The politics and contradictions of children's sexual subjectivities

In Western societies, contemporary childhood has become the most intensely governed period of personal existence. It is a period of extreme surveillance in which the child has become the target of social, political, educational and legal regulations that constitute children as the powerless and dependent Other in relation to adults in society (Rose 1999). Parents have also been subjected to a similar regime of governance in relation to the child. This surveillance has been primarily constituted in the name of *protection* – largely of the *innocence* of childhood – but it has also been instrumental in constituting, regulating and maintaining adult/child and broader socio-cultural relations of power in society. The discourse of protection, often framed as being *in the best interests* of the child, is perpetuated not just through social practices, but also through government policies and legislation that impact on the way that children are viewed and treated in the family, in schools, and in society more broadly. This process of governance acts as a powerful social control, establishing commanding 'regimes of truth' that act to classify, discipline, normalize and produce what it means to be a child, and, in addition, what it means to be an adult, a good parent, and a good normative adult citizen-subject (Foucault 1977, 1978). Although it is important to have effective social and legal regulations in place to protect children from harm and exploitation, the ways in which this process of governing the child frequently loses sight of children's realities and best interests is explored. What is considered as being in the best interests of the child is often in conflict with those of adults and of the state, and with what is generally considered the natural order of things in society.

Nowhere has the governance of childhood and adults – and the use of 'the child' as a technology of power – been more obvious than in the area of sexuality. This governance, especially in relation to children's sexual subjectivity and the construction of children's knowledge of sexuality, is central to the focus of discussion in this book. Over time, children's sexual subjectivities have been constituted through a range of competing and contradictory discourses in Western societies. These discourses ('children are asexual and innocent'; 'children's sexuality is dangerous to society and needs to be regulated'; 'children's sexuality is normal and critical for the development of a creative and vibrant society'; 'sexuality is dangerous to the moral development of the child'; and 'children are vulnerable to abuses and exploitation by adult sexuality and need to be protected') have all impacted the ways in which children have been and continue to be viewed and treated as sexual subjects. An additional discourse around children's sexual subjectivity that is critical to processes of regulation is that children are *naturally* heterosexual. The 'queer' child, 'whose play confirms neither the comfortable stories of child (a)sexuality nor the supposedly blissful promises of adult heteronormativity' (Bruhm and Hurley 2004: ix), often manifests in social panic. The discussions in this book are primarily concerned with the politics of children's sexual subjectivities and the power relationships that operate around these competing discourses. Also of concern are the contradictions that prevail around childhood and sexuality – contradictions that are often rendered invisible through processes of normalization, and operate not just to regulate the child and the adult but also the dominant relations of power in society.

Since the 1980s, adults' fears and anxieties around potential threats to the child and to the nature of childhood itself have intensified. This is reflected in the media and in an increase in government and community organizations and events that focus on protecting the child. For example, in Australia, organizations such as The Child Protection Society and the National Association for Prevention of Child Abuse and Neglect (NAPCAN) actively campaign to increase awareness of children's vulnerabilities and need for protection. These fears and anxieties have been linked to a range of factors. First, there has been an increased awareness of the extensiveness of child sexual abuse in the home since the 1980s, largely as a result of feminist agitation in this area. However, community and media focus on child abuse has been primarily on 'stranger danger', or the paedophile, as the central threat to the safety and wellbeing of children. Second, adult fears and anxieties have intensified due to children's increased access to information and communication technologies, such as the Internet and mobile phones. This uneasiness is linked to concerns about children having unlimited and easy access to 'inappropriate' adult information; to parental concerns about children's increased vulnerabilities to paedophiles through the Internet; and to the perception that children are easily exploitable targets of unscrupulous advertisers. Anxieties and fears have also intensified as a result of what has commonly become termed the 'sexualization' and 'adultification' of representations of children (Postman 1982; Rush and La Nauze 2006; Levin 2009; Olfman 2009), especially girls, in popular culture, media and advertising. All of these issues are central to current social and political debates in countries such as Australia, the USA and the UK, and are perceived by many to be placing Western children 'at risk' and destroying what is popularly understood as childhood. Many parents also feel that they are being left behind in terms of technological advancements and new media, which have become so much part of the everyday lives of their tech-savvy children. Concerns about the 'disappearance of childhood' through its increasing commodification and the breakdown of traditional characteristics that have distinguished childhood from adulthood, such as children's access to adult 'secrets' or knowledge (e.g. sexuality) and to adult language (e.g. 'dirty' words), have resulted in the widespread perception that childhood is in crisis (Postman 1982; Winn 1984; Rush and La Nauze 2006; Levin and Kilbourne 2008). Catch-cries of 'Let children be children' ring loud in these debates, as do calls for increased regulation of media and popular culture, reflecting parents increasing concerns about how best to 'protect' their children in a changing world where they themselves often feel they are losing control.

This book offers a contribution to these international debates, critiquing among other issues the lack of children's and youths' voices, the dismissal of children's agency as sexual subjects, and the inadequate analysis of the broader discursive relationships between childhood and sexuality that significantly influence the ways in which discussions around this subject have played out. Fear and anxiety about children's and youths' sexual agency, particularly the sexual agency of girls, continues to prevail in these debates: dominant discourses around childhood and children's relationships with sexuality assert that sexuality lies – or should lie – inherently outside of the child's domain, resulting in practices such as censorship and policing of children's environments by adults in order to protect children. However, this logic and behaviour is in fact *counter-productive* to the protection of children. Rather than sheltering children, I argue that developing their critical literacy and fostering their competencies, knowledge and agency will do far more to support their health and wellbeing. Agency, understood here as the power of an individual to actively engage in the construction of their self (or *subjectivity*), is not inherent in the subject but is an element of signification and repetition. Individuals do not entirely devise their own subjectivity, as agency is always constrained by discourses such as cultural norms, taboos, conventions, laws, age and social class that 'invest our bodies with meaning' (Lloyd 2007: 58). Judith Butler (1990, 2004), taking up a Foucauldian framework, points out that the socio-cultural and political practices that produce gendered subjects (or other aspects of subjectivity) are also the sites where critical agency is possible: they become spaces of potential transformation through resistance.

Childhood innocence as a regulatory tool

The primary influence on the precarious relationship between childhood and sexuality has been the humanist concept of childhood innocence – the most important signifier of the socio-culturally-constructed differences between adulthood and childhood in Western societies. Childhood innocence has been historically manufactured as a means of regulating the lives of both children and adults. It continues to be a major force – albeit in the name of protection – in the subjugation of children's lives, and underpins the dualistic relationships of *the world of adults* and *the world of children*, and of *adults' knowledge* and *children's knowledge*, which function to maintain relations of power in Western society (Meyer 2007). The regulation of children's access to what has become *adults-only* knowledge stems largely from adult fears of children's perceived loss of innocence. The justification for this regulation has been linked to the perception that accessing this knowledge too early may impact on children's normal and healthy emotional and physical development, scarring them for life.

In the context of sexuality, the use of childhood innocence as a tool of censorship has done little to help protect children. Rather, I argue, it has contributed significantly to children's vulnerability in several ways. First, childhood innocence has been mobilized to justify the regulation of children's access to important knowledge, which has undermined their development as competent, well-informed, critical-thinking and ethical young citizens. Second, it has been employed to deny children's sexual subjectivities and desires – that is, their sense of self as sexual beings. The perception that sexuality is irrelevant to young children dismisses a core component of what makes up their subjectivities, or selves. Young children are engaged on a daily basis in constituting their subjectivities and negotiating the discourses of ethnicity, social class, gender, sexuality and so on that are available to them across the different social fields in which they operate (Davies 1989, 1993). They are given little critical guidance in negotiating the various and contradictory discourses they encounter, particularly in relation to sexuality. Third, childhood innocence has been deployed in the censorship and regulation of sexuality, with the result that sexuality has become a taboo subject, particularly for children. This has contributed to the fetishization of the child and of childhood innocence as a focus of desire for some adults (Kincaid 1998). Socio-cultural taboos around sexuality have resulted in its being viewed as *difficult knowledge* – that is, knowledge that many adults find challenging to address in their own lives, but especially with children. Childhood innocence can function as a convenient excuse for adults/parents not to address sexual knowledge with children. Children learn early that you do not talk about these issues with adults, or even parents.

Discourses of childhood and childhood innocence have constituted and regulated the normative adult citizen-subject in Western contexts. This normative adult citizen has historically been represented as white, middle-class, heterosexual, and upholding of Christian family morals and values (Berlant 1997; Bell and Binnie 2000; Richardson 1998). Politicians and 'moral entrepreneurs' (Becker 1963) have successfully utilized fears of the perceived disappearance of childhood to rally public sentiment and support for largely conservative social, political and economic policies and reforms. But the governance of children, their sexual subjectivities and knowledge of sexuality is not just about maintaining the discourse of childhood innocence or hegemonic understandings of childhood. Rather, this governance, I argue, is also about constructing children as heteronormative citizen-subjects. Discourses of childhood and childhood innocence underpin everyday technologies of power, and regulate children's early educational experiences in order to maintain the hegemony of heteronormative subjects. The production of the 'good', normative adult citizen-subject has important implications for what is considered appropriate education for children and their constitution as *future* heteronormative citizens. Thus, while the discourse of childhood innocence constructs children as asexual subjects and positions knowledge of sexuality as developmentally inappropriate, it is not utilized in the same manner to disrupt and intervene in the construction of children as heterosexual subjects. Contrary to the position of sexual knowledge as detrimental to children, the heteronormalization of children is not viewed as problematic and is a process that is largely rendered invisible through the ubiquity of heteronormative models in children's literature, play, early educational curricula and discourses of child development (Robinson 2005c).

The changing nature of children's lives

It seems that one of the greatest reasons for adults' fears and anxieties around childhood is that children *are* changing. Childhood has changed – indeed, is ever-changing – and children on the whole seem to adapt more successfully to these changes than adults. Like adulthood, childhood changes in response to shifts in socio-cultural, political and economic conditions over time. The reality for many children is that they are living in a world that is increasingly different from that of their parents and grandparents. It is a world in which parents, grandparents and other generations of adults cling to a nostalgia that idealizes and romanticizes a perception of childhood as happy, carefree, naïve and innocent. In reality, this perspective rarely reflects their own, or their child's, experiences – or those of most children in non-Western cultures. Western 'tween' culture (ages 8–12) for example, is a representation of socio-cultural and economic changes in children's lives, especially in the lives of girls. Tween girls' interactions with popular culture and consumerism, and their quests for agency, raise adults' concerns and anxieties. The construction of 'the teenager' decades prior roused similar adult concerns, anxieties and calls for censorship in popular culture – especially surrounding music, which was viewed as potentially dangerous and corrupting of girls' 'innocence' and 'virtue', as well as to the morals of society more generally (Austin and Willard 1997). The construction of the teenager was as much a representation of historical socio-cultural changes such as transformations in economies, consumerism, family structures and childhood as it was of popular culture (Jackson 2006).

More recently, changes in socio-cultural and political discourses around diverse sexualities, same-sex relationships and families in some Western countries, for instance, have meant that many children and young people are increasingly experiencing different views, choices and options about sexuality than those experienced by previous generations. These changes are also an indication that more are openly living in same-sex families. In addition to these socio-cultural and political changes, scientific progress in reproductive technologies is now challenging normative narratives of sexual reproduction. Many children, regardless of the gender and sexuality of their parents, are increasingly born through supported reproductive technologies. Against this background, current understandings of children's sexual subjectivities and approaches to children's sexuality education are out of step with the reality of many children's lives.

The importance of children's voices in current debates and in constructing knowledge of children's sexual subjectivities

Significantly, this book contributes to filling a critical gap that exists in relation to the inclusion of children's perspectives and voices around sexuality, relationships and their own sexual subjectivities. Understanding and perceiving children as active knowing agents in the construction of their own – and the policing of others' – sexual subjectivities is a controversial subject. The controversial nature of this topic contributes to the limited research in this area (Jackson 1982; Renold 2005; Blaise 2010; Robinson and Davies 2010; Davies and Robinson 2010; Robinson 2012a). The discourse of child protection has intensified the cautiousness and regulation associated with children's participation in research, especially research of this kind. There are also fears about the vulnerability of children to exploitation in the research process, which rightly results in strict ethical and legal regulations governing researchers. Ken Plummer, a US sociologist, pointed out more than 20 years ago that there is a lack of information and understanding around children's perceptions of sexuality. This is still the case today. Plummer comments:

> What is important is the mode of approach: looking at sexuality through the child's eyes to grasp how [the child] actively has to construct a sexual world. What matters is how the child interprets sexuality. Of this we know very little.
>
> (Plummer 1990: 240)

The vulnerability of researchers in this area to becoming personal targets of moral panic initiated by conservative and right-wing individuals and groups is a further issue impacting on the lack of children's voices and perspectives on this topic. It is not uncommon for academics and other professionals to self-regulate and move away from doing this research out of fear of the technologies of power that they can be subjected to, particularly through the media.

Constructing the vulnerable child

The constitution of innocence, pivotal in the hegemonic definition of childhood, along with the moral panic often associated with children and sexuality, increases children's vulnerabilities to exploitation and abuse. This occurs primarily through the way these discourses contribute to children's lack of language, knowledge, voice and agency to negotiate more effectively the experiences, situations and incidences they encounter in their early lives (Corteen and Scraton 1997; Kitzinger 1990; Plummer 1990; Robinson 2005b, 2005c, 2008; Hawkes and Egan 2008). Children are rarely given the vocabulary to talk about their sexual bodies, or the permission to talk about sexual matters (Gittins 1998; Robinson 2005b; Robinson and Jones Díaz 2006; Egan and Hawkes 2008, 2010). Denying children access to knowledge – and to frank and open discussions around the questions they have in relation to their bodies, sexuality and relationships – leave children 'to sort out their scripts with peers, media or alone in secretive and dark corners' (Plummer 1990: 239). To increase children's resilience, it is critical that children are given the appropriate tools – including knowledge, critical thinking skills and language – to become competent individuals and negotiate more effectively and ethically their everyday interactions, relationships and experiences with peers and adults (Robinson 2005a).

Building ethical relationships around diversity and difference early in children's lives

It is also important that young children (and adults) are aware of and able to build a critical understanding of diverse sexed bodies, sexualities and genders. Some people are born as intersex – that is, with a reproductive or sexual anatomy that does not seem to fit the typical definitions of female or male. For example, a person may be born with genitals that seem to be in-between the usual male and female bodies. Decisions by doctors and parents are made at birth about the construction of the child's sex. Others can experience changes in their sexual anatomy at puberty which impact on their assumed gender identities at birth and can have serious implications for the child and their families (Intersex Society of North America 2012). The constitution of the sexed body as fixed in the male and female binary marginalizes those who have different experiences of their sex. It is also important for children and adults to understand the fluidity of gender; that is, that performances of masculinity and femininity are not always aligned with constructed male/female norms (Butler 1990; Halberstam 2005). Some females take up masculinity as their preferred expression of gender subjectivity. Equally, some males' performances of gender are not aligned with hegemonic masculinity, but are instead infused with characteristics that have been constituted as feminine. In both instances, such non-conformance is generally met with adult concerns, anxieties and the regulation of children's behaviours to adhere to gender norms. Children need to be aware that sexuality is not fixed, but fluid. For many young people, negotiating desires for another person outside the boundaries of heternormativity can be extremely difficult, and can have dire consequences if they have to do this negotiating alone. Children's critical awareness of sexuality is important in order to foster ethical relationships around diversity and difference early in life, and to counteract, for example, the homophobia and heterosexism encountered by non-heterosexual and gender non-conforming subjects. The stark realities of homophobia and heterosexism in children's and young people's lives are reflected in the high rates of suicide and suicide ideation amongst gay and lesbian youth who grapple with discrimination (Denborough 1996; Mac An Ghaill 1994). This is not just an issue faced by young people who identify as non-heterosexual, but is also faced by all children and adults who are perceived by others to be transgressing normalized, heterosexualized gendered identities, regardless of their actual sexualities. A large percentage of hate crimes perpetrated against gays, lesbians and those perceived to be non-heterosexual as a result of their gender non-conformance are enacted by male youth (Mason and Tomsen 1997; Chasnoff and Cohen 1997). Such fear and hatred does not just happen one day at puberty, but is formed through the construction of children's gendered and sexual subjectivities, framed and policed within the rigid boundaries of historically, socially and politically specific practices (Epstein and Johnson 1998; Renold 2006).

The social construction of childhood

Understanding childhood as a social construction which is fluid and changing across time and space is foundational to the arguments presented in this book. Children are not inherently innocent and unknowledgeable, but rather are engaged in making meaning in their everyday lives and, as mentioned earlier, actively negotiate competing discourses that they encounter in order to constitute themselves as intelligible subjects (Davies 1989, 1993). Children make choices in their lives, but these are always limited by their knowledge and by the specific socio-cultural relations of power that constrain their possibilities, options and agency. These understandings of childhood – theoretically located within poststructuralist frameworks – are in stark contrast to traditional humanist perspectives of childhood, which emerged within the Western historical context of the Enlightenment and positioned adulthood and childhood as oppositional entities.

Normative narratives of time and space are constituted within universalized Western Enlightenment discourses of what it means to be human. The Enlightenment fostered the notion of a universal human history united by the common ideals of human reason and rationality, and progress and perfection – all reinforced by and founded on scientific 'truths' and Western philosophical ideals (Erickson and Murphy 2003). Western psychological discourses of human development emerged from these humanist, modernist perspectives, constructing childhood, adolescence and adulthood as linear and framed by categorical biological markers of human maturation. Within humanist frameworks, these life stages are rigidly separated from each other according to age and stages in cognitive and physical development, which inflexibly define what it means to be a child, adolescent or adult (Piaget 1973 [1929], 1959; Durkheim 1956). Overlapping this process of development are other biological and cultural life markers that also operate as signifiers of maturation along this linear pathway to adulthood, such as schooling, sexual maturity, starting work, voting, marriage, reproduction and retirement. Simultaneously, these markers not only constitute and reinforce culturally-defined boundaries between childhood, adolescence and adulthood, but also function as hegemonic socio-cultural, political and economic organizing principles of human relations in society.

In discourses of human development, the adult/child binary constitutes childhood in opposition to adulthood, with the child viewed as inherently different from adults. Binary relationships are representative of hierarchical power relationships: in this case, the child is subordinate to the adult, and becomes the Other in the adult/child relationship. As Elliott (2010: 196) aptly points out, 'binaries provide ideological justification for social inequality'. Within this culturally constructed adult/child relationship, the differences between adults and children are perceived as logical and natural, and children's dependence and powerlessness is assumed. This 'common-sense' knowledge about adults and children prevails, and the differences are regulated in daily interactions and in language. For example, the practice of chastising adults with phrases such as 'Don't act like a child', or disciplining children for behaving like adults and acting beyond their age, operate to maintain the binary relationship between adults and children.

Despite the critiques and shifts to post-developmentalist perspectives in studies of childhood internationally, the discourse of developmentally-appropriate practice continues to dominate rationales for increased regulations and censorship around children's learning, access to knowledge and popular culture, and for dismissing and/or trivializing children's active involvement in decision-making in both their own lives and in broader socio-cultural political arenas in many Western countries. As is demonstrated throughout this book, children at very young ages are already actively making decisions about their identities, and engaging in behaviours, processes and practices that many adults consider developmentally inappropriate or irrelevant to children's lives, especially with regard to politics, gendered relationships and sexuality.

Defining sexuality

From feminist poststructuralist and queer perspectives, sexuality is a socio-cultural construction that intersects with the body. Sexuality is viewed as being a fluid, non-linear, multifaceted, complex, contradictory and unstable aspect of human subjectivity that varies across cultures and over historical periods of time (Britzman 1997; Foucault 1977; Weeks 1986). These theoretical frameworks are in contrast with more traditional humanist perspectives, which consider sexuality to be a fixed, biologically inherent aspect of the human subject that largely emerges at puberty as part of the process of human development. Biologically determinist readings of sexuality produced by the humanist school have been challenged in recent times by critical social theorists, who have argued that sexuality and sexual desire are discursively constituted and are the result of social relations of power (Foucault 1977; Weeks 1986; Butler 1990). Jeffrey Weeks, a UK sociologist points out that sexuality exists through social forms and social organization, and this perspective influences the way that sexuality is viewed in this book. Weeks argues:

> Sexuality is something which society produces in complex ways. It is a result of diverse social practices that give meaning to human activities, of social definitions and self-definitions, of struggles between those who have power to define and regulate, and those who resist. Sexuality is not a given, it is a product of negotiation, struggle and human agency.
>
> (Weeks 1986: 25)

Foucault points out that sexuality is the 'precise point where the disciplinary and the regulatory, the body and the population, are articulated'

(Foucault 1997: 252). Sexuality not only operates as a regulatory and disciplinary technology of the self, but is also a critical point through which the 'massifying' of power is articulated – that is, the process through which technologies of power are extended to the social body, regulating and governing populations. This is what Foucault terms biopower, or the 'biopolitics of the human race' (1997: 243). Biopolitics deals with the population as a political problem and as 'power's problem' (1997: 245). It incorporates the use of regulatory State mechanisms (e.g. forecasts, statistical estimates, overall measures) that counteract and control the randomness of populations in order to 'optimize a state of life' (1997: 246). Foucault argues that sexuality in the nineteenth century became a field of vital strategic importance for two main reasons: first, for the purposes of social sanitization. The undisciplined sexual body, according to Foucault's analysis, is open to disease and degeneracy; this link historically precipitated the regulation and disciplining of individuals' sexual behaviours through constant surveillance. Second, the field of sexuality was strategically important in order to regulate and discipline the biological processes of procreation in populations, with a particular focus on hygiene and the medicalization of reproduction. The mass perpetuation and regulation of the heteronormative sexual subject and the good citizen-subject is dependent on the perpetuation of hegemonic discourses of childhood and childhood innocence.

Sexuality has been primarily constituted and regulated within the context of a heterosexual/homosexual binary relationship, in which heterosexuality is considered the norm and a natural expression of sexuality, while all non-heterosexual identities are defined as deviant and unnatural. The privilege and power associated with heterosexual relationships is perpetuated both systemically (for example in legal, medical and education systems, as well as across various religious faiths) and through the micro-relationships of everyday interactions between individuals. Lesbian, gay, bisexual, transgendered, queer and intersex (LGBTQI) subjects have had to struggle for recognition and access to civil and human rights, and to resist the marginalization imposed on them. The critical socio-cultural and political recognition of same-sex relationships and rights to marriage achieved by gays and lesbians in recent times in many Western countries has challenged the marginalization produced by this binary relationship of power, but inequities and experiences of violence still persist. The construction of the homosexual subject in relation to the child continues to be fraught, as conservative moral entrepreneurs and politicians mobilize myths about paedophilia and 'folk devils' (Cohen 1972) to undermine the gains made by non-heterosexual subjects. This moral panic is explored in Chapter 3. I share Canadian educationalist Deborah Britzman's (2000: 37) view of sexuality as 'a human right of free association' and as a *force* that is vital to human passion, interest, explorations and disappointments. As I point out in this book, children, in their own ways, share in experiencing this force in their early lives. However, this force is undermined and contained through strict regulatory practices that have not only operated to construct the sexual child, but have significantly defined the 'good' adult sexual citizen and the 'good' parent. These regulatory practices have not only defined what children should or should not be, or should or should not know, but they have also defined what adults should/should not be, and what, when and how they should or should not educate children about sexuality and other difficult knowledge.

Pepper Schwartz and Dominic Cappello (2001) define sexuality in broad terms, referring to the sum total of our sexual desire, behaviour and self-identity. It is this perception of sexuality that is encompassed in this book. Sexuality is experienced and expressed in multiple ways, and our emotions, desires and relationships are constructed by the cultures in which we live. This approach contrasts with reductive views, which narrowly define sexuality by the physical sexual act, thus contributing to the perception that sexuality is irrelevant to children (Robinson 2005a, 2005b). Sexuality does not only relate to the physical embodiment of sexual feelings and who one chooses to do what with, but it is also about one's subjectivity and how one performs being a sexualized subject. Sexuality is equally as important to children's subjectivity as other components such as ethnicity, gender and social class. Sexuality is not the exclusive realm of adults, but also belongs to children's experience: like adults, children constantly negotiate the discourses of sexuality available to them, and constantly try to understand themselves as sexual beings (Blaise 2010; Jackson 1982; Goldman and Goldman 1982; Renold 2006; Davies and Robinson 2010). Children's understandings and emotional and physical experiences of sexuality may be different from those of adults, but they nonetheless engage in the construction of their sexuality and sexual desire early in life, as is demonstrated in Chapter 5. It is in this context of the social construction of sexuality and childhood that we can view the ways in which sexuality has been culturally and historically defined as adults-only, and children have been largely excluded from this knowledge. Developmentalist discourses have constituted children as too young to have an understanding of 'adult' concepts such as sexuality. This perception is intimately linked with and reinforced by dominant religious and moral values (Gittins 1998).

The social construction of the relationship between childhood and sexuality

Within humanist discourses of sexuality, physiological sexual maturity has represented the boundary between adulthood and childhood (Gittins 1998). Sexuality is generally considered to begin at puberty and mature in adulthood, and children's sexuality within this discourse is considered immature or non-existent. Childhood innocence is most frequently equated to purity and naïvety, which is positioned in contrast to sexual knowledge. This innocence is perceived as natural and normal in the child, who is essentially constructed as asexual – which is ironic considering the great lengths adults have historically gone to in order to curb the sexual tendencies of young children (Wolfenstein 1998). Sigmund Freud was one of the first to offer a different perspective from the humanist construction of children's sexuality when he argued that sexuality is an active and normal part of children's lives. Freud believed that children's initial feelings connecting them to the world (especially to the mother) were sexual in nature, and upheld that the repression of children's sexuality could result in various psychoses in adulthood. Despite the critiques of Freud's theory of children's sexuality (e.g. lack of empirical evidence; feminist concerns around the seductive child; and sexual abuse that perpetuated 'blaming the victim'), his perspective provided a counter-discourse to children as asexual or as dormant sexual subjects, and offered an alternate perspective of children as engaged sexual beings with desire. Still, children's sexuality has remained taboo in Western culture. Expressions of children's physical sexual desires are highly regulated and hidden away, especially from public display: they are rarely spoken about in public; they are under-researched, as I pointed out earlier; and have largely been repressed and rendered invisible through the discourse of childhood innocence and regulations stemming from cultural values, morals and taboos. Through this regulation, sexuality has become constituted as an exclusive realm – a world in which children have been constituted as vulnerable and in need of protection from predatory adults.

Children's desire for knowledge of sexuality

Children become frustrated when they do not get information or find a meaning through which they can come to terms with and understand their sexuality. Ron Goldman and Juliette Goldman (1982) argue that adults must be honest when discussing sex with children. Schwartz and Cappello (2001) also point out that it is necessary for adults to discuss sexuality with children in order to deconstruct and reconstruct children's understandings around the difficulties often encountered surrounding their sexuality. Goldman and Goldman (1982) conducted two major studies on children's sexual thinking and experiences. Based on their findings, they recommended that the subject of sexuality should be introduced to children early in their lives. They argue that if this information is not made available to children early, they tend to complete the picture of sex differences, sexual relations and other sexuality information from their imagination or by shared ignorance with friends (see also Davies and Robinson 2010). Goldman and Goldman (1982) also point out that as children get older and become more aware of the socio-cultural values that predominate around sexuality, it becomes more difficult for adults to introduce and discuss sexuality with children. In their study, teenagers reported that they wished they had had access to sexual knowledge much earlier in their lives. This way, they would have avoided the bewilderment surrounding their sexuality, especially due to the changes which occur during puberty. This desire for knowledge around sexuality was reiterated in research conducted with children by Chasnoff and Cohen (1997). However, in this later research, children extended this desire for knowledge to include information around differences in sexual orientation. It is important to include children's voices and perspectives on sexuality (Rademakers *et al.* 2000) in order to understand more about children's sexual subjectivities and to provide more effective sexuality education for all children. Children's voices are rarely part of such discussions, largely as a result of the regulatory practices that this book addresses. The inclusion of children's voices, as well as those of their parents, can offer valuable insight into how children view sexuality, construct their own sexual subjectivities, and regulate those of other children.

Key arguments in this book

To conclude this introductory discussion, I want to reiterate the arguments that are key to this book. The social construction of childhood innocence which prevails in Western countries, and in some developing countries, is detrimental to children's wellbeing and their development as competent, responsible, resilient, critical-thinking subjects with agency in their lives. Childhood innocence is mobilized to regulate children's access to certain knowledge constituted as adults-only, with sexual knowledge the most controversial of these areas of regulation. Through the denial of accurate information and open discussions in the area of sexuality, often in the name of protecting children's innocence, adults have intensified children's vulnerability to exploitation and abuse and to the undermining of their health and wellbeing more generally in the area of sexuality. In light of the changing nature of childhood in the twenty-first century, it is critical to find ways to work with children that provide them with the skills and agency to negotiate the broad socio-cultural changes occurring in their lives. However, normative representations of the child and childhood innocence have a broader role in society in that they have been utilized to regulate dominant relations of power and constitute the heteronormative adult citizen-subject. The child is used as a powerful tool for perpetuating particular political agendas that maintain certain social inequalities.

Chapter overviews

The chapters in this book constitute an in-depth exploration of the relationship between childhood and sexuality; of children's sexual subjectivities; of the mobilization of childhood innocence as a regulatory tool; of knowledge and power; and of the debates that prevail around censorship and contemporary childhood. Following is a brief overview of the focus of each chapter.

Chapter 2 provides a discussion of 'difficult knowledge', 'subjugated knowledge' and a *hierarchy of difference*, examining the relevance of these concepts to the construction of knowledge in childhood and to the maintenance of the Western binary relationship of adult/child. This binary is crucial to the regulation of children's participation in society and the transfer of knowledge across generations, as well as to how children's production of knowledge is subjugated in Western societies. This chapter also examines children's relationships with discourses of citizenship in Western societies, particularly sexual citizenship. Children's relationship to sexual citizenship is explored in two main ways: first through the ways in which the concepts of *childhood* and *innocence* have been utilized to regulate children's access to knowledge of sexuality and to deny their relevance and access to sexual citizenship; and second through the ways in which these two concepts are intimately connected as a means of constituting and governing the 'good' normative adult citizen-subject. I propose that the constitution of the heteronormative adult citizen-subject has critical implications for what is considered appropriate education for young children, who are constituted as *future* heteronormative citizens.

Chapter 3 provides a brief historical overview of the construction of children's sexuality and the constitution of sexuality as dangerous to children. This discussion incorporates how innocence has become discursively synonymous with childhood, contributing to the discourse of sexuality as dangerous and to the construction of children as vulnerable subjects. It explores how society's endeavours to protect children's innocence by operating 'in the best interests of the child' have ironically made children far more vulnerable through the regulation of children's knowledge, especially sexual knowledge. Childhood innocence is examined as a social construction defined within the binary relationship of adult/child and regulated by broad socio-cultural and political practices. In addition, the chapter explores how childhood innocence is employed by politicians and social conservatives to instigate moral panic in order to maintain the hegemonic discourses of childhood and the normative social order in societies. The discussion includes a focus on moral panic and censorship relating to children and sexuality, and an overview and critique of the contemporary international debates about the sexualization of childhood in the media, advertising and the arts which have called for increased censorship. A critical consequence of censorship – the repression of children's sexuality over the centuries and the insistence of childhood innocence – has been the commodification and fetishization of the child and of childhood innocence.

Chapter 4 examines the technologies of power operating in schools that regulate children's access to knowledge of sexuality and also regulate the behaviours of teachers. The constitution of the child as a heteronormative subject is central to this regulation. Foucault's knowledge/power nexus is used to frame how schooling policies, practices and curricula maintain binary relationships between adults and children, and between heterosexual and homosexual subjects, in order to maintain hegemonic, heteronormative power relations. In this chapter, I provide an overview of such regulation in selected Western countries, including Australia, New Zealand, the UK and the USA, and demonstrate how discourses of risk and moral panic constitute and instil understandings of the heteronormative citizen-subject early in children's lives.

Chapter 5 includes an exploration, based on qualitative research with children (and their parents), of the construction of children's sexual subjectivities and of their desires. The hegemonic discourses which children mobilize in this process of subjectification are examined, as are the discourses they utilize to construct their knowledge of relationships, intimacy, love and sexual subjectivity. A particular focus is given to the ways in which children often construct themselves as heteronormative subjects and how they police the normative construction of gender and sexuality in the lives of their peers. However, childhood as a counter-public, or a space in which non-normative performances of childhood and gender are possible, are also discussed.

Chapter 6, based on qualitative research with parents, explores the construction of parents' sexual subjectivities in childhood, and how their experiences as children and young adults have impacted on their perspectives of their children's sexual subjectivities and their approaches to educating their children about sexuality. The anxieties that many adults experience around their children's sexual subjectivities and with talking about sexuality with their children are examined. Through their inability and/or discomfort in dealing with sexuality issues with children, many parents reinforce social taboos associated with speaking about sexuality. Many adults are highly anxious about addressing sexuality with children and often struggle to know when and how to approach this subject. Despite many parents' negative childhood experiences surrounding sex education and their aims to do it differently with their own children, many parents are unskilled and lack the confidence to educate their children effectively in this area. The chapter also examines the tensions between normative narratives of gender and sexuality that prevail in children's lives and the alternative narratives that some parents wish to convey to their children.

Chapter 7, the concluding chapter, is a summation of the central issues raised and of the main arguments in the book. This chapter provides practical strategies for approaching children's sexual subjectivity and sexuality education, based on the issues and arguments raised throughout the book. These strategies are intended to support educators and other professionals working with children – as well as parents – in their efforts to deal with children's sexuality education more productively.

Chapter 2

Difficult knowledge and subjugated knowledge

Adult/child relations and the regulation of citizenship

Introduction

This chapter examines the concepts of difficult knowledge (Britzman 1998) and subjugated knowledges (Foucault 1980) and how they relate to the construction of knowledge in childhood. Each of these concepts are from different theoretical paradigms – difficult knowledge from a psychoanalytic framework, and subjugated knowledge from a discursive framework – and each provides critical insights into the way that knowledge is constructed, encountered and adopted by individuals. These paradigms allow for an analysis of how knowledge operates, both at the emotional level and as a socio-cultural and political technology of power at the micro and macro levels in society, structuring social life and regulating individual subjectivities. Foucault (1980) points out that the dismissal of certain knowledge, and the constitution of particular knowledge as difficult, is bound up in struggles for power exercised through the competing discourses that constitute the object of which they speak. Stephen Ball, a sociologist of education in the United Kingdom, says of discourse:

> [Discourses are] about what can be said and thought, but also about who can speak, when, and with what authority. Discourses embody meaning and social relationships, they constitute both subjectivity and power.
>
> (Ball 1990: 2)

The discourses in which individuals are invested and located effect the version of events or knowledge they understand as their 'truth', and are also constitutive of their subjectivities. Difficult knowledge can be linked to subjugated knowledge, which is knowledge or worldviews associated with subordinate groups in society that differ from the knowledge and perspectives perpetuated by more powerful colonizing groups. The knowledge associated with non-heterosexual subjects' life experiences, for example, is disqualified and marginalized as a result of their subjugated position in society. The social taboos surrounding sexuality, especially associated with children, result in sexual knowledge being viewed by many as difficult knowledge. As a subordinated group in society, the knowledge of non-heterosexuals and about their lives also becomes subjugated knowledge.

The concept of a *hierarchy of difference*, and how it impacts on the way individuals perceive, interact with and transfer knowledge associated with the Other is examined in this chapter. This concept, which emerged from research undertaken with early childhood educators and pre-service teachers, relates to individuals' comfort levels (and tolerance levels) associated with educating children around difference and identity (see Robinson and Jones Díaz 2000, 2006). This hierarchy is also reflective of the binary construction of knowledge into adults' knowledge and children's knowledge, which contributes to the mutually exclusive discourses of the world of adults and the world of children. Within this context, children's lives have been largely relegated to private spaces, such as the family and the home. Children's participation in public spaces in Western societies has traditionally been minimal, although there has been a greater focus on children's and youths' participation in public life and politics in more recent years in both Western and non-Western countries. The absence of children in discourses of citizenship – especially sexual citizenship – not just in Western countries but globally has important implications for public health. This can be seen in the high incidences of sexual abuse in childhood internationally; of teenage pregnancy and sexually transmitted infections amongst teenagers in some Western Countries (UK, USA, New Zealand and Australia); and of HIV and AIDS infections through sexual transmission in South Africa. Children's lack of access to sexual knowledge due to cultural politics is contributing to a rise in children's sexual health problems, which are carried on into adolescence and adulthood – if the affected children survive (Bhana 2010; UNESCO 2009). Children's access to sexuality education is an equity and civil rights issue. All children require the knowledge and skills to take some responsibility for their bodies to help increase their chances of positive physical and mental health and wellbeing, and to help prevent issues such as those raised in the example above. Children's relationship to citizenship and sexual citizenship is explored in this chapter not just as an issue relevant to sexuality education but also as a civil rights issue.

Difficult knowledge and children

Deborah Britzman, the Canadian educational philosopher, developed the term *difficult knowledge* in her book titled, *Lost Subjects, Contested Objects: Toward a psychoanalytic inquiry of learning* (1998). In this work, Britzman argues that the critical relationship between difficult knowledge and learning is important for educators engaging in affective pedagogy. Taking up a Freudian psychoanalytical framework, Britzman maintains that learning is a psychic event charged with resistance to knowledge. This resistance is considered 'a precondition for learning from knowledge and the grounds of knowledge itself' (Britzman 1998: 118). Difficult knowledge is the key to learning through the way that it challenges one's subjective reality in the world, provoking 'a crisis within the self', which 'is felt as interference or as critique of the self's coherence or view of itself in the world' (Britzman 1998: 118). Britzman's argument that for learning to occur there must be a point of self-crisis and resistance to knowledge is critical to informing pedagogies. Building on Britzman's understanding of difficult knowledge, I incorporate a Foucauldian perspective, arguing that this term also encompasses the tensions that exist around the relations of power inherent in knowledge – that is, Foucault's power/knowledge nexus.

Difficult knowledge is very much determined by adults. Bodies of knowledge pertaining to issues such as sexuality, death, war, poverty, violence and politics have been socio-culturally and politically constructed as difficult, particularly in relation to children. The impact of these bodies of knowledge being understood as 'difficult' has frequently resulted in censoring this information in children's early education. It is knowledge that is often constituted as adults' knowledge in Western contexts. These are topics considered by many adults to be unsuitable for general discussions with children or irrelevant to their lives. This censorship is significantly linked to Western ideals of childhood innocence and its intersection with the discourse of child development, constituting children as too young to deal emotionally and cognitively with concepts fundamental to narratives of struggle, survival and procreation. There is a prevailing perception that children should be sheltered from this knowledge for as long as possible in order to avoid any stress or trauma that might be associated with *premature* access to this information.

Difficult knowledge tends to be associated with topics that pose the greatest challenges for adults in their own lives – bodies of knowledge that are often linked to powerful affective responses, such as those identified by Silvan Tomkins. Tomkins, a US psychologist who was seminal in the development of affect theory in the 1950s, identified several affects, including interest, surprise, shame, fear, anger, joy, distress, disgust and contempt (Sedgwick and Frank 1995). Sexuality is an area of difficult knowledge for many and is often linked to shame. Sara Ahmed (2004), a race and cultural studies theorist, points out that shame is crucial to moral development and is infused with norms of sexual conduct. Ahmed argues, 'in order to avoid shame, subjects must enter the "contract" of the social bond, by seeking to approximate a social ideal' (2004: 107). Consequently, shame 'can be experienced as the affective cost of not following the scripts of normative existence' (2004: 107). Sedgwick and Frank (1995: 22) reiterate Tomkins' belief that 'without positive affect, there can be no shame: only a scene that offers you enjoyment or engages your interest can make you blush'. Shame can occur when enjoyment is experienced, or when one is involved in behaviours considered inappropriate according to sexual conduct norms. Sexual taboos and shame associated with sexual conduct can operate to shut down or repress behaviours and conversations around sexuality, which in turn reinforce taboo and shame. This shame and discomfort influences how adults approach these issues with children. Children can learn early in their lives the taboos and shaming that operate around sexuality and sexual conduct, which can result in them not discussing these issues with their parents (and other adults), despite parents' contrary practices of trying to build positive communication links with their children.

Jonathan Silin, in his book *Sex, Death and the Education of Children: Our passion for ignorance in the age of AIDS* (1995), also critiques traditional approaches in young children's education that consider certain knowledge as developmentally inappropriate for children. Discussing the lack of education around death and sexuality in children's early years, Silin argues that it is the 'passion for ignorance' that underpins the way this knowledge is silenced in children's education. Children are generally kept in a state of ignorance due to adults' fears and discomfort. Silin comments:

> Denied choices, unable to make an impact on the environment, children do not learn who they are and what they can do. A sense of authentic time, of the role of death in life, is essential to our becoming active, intending participants in the world rather than passive victims of circumstances in a one-dimensional present.
>
> (Silin 1995: 43)

Childhood innocence and its intersection with the discourse of child development becomes a powerful mediator/regulator of what is included and excluded from children's early education. I agree with Silin that the development of children as aware and competent subjects and active citizens is undermined through lack of meaningful discussion around issues that are as pertinent to children's lives as they are to adults' lives. For example, not talking with children about ethical relationships early in their lives, when they are forming understandings of their sexual and gendered subjectivities and relationships with others (see Chapter 5), can perpetuate dominant discourses around unethical gendered relationships inherent in hegemonic masculine cultures. One example of this is the alleged rape of a 12-year-old girl at a Christmas Eve party in Western Australia by three boys aged 11, 13 and 14, which demonstrates that this culture of violence, unethical sexual behaviour and disrespectful relations begins early in life (Australian Associated Press 2009). Research conducted in Australian schools also indicates that sexual harassment is acculturated in schooling and young people's lives (Clark 1989; Robinson 1996, 2005d). A further example can be seen in South Africa, where primary school children are not provided with sexuality education around HIV/AIDS due to cultural attitudes about childhood innocence, thus increasing the risk of unsafe sexual practices when these children become sexually active. As these examples show, much of adults' censorship and shutting down in conversations with children, often done in the name of protection of childhood innocence, is not necessarily an effective form of protection at all.

Hierarchy of difference

Difficult knowledge is also linked with another concept – a hierarchy of difference. This describes the ways in which individuals, and society more broadly, preference certain areas of identity – race, ethnicity, social class, gender, sexuality and/or (dis)ability – in terms of respect, acceptance and inclusivity over others. This concept emerged out of research undertaken with early childhood educators, parents of young children and pre-service teachers, which examined the policies and everyday practices associated with diversity, difference and inclusion in early childhood educational settings and in the education of young children (Robinson and Jones Díaz 2000, 2006; Robinson 2005d). A hierarchy of difference reflects the comfort/discomfort, tolerance/intolerance, and/or the level of commitment individuals have to engaging personally and professionally with certain areas of cultural diversity and difference (Robinson and Jones Díaz 2006). This hierarchy is linked not only to individuals' subjectivities, personal experiences, biases or fears of approaching certain issues with children, but also to perceptions of what knowledge is relevant and considered developmentally appropriate to address with them. Varying levels of comfort around diversity issues may be related to a number of other factors, including an individual's own identity; their experience or lack of experience with difference; their knowledge about difference; their religious and cultural values; and their positioning in sexist, heterosexist, homophobic and racist discourses. The educators and pre-service teachers who participated in this research, for example, considered multiculturalism (as well as biculturalism and bilingualism) to be the most relevant and important area of cultural diversity and difference in children's lives, and they felt most comfortable dealing with these concepts with children. Areas considered more personally difficult and uncomfortable by educators and pre-service teachers were also considered more difficult to address professionally with children, and less relevant to children's early education. Such matters included: single-parent families (related to family breakdowns, divorce and death); socio-economic issues (related to poverty, and socio-economic and class disadvantage); Indigenous Australian concerns (related to racism, dispossession, genocide and economic, political and social discrimination); and sexuality (related to identity and discrimination) and same-sex families. Without exception, issues surrounding sexuality and same-sex families were considered the most difficult to address with children, eliciting the most discomfort and even hostile responses from some participants.

Educating children around multiculturalism generally involves a touristic approach in which understandings of identity are constructed as fixed, and pedagogies are focused on developing tolerance of ethnic diversity through celebrating superficial cultural differences like food, clothing and artefacts. Multiculturalism is a discourse of cross-cultural co-existence that does not challenge existing cultural hegemonies – that is, the social and institutionalized inequalities that are legitimized around difference. The discourse of multiculturalism is depoliticized within liberal humanist perspectives of tolerance and intercultural understandings (Rizvi 1991), unlike anti-racism and anti-racist education, which aims to disrupt dominant relations of power and privilege in society (hooks 1997; Luke and Luke 1998; Kincheloe and Steinberg 1997; Robinson and Jones Díaz 2006; Robinson and Ferfolja 2001). In the liberal humanist context, multiculturalism is considered developmentally appropriate knowledge to address with children and, as we have seen, is an area that educators, parents and other professionals generally feel personally comfortable discussing with children. It is considered relevant to children's lives due to the obvious existence of ethnic diversity in children's cultural backgrounds, as well as those of their peers, and in the communities in which they live. Its inclusion in children's early education is further legitimized through the sanctioning of multiculturalism in official social, political and educational policies and practices in Australia and other Western countries. However, the effectiveness of pluralistic multicultural education with children has been questioned in recent years, largely as a result of the failure of this pedagogical approach to acknowledge and challenge young children's practices and positioning in racist discourses that perpetuate inequalities and discriminatory relations of power (Robinson and Jones Díaz 2006; Davies and Robinson 2012). In this way, while the idea of *tolerance* towards ethnic diversity is sanctioned in the discourse of multiculturalism and in related government policies, discourses of *equity* continue to be marginalized, not just around ethnicity, but also in relation to other sites of cultural diversity.

Cultural diversity and difference issues related to lesbian and gay identities, for example, remain subjugated in the political and public arena. Issues surrounding non-heteronormative sexualities pose the greatest concern and discomfort for educators, parents and carers because they are considered developmentally inappropriate knowledge, and are perceived to be the least relevant to children's lives. This perceived irrelevance and discomfort is linked to a number of factors. One is the prevalence of homophobia – the prejudice, discrimination, harassment or acts of violence perpetrated against people from diverse sexuality backgrounds, or those perceived as non-heterosexual based on their gender non-conformance. Another is discourses of heterosexism and heteronormativity, in which children are assumed to be latent heterosexuals, and in which heterosexuality is considered the superior, natural and normal sexual orientation. Heteronormativity expresses how everyday interactions, practices and policies construct normative subjects as heterosexual, and non-heterosexual subjects as abnormal, deviant and unnatural. These beliefs are frequently framed within religious values. Discomfort also arises due to fears that introducing diverse genders and sexualities to children might encourage their curiosity and interest in experimenting with these behaviours. Further, discomfort also stems from the social taboos associated with sexuality, and the construction of sexuality – including discussing and deconstructing homophobia, heterosexism, heteronormativity and their consequences with children – as difficult knowledge.

The fears and discomfort that educators and parents feel around addressing diverse genders and sexuality issues with children, beyond the obvious discourses of childhood innocence and those issues raised above, can come from their own lack of confidence and knowledge of the issues. For the majority of educators and parents in this research, addressing sexuality and same-sex families with children, despite children asking questions, was only ever done 'if it became absolutely necessary to do so', in the words of one early childhood educator. Most often, children's questions were minimally discussed, sidestepped or ignored. The premise behind child-centred pedagogy and the curriculum that predominates in early childhood education is that issues and topics emerging from children's questions and play pedagogically direct curriculum planning and teachers' discussions with children. However, this does not seem to be the case with questions and play that involve sexuality. Many early childhood educators and pre-service teachers who participated in this research prided themselves on being strong social justice advocates on issues such as multiculturalism, additional needs and gender, but the same level of professional commitment was not given to sexuality issues and same-sex families. Feminist poststructural theory points out that subjects can shift discursively according to different contexts and across periods of time, based on the investments they personally or professionally locate in some discourses rather than others (Weedon 1987; Robinson and Jones Díaz 2006). In this light, it is not surprising that many of the research participants evinced such complex, fluid and contradictory subjectivities.

The discourse of childhood innocence, reinforced by the discourse of developmentalism, operates to construct children as politically unaware. Children's early education is depoliticized and children are constituted as too young to have an interest in, understanding of, or opinion on broader social issues. Rather than taking up a critical pedagogical stance with children in order to counteract racism, sexism, homophobia, classism and other discourses of bias that children encounter and engage in daily, much of children's early education does little to challenge their participation in perpetuating these dominant relations of power and inequality. Educators do not adequately challenge children around the ways in which children's practices of power are linked to broader socio-cultural, political and economic discourses that underpin inequities. Educators and parents often comment that children do not see differences like adults do, exemplified in this research by one educator's statement that 'children aren't aware of these things unless it is pointed out to them by adults'. This perception suggests that recognition of difference, and the negative connotations that can go with it, is not part of children's experiences and understanding of the world around them. Children's views of the world are often thus romanticized within ideals of childhood innocence and perceived as easily corrupted by the inflictions of adults' concepts (Gittins 1998). On the contrary, however, research has demonstrated that this romantic view of childhood is far from the reality of children's lives, and that young children engage daily in relations of power that perpetuate social inequalities associated with differences, such as race, gender, sexuality, class and disabilities (Davies 1993; Robinson and Jones Díaz 2006; MacNaughton 1993; Kilodavis 2010).

Subjugated knowledge

Subjugated knowledge is a Foucauldian concept that refers to historical content and ways of knowing that have been 'buried and disguised in a functionalist coherence or formal systemization' (Foucault 1980: 81) – that is, buried under the dominant forms of knowledge that have developed in fields such as science, history and government as part of a colonizing process. Subjugated knowledge refers to knowledge that has been historically and politically dismissed, disqualified, considered naïve and inadequate, and located on the lower levels of the hierarchy of knowledge, 'beneath the required level of cognition or scientificity' (Foucault 1980: 82). Despite being dismissed through this process, subjugated knowledge gains power through the force by which it is opposed by everything surrounding it. Subjugated knowledge is maintained through relations of power, which authorize certain knowledge as *truth*. This knowledge maintains its hegemonic position of power through socio-cultural and political practices and policies, including the everyday interactions of subjects who take up this knowledge as their own truth. Through this process, subordinate groups become the Other, dismissed as inferior, primitive or non-normative. For example, the cultural knowledge of Indigenous peoples throughout the world has been subjugated through colonization. Aboriginal and Torres Strait Islander peoples in Australia have subjugated knowledge that provides an understanding of the world from an entirely different perspective from that given in Western science. Within a 'hierarchy of knowledge' (Foucault 1980), the hegemony of Western scientific knowledge prevails as a result of white colonialism – a position that has continued in many instances to the present day. Still, the subjugated knowledge of Aboriginal and Torres Strait Islander peoples operates to sustain the struggle of these cultures under colonialist regimes. The dismissal and disqualification of women's history and knowledge through the colonizing system of patriarchy is another example of subjugated knowledge.

The subjugated knowledge of children and non-heterosexual subjects are two important examples of this process, which are particularly relevant to discussions of the construction of childhood and its relationship to knowledge. The subjugation of children's knowledge – or how children view and experience the world – is discussed in depth below, but first I will provide some focus on the latter example. In Western society, the knowledge embodied by non-heterosexual subjects and their lives has been disqualified and marginalized through the colonizing principles inherent in heteronormativity. Official denial of the lived experiences of non-heterosexual subjects has functioned to disavow the lives of many children who live in same-sex families, and negate or dismiss the experiences of children with relatives and/or close friends who identify as queer. Conservatives have traditionally viewed the child as 'at risk' from non-heterosexual and queer subjects, who have been mythologized either as paedophiles, or as out to 'recruit' children and young people into the 'gay lifestyle' (Kincaid 1998). The same-sex marriage debates that have been occurring in many Western countries in recent years demonstrate this process well. In an effort to counteract any political gains made by gay rights activists in this area, the conservative right in Australia – with the assistance of anti-gay marriage advocates from the US – in a campaign with the slogan 'Don't meddle with marriage', have taken up scaremongering to try and reignite a moral panic associated with same-sex marriage, linking some people's fears of homosexuals to old myths. Calling for Australians to join her in a 'war for the future of the human race', the US advocate Rebecca Hagelin opined that there was 'no greater evil' than legalizing same-sex marriage, asserting that 'It won't stop at homosexual marriage – look for polygamy and marriage between adults and children to be legalized. There is no greater dream for a paedophile than to be able to legally acclaim [*sic*] a child as his lover.' (Farrelly 2011; Rout 2011). The emotional capital inherent in the child is a most effective strategy, in which the homosexual subject is dismissed, disqualified and demonized for disrupting the perceived natural order of things in society according to these conservatives. The apolitical child thus becomes an effective political tool.

Children's subjugated knowledge

Children's production of knowledge has been dismissed and disqualified as local and naïve and unsophisticated. Children's knowledge has been subjugated through Western scientific discourses, such as philosophy and psychology, that have given credence to the authenticity of mature adult knowledge and experiences as rational and logical, over the perceived irrationality and naivety of children and young people. Hegemonic discourses that construct knowledge of childhood and constitute what it means to be a child have privileged and normalized white, Western, middle-class images, values and perceptions as underpinning the *true nature* of the child and of childhood.

Utilizing a postcolonial lens, adults have signified the child in Western Enlightenment and colonialist discourses as the Other, scrutinizing them under a scientific gaze and a process of colonial surveillance that has constituted children as inherently different from adults (Cannella and Viruru 2004; James and Prout 1990). The knowledge gained through this process has legitimated systems of governance at both macro and micro levels in society that control children's lives, bodies and access to knowledge. As pointed out by Gaile Cannella and Radhika Viruru:

> [T]hose who were labelled as children have been consistently seen as the same as the colonized, exotic beings who were different from adults and interesting only to the extent that they could be analysed for who they would become.
>
> (Cannella and Viruru 2004: 84–85)

These perceptions of the child and of the colonized are inherent in humanist Enlightenment discourse. The Enlightenment was a period emerging out of the Dark Ages, beginning approximately in the mid-seventeenth century. It is represented as an intellectual awakening sparked by geographical discoveries and the scientific revolution, which resulted in new knowledge associated with mathematics, astrology, physics, biology and anthropology. The scientific revolution changed the way the world was viewed, with scientific *facts* and *truths* repositioning and privileging *man* within the universe and challenging the centrality of god as the creator of the universe. It was a period in which the emergence of Western philosophy extended thought from a greater understanding of the natural world into the social realm of human relationships and interactions. Within Enlightenment discourse, it was perceived that not only could science discover the natural order of the world and the laws that governed it, but that such knowledge could also be discovered about man and what it meant to be human. From within this context, positivism emerged – a perspective that promoted objective, value-free science as the model for social and scientific enquiry. The insistence that human beings have the capacity to engage in reason and rationality, progressing to moral and intellectual perfection, formed the ideals behind humanism and the foundations of modernist thought.

During this time, the separation of the child from the adult reflected the dichotomous thought that distinguished and privileged certain knowledge, subjectivities, and ways of being over others – for example: mind/matter, adult/child, innocent/knowledgeable, man/woman, heterosexual/homosexual, rational/irrational, rooted in Western logic/primitive, and good/evil. Along with the representation of Western logic as the epitome of human progress, Charles Darwin's evolutionary theory placed white, Western man (there was an assumed heterosexuality in this ideal) at the pinnacle of human evolution (Darwin 1859, 1871). The child, women, the homosexual (considered more female-like) and non-Western cultures (primarily colonized people of colour) were considered more aligned with *nature* than man, as they were perceived to lack the rational and reasoning qualities of the Western adult (heterosexual) male. These theories legitimated the separation of the child from the adult and the colonization of non-Western cultures, considered to be more primitive. The child has thus been positioned as the immature and powerless Other to the adult, who has come to represent the pinnacle of human development, marked by physical and emotional maturity and the ability to engage in abstract and hypothetical thinking. Consequently, the child has been perceived as not being fully human (due to its stage in biological development), but rather as being in the process of *becoming* human – as professed by the French sociologist Emile Durkheim in the late nineteenth century:

> In everything the child is characterized by the very instability of [its] nature, which is the law of growth. The educationalist is presented not with a person wholly formed – not a complete work or finished product – but with a *becoming*, an incipient being, a person in the process of formation.
> (Durkheim 1982: 150)

The child (like the adolescent) does not become a citizen, a fully-fledged human, until it becomes an adult – and the child is encouraged to become a particular kind of adult citizen (discussed below, and also in Chapters 4 and 5). Positioned as oppositional to the adult, the child is viewed as lacking as a subject and is thereby relegated to the margins of public life. This modernist paradigm has been instrumental in artificially creating the separate, distinct and often mutually exclusive spaces which have become known as *the world of adults* and *the world of children*.

The child, viewed as lower on the evolutionary scale, was considered to be progressing toward the pinnacle of rationality – epitomized by the adult. This is similar to the colonizing discourses surrounding non-Western cultures and people of colour, which constituted them as requiring Western intervention in order to set them on the path to modernization and progress (Westernization). The notion of universal human development led to belief in a natural truth – or laws that determined the linear progress of the human from birth to adulthood – which could be discovered through observing the development of the child. The Western, white, (heterosexual) male child became representative of the norm from which this progress was to be measured. This constitution of child development as progressing in chronological stages according to age is exemplified in Piagetian theory (Piaget 1973 [1929], 1964, 1968). The critical point to be made here in terms of subjugated knowledge is that, in Western society, there has historically been little interest in the child's knowledge, experiences and ways of being in the world; interest has only lain in observing and analysing how the child's development informed 'truths' about the mature adult mind and body.

While the subjugation of children's knowledge has largely continued into the present, an interest in the child in its own right has emerged in recent times with the reconceptualizing childhood movement. Canella and Viruru (2004: 97) point out that scientific discourses, especially those in psychology, have created children as the 'perfect objects of Empire'. Children in Western societies have tended to be defined, described, constituted and regulated through a process of colonialism that has dismissed their knowledge of the world. However, the subjugation of children's knowledge is not the norm in all cultures. Therefore, a global perspective of childhood is important in opening up the possibility of counter-discourses around children's production of knowledge and citizenship to those prevailing in Western cultures (Katz 2004).

Children, citizenship and knowledge: constructing the apolitical child

Access to knowledge, participation in knowledge production, and independent thinking and decision-making are important civil rights issues. The United Nations' *Convention of the Rights of the Child* (United Nations General Assembly 1989) goes someway to acknowledging this point in clause 13, which states that children have the right 'to freedom of expression, including freedom to seek, receive and impart information and ideas of all kinds, regardless of frontiers, either orally, in writing or in print, in the form of art, or any other media of the child's choice' (Alderson 2000: 40). However, as with many of the clauses in this convention, articulation into children's social and public lives or into institutionalized laws is often limited, if not non-existent. This does not just stem from the construction of childhood and adult/child relations of power, but also from the ways in which these rights are imbued with geographical, racialized, classed, gendered and sexualized inequalities. Pursuing children's rights spotlights and challenges the subjugated position of children inherent in the adult/child binary, and raises questions about the nature of childhood and of rights more generally in society. However, it remains difficult to locate children in dominant discourses of citizenship in Western countries due to traditional understandings of childhood, children's lack of status and agency, and perceptions of age and competency.

As the vast range of research on children and citizenship highlights, children are predominantly considered citizens *in potentia*, rather than current citizens in their own right (Harris 1987; Landsdown 1994; John 1995; Roche 1999; Hultqvist and Dahlberg 2001; Kulynych 2001; Marc 2004; Dahlberg and Moss 2005; Howe and Cavell 2005; Mayo 2006). Children's citizenship is always in tension with adult/child relations of power, as is adults' citizenship, and adult sovereignty or governance over childhood is often considered fundamental to the maintenance of the status quo in society (Howe and Cavell 2005). Making decisions for, and in the best interests of, children is seen as one of the key roles of parents in Western society. In the absence of parents, these decisions are made by state authorities based on welfare regulations which seek to define and standardize the best interests of children. Children's dependence on adults is generally viewed as a natural and essential social arrangement, which is reinforced through law and policy discourse (Goldson 1997). Berry Mayall (2006: 11) points out that the child is 'firmly placed as the object of intervention by the state and family'. The more control and regulation that is enforced on children either through the family or the state, the less chance children have to develop responsibility skills or to demonstrate what they are capable of achieving; adults are also less likely to develop more trust in their children (Dauda 2010; Mayall 2000; Qvortrup 2005). Jens Qvortrup (2005: 7) comments that 'participation and protection are offset against one another often severely circumscribing the agency of children and youth'. Rights given to children are only ever partial and/or conditional on broad socio-cultural and political regulations. Within these relations of power, the reality is that children's access to citizenship is generally limited, and their inclusion and participation in social, economic, political and educational decision-making is minimal. Even so, they are often central to political rhetoric about the need to consider the *future* lives of children when making decisions today.

The concept of citizenship is strongly contested across disciplines, and the debate encompasses a broad range of perspectives. Within this scholarship, perspectives on citizenship range from 'normative commitments to an ideal of citizenship' and 'the promise of personal fulfilment, community wellbeing, and democratic fulfilment', to 'citizenship as a discourse of self-governance, in which subjects are transformed into citizens through technologies of citizenship' (Cossman 2007: 4–5). However, across these perspectives generally is the notion of citizenship as membership, belonging and fully participating in a national culture (Turner 1993). Brenda Cossman's view of citizenship provides a useful framework for understanding this concept that is reflective of my own perspectives and relevant to my research. Cossman states that citizenship invokes:

> A set of rights and practices denoting membership and belonging in a nation state ... including not only legal and political practices but also cultural practices and representations ... also ... invoking the ways that different subjects are constituted as members of a polity, the ways they are, or are not, granted rights, responsibilities, and representations within the polity, as well as acknowledgement and inclusion through a multiplicity of legal, political, cultural, and social discourses.
>
> (Cossman 2007: 5)

Citizenship in this framework has some connection and relevance to the lives of children through its focus on *membership*, *belonging* and *participation* across social, cultural, political and legal spaces. These issues in particular have been at the core of advocacy for greater recognition of children's citizenship (Kulynych 2001; MacNaughton *et al.* 2008; Marc 2004; Mayo 2006). Of particular interest in Cossman's citizenship framework is the perception of citizenship as *a process of becoming* (Cossman 2007: 2): that is, all subjects – not just children – are perceived as being in a process of *becoming* citizens. This view has important implications for disrupting the adult/child binary, which is mobilized to regulate the behaviours of adults and children, as well as to justify broad socio-cultural and political practices engaged in maintaining dominant relations of power in society – including those around citizenship. Cossman (2007: 2) argues that 'The process of becoming citizens is one that operates its own technologies of inclusion and exclusion and constitutes subjectivities through these technologies'. This perspective of becoming citizens highlights citizenship as a regulatory process involving the production of the quintessential citizen-subject. Viewing citizenship in this manner raises the questions of what is considered to be the quintessential citizen and what are the norms of good and bad citizenship. These questions become critical in relation to the production of children as normative citizen-subjects.

Children's access to knowledge and their participation in the production of knowledge locally and globally is an important social justice issue for children as citizens. It is foundational to children's good health and wellbeing, and to the development of resilience, competency and agency in their lives as children and later as adults. A dualistic approach to knowledge has emerged in many Western societies, represented by the adults' knowledge/children's knowledge binary, which is maintained largely through the perpetuation of discourses of childhood innocence and protection (James and Prout 1990; Jenks 1996; James *et al.* 1998; Dahlberg *et al.* 1999; Davies 1989, 1993). What has been constituted as children's knowledge is constitutive of childhood itself – a period of time in which the child subject is constructed as being primarily apolitical and a proto-citizen. The construction of adults' knowledge and children's knowledge has also been constituted in the public/ private binary relationships of power, in which the public world of politics and economics, and the knowledge thereof, has been separated from the private sphere of the home, family and personal relationships. This binary is also representative and constitutive of broader adult/child and gendered power relationships in Western society. The public world and the experiences and knowledge gained therein has been historically associated with adults, especially men and masculinity, and is considered as having a more critical, prestigious and authoritative role to play in society. Comparatively, the private sphere of the home, family and personal relationships, and the experiences and knowledge gained in these contexts, is constituted in opposition to the public world. The private sphere has been associated with women, femininity and the child. Women's entry and acceptance into the public sphere of politics and economics has thus historically been a battle against humanist discourses which have constructed women as naturally childlike, lacking the *personality,* aggression, authority and physical strength to successfully take up similar roles to men in the public world.

The political philosopher and theorist Hannah Arendt (1961) vehemently opposed children's politicization, believing that they should remain protected in the private space of the family from the politics of the public world that plagues and corrupts the lives of adults (Kulynych 2001). This sentiment echoes the humanist philosophical beliefs of Jean-Jacques Rousseau, who considered children to be naturally saintly, virtuous and unspoilt, and distinctly different from adults in their limited experiences of life (Rousseau 1992 [1762]). An important aspect of this interpretation of the child was sexual innocence, which seemed threatened by participation in the social, economic and political worlds of adults. Judith Levine points out:

> The child's innocence was threatened by the very act of growing up in the world, which entailed partaking in adult rationality and politics ... the child was clean not just of adult political or social corruption, but ignorant specifically of sexual knowledge and desire. Ironically, as children's plight as workers worsened, adults sought to save them from sex.
>
> (Levine 2002: xxviii)

For Rousseau, the child's inherent goodness and purity was vulnerable to corruption through political and cultural practices. *Saving* the child's goodness and innocence from corruption was tantamount to saving humankind and producing the good and worthy citizen-subject.

Sexual citizenship and the child

The relationship of childhood to sexuality is fraught with difficulties, controversies and complexities; it is one openly and officially based on exclusion, with children constituted as requiring protection from sexuality – considered an adults-only domain, dangerous to children. Children's relationship with citizenship is even more problematic in the context of *sexual citizenship*. Children's sexual citizenship is not only seen as problematic in terms of the ways in which childhood is primarily perceived and constructed as a period of innocence and asexuality. There are two other critical points operating here. First, discourses of childhood and innocence are utilized to regulate children's access to knowledge of sexuality and to dismiss children's sexual agency, resulting in the perspective that sexual citizenship is irrelevant to children's lives. Second, discourses of childhood and innocence are mobilized to produce 'good' normative adult citizen-subjects – that is, white, middle-class, heterosexual adult citizens upholding of Christian family morals and values (Berlant 1997; Bell and Binnie 2000; Canaday 2009; Cossman 2007; Richardson 1998; Davies 2012). Within this context, the girl child in particular has traditionally personified innocence and vulnerability to sexual abuse and exploitation from predatory male adults (Australian Bureau of Statistics 2006; Mouzos and Makkai 2004; World Health Organization 2002). As Lauren Berlant, so aptly argues, 'It is in her name [the girl child] as future citizen that state and federal governments have long policed morality around sex and other transgressive representation' (Berlant 2004: 61). Berlant highlights the importance of childhood innocence in this regulation, as well as its gendered nature, in that girls and women are the most vulnerable to sexual violence.

What is sexual citizenship? Within the resurgence of interest in citizenship in the 1980s, and its broad inclusion of political, economic, social, legal and ethical realms, sexual citizenship came to be viewed as a useful concept for articulating and agitating for sexual politics (Bell and Binnie 2000). There are many different forms of sexual citizenship, but as David Bell and Jon Binnie (2000) state, 'all citizenship is sexual citizenship, in that the foundational tenets of being a citizen are all inflected by sexualities' (2000: 10). However, within the mainstream politics and legal foundations of citizenship, there is an inherent representation of the normal and natural citizen as heterosexual (Bell and Binnie 2000; Richardson 1998; Berlant 1997; Cooper 1993; Duggan 1994). Sexual *Others*, such as gays, lesbians and the transgendered, have a different and difficult citizenship status (Bell and Binnie 2000). A range of issues central to critical discussions of sexual citizenship include: a focus on the material construction of the sexual citizen in a consumer market (Evans 1993); the place of love, family and the social in relation to citizenship (Bell and Binnie 2000; Berlant 1997; Cooper 1993; Richardson 1998; Plummer 1995; Weeks 1998); the globalization of sexual identities and politics (Bell and Binnie 2000; Weeks 1998); and the impact of AIDS and the New Right on the reinvestment in (hetero)normative family life (Berlant 1997; Evans 1993). All of these issues have relevance to children, as I argue later in this discussion.

Bell and Binnie (2000) note the ambiguities and tensions associated with the concept of sexual citizenship, arguing 'Many of the current nodes of the political articulation of sexual citizenship are marked by compromise'. In other words, an acceptable sexual citizen-subject position is one that is 'privatized, de-radicalized, de-eroticized and confined in all senses of the word: kept in place, policed, limited' (2000: 2). Citing and critiquing Jeffrey Weeks (1999: 37), who upholds that the 'moment of citizenship' represents the only way that 'difference can [ever] find a proper home', Bell and Binnie point out that there must be some questioning of who defines what a 'proper home' is for the sexual citizen (2000: 3). They believe that rights claims for the sexual citizen operate to reinforce 'phobic arguments that grant sexual rights only on the understanding that they will be kept private: that is invisible' (2000: 5). Davina Cooper (1995) echoes this point, raising concerns around the tensions in public-versus-private narratives of sexuality. She argues that sex is either considered inappropriate to the public or its privacy is seen as in need of protection from encroaching public scrutiny.

Diana Richardson (1998: 90) also argues, 'lesbians and gay men are granted the right to be tolerated as long as they stay within the boundaries of that tolerance, whose borders are maintained through a heterosexist public/ private divide' – that is, gay men and lesbians can be citizens only if they can be *good* citizens and uphold heteronormative values.

In addition to childhood being a technology of power in the production of the normative citizen, sexual citizenship is relevant to children in other important ways. First and foremost, children's inclusion in sexual citizenship discourse is critical to the acknowledgement of children's sexual agency and is a matter of social justice. Sexuality is a component of children's subjectivities: it matters to children and young people, since they actively engage in constructing their sexual identities from very early ages. Providing children with relevant and accurate sexuality education is imperative to supporting them in this process. It is also important that children's voices and perspectives are included in knowledge production and debates around children's sexual subjectivities. For example, debates in Western countries such as Australia, the USA and the UK focusing on the sexualization of children in commercial consumer cultures and the media have tended to dismiss children's sexual agency and limit children's perspectives and contributions to these debates. The views that have dominated reflect an anxiety around children's sexual agency – particularly that of girls – and have tended to call for greater censorship (Papadopoulos 2011; Levin and Kilbourne 2008; Rush and La Nauze 2006; American Psychological Association 2007).

As pointed out previously, sexual citizenship in Western contexts is infused with binary politics of private/public spaces, in which the heteronormative family is considered the normalizing space of the *good citizen-subject*. The *good child*, as the future good citizen, is largely constituted as an innocent, conforming, middle-class subject growing up in the normalizing space of the heteronormative family – and assumed to be a heterosexual subject herself or himself. Within this framework, socio-cultural issues of love and family become contentious when individuals transgress heteronormative boundaries. Regulatory socio-cultural and political practices operating around queer subjects and their families impact children's lives, concepts of self, and perceived future choices (Mayo 2006). The impact of these regulatory practices can be seen in the disturbing level of addiction, suicide and homophobic violence experienced by queer youth (Donaghy 1997; Davies and McInnes in press 2012).

Children's education for sexual citizenship (and citizenship more generally) is framed within heteronormative discourses, and debates around this education are steeped in the politics of private/public spaces. Concerns around what is considered appropriate knowledge for children in regards to sexuality education is followed by the equal concern of who are the appropriate people to impart this information to children – parents or educators (Jackson 1982; Walker and Milton 2006; Robinson and Davies 2008b; Davies and Robinson

2010)? Despite schools playing a role in the sexuality education of children and youth, it is still perceived largely as a private matter best handled by families, especially with younger children. This view prevails particularly in terms of sexuality education around non-heterosexual relationships, which is considered more risky as a result of the deep-seated moral and religious values that surround this topic.

Sexual citizenship is also relevant to children as it relates to the health and wellbeing of subjects, especially in terms of bodies, desire, relationships and identity. Knowledge of bodies and sexuality is important to all children in developing a sense of control and responsibility about who they are as sexual subjects across their life span. Children are sexually active earlier in some cultures compared to others, so appropriate sexual health education early in children's education is imperative in terms of children's awareness of contraception, sexually transmitted infections (STIs), HIV and AIDS. However, this information is important to all children as sexual subjects, regardless of whether they are sexually active or not. There is a critical need for sexuality education in developing countries – particularly in regions such as Africa – to intervene effectively in the spread of STIs, HIV and AIDS in poor communities, particularly amongst children (Bhana 2010; UNESCO 2009). Globally, socio-cultural factors, such as discourses of childhood innocence, can impede positive interventions through children's early education (Bhana 2010). Cultural myths associated with childhood innocence can also increase young children's risk of contracting HIV and AIDS through sexual assault. For example, having sex with a virgin child is believed in some South African cultures to cure AIDS, resulting in an increase of child sexual abuse in some communities (Meel 2003; Groce and Trasi 2004).

Children' s resistance and active citizenry

Many children resist being confined to passive representations of childhood and citizenship, and there are many examples of children's political engagement in actions for social change. Many initiate and participate in a range of schooling activities, community events and demonstrations, as well as take responsibility for organizing local, national and global projects – including research – that aim to make a positive difference in social, environmental, political, economic and educational spaces (Hart 1992; Kellet 2009). In recent years, researchers have challenged the hegemonic position of developmental theory in determining children's capabilities for understanding and building competencies around complex concepts (James and Prout 1990; Alderson 1999, 2000; Hultqvist and Dahlberg 2001). Alderson (2000: 57) argues that Piaget's theories of children's cognitive and moral immaturity, for instance, have perpetuated the belief that children have a false sense of reality and identity and that they cannot distinguish that their view is one among others. Consequently, their accounts of events are considered unreliable.

Alderson's (1999) research with children aged seven to seventeen refutes this claim, indicating that they have higher abilities to deal with spatial, moral and other issues than the works of Piaget suggest. Children operate in discursive frameworks that incorporate understandings of values and they have the ability to make moral choices. Therefore, they need to access a broad range of knowledge relevant to their lives in order to engage effectively and productively in decision-making (Dunn 1995).

The emergence of children's parliaments across the world (e.g. India, Pakistan, UK, Scotland, Nigeria and Zimbabwe) is a demonstration of children making political choices and putting these into action. Children in these contexts work at the community grass-roots level, often with disadvantaged families, to enact change in their own and other children's lives. They also advise governments and other organizations on matters important to children and youth in order to improve their futures. Gay/Straight Alliances in schools are an example of young people engaging in sexual citizenship, working together to counteract homophobia and heterosexism to improve the social and educational experiences of queer youth (Walls *et al.* 2010). Children and youth growing up in same-sex families often support the civil rights of their families, as do their friends living in normative family structures. They do this through marching in political rallies or being involved special public events, such as Gay Pride days or the Lesbian and Gay Mardi Gras, which is an annual event in Sydney, Australia. However, children's agency in these events is often dismissed.

Children's active citizenship – demonstrated through their membership, belonging and active participation in communities – is highlighted in the research of Cindi Katz (2004). Katz' research in a Sudanese village that she calls 'Howa' reveals a very different experience of children's citizenship to that experienced in most Western countries. It is an experience in which children's autonomous participation in everyday life is integral to the socio-cultural, political and economic success of the village community, and the exchange of knowledge across generations is couched in practice that begins in early childhood. Katz (2004: 46) points out that children in this environment grew up 'learning to negotiate and to be accomplished in the multiple political-economic and political-ecologic terrains that composed their everyday environments'. Katz goes on to say that:

> [Children's] routine activities and everyday interactions – both work and play – offered opportunities to acquire, try out, use, master, remagine, and alter environmental knowledge. Each of these material social practices was important for the continuation of village life and helped shape the children's impending adulthood. Work and play were key and critical means through which children reproduced themselves and social and economic life of their village.
>
> (Katz 2004: 60)

Katz' research is important in demonstrating the multiplicities of childhood experiences and the possibilities of children's citizenship, providing counter-discourses to those that prevail in Western contexts. It is not easy to transfer these discourses and experiences across different socio-cultural, political and geographical contexts, but it does open up the possibility of different narratives for children's active citizenship in other locations.

Key points in this chapter

Citizenship and sexual citizenship encompass a broad range of issues relevant to the lives of children and critical to their early education. These concepts are constituted in intimate relationships, issues of identity, knowledge of bodies, sexual health and wellbeing, social responsibility, ethical and respectful relationships, values, and family diversity. All of these issues are concerns of everyday politics in the lives of both adults and children, and understandings of how power and resources are dispersed. Children's relationship to citizenship, especially sexual citizenship, has been fraught with difficulties, and citizenship is almost impossible to articulate into children's lives as a result of adult/child relations of power that constitute who children are as subjects. Children's difficult relationship to citizenship is intensified by the volatile relationship between sexuality and childhood. The controversial and moralistic frameworks in which the relationship between children and sexuality is constructed operate to regulate children's lives and maintain dominant relations of power more broadly in society by helping to uphold the normative citizen-subject. Childhood innocence is often employed to fuel moral panic when heteronormative boundaries are transgressed in both children's and adults' lives, and is also regularly invoked to justify regulatory and protectionist actions – such as the censorship of sexuality from children's domains, including the domain of education. However, openness about sexuality has the potential to be a far more constructive mode of protection. Children's access to sexual knowledge and to open honest discussions around sexuality is critical to their health and wellbeing throughout their lives. It is equally essential for the foundations of a sustainable culture of sexual ethics and respectful relationships to be established in society more broadly (Carmody 2009), and for these to be considered a major foundational component of citizenship education for all.

The discourse of children's rights, for many adults, is often framed by the notion that giving children more power means adults losing their power, potentially resulting in unruly children who do not respond to adult authority. Consequently, children's political roles in society are limited, and children's relegation to the private space of the family prevails. For a few, children's agency is at best negotiated within flexible parent/child relationships, and for most, at worst, it is non-existent within the discourse of enforced dependency on parental decisions made in *the best interests of the child*. As a consequence of the colonized position of children in society, there is a lack of children's voices around issues relevant to their lives, as they have not generally been viewed as competent and worthy sources of knowledge. Children's ideas have traditionally not been viewed as legitimate, and their perspectives have been given little credence beyond tokenism in many cases. Children have predominantly been the objects of research and the focus of narratives developed by adults, rather than subjects with ideas and perspectives to offer to the production of knowledge in society. In recent years, these views have been increasingly challenged (Mason and Fattore, 2005; Kellet 2010, 2009). It is critical that children's voices are included in discussions around difficult knowledge, particularly sexuality. However, discourses of innocence and protection have resulted in strict regulations around including children's voices in research related to sexuality and other areas of difficult knowledge. The limited inclusion of children's voices in research often stems, and rightly so in some instances, from concerns associated with adults' potential exploitation and abuse of children. Those wishing to explore children's knowledge about sexuality have to negotiate an array of social barriers, professional ethical approval procedures and cultural fears that place the researcher under suspicion regarding their motives. These hurdles are important in many respects, but we must find a balance in this process. It is crucial to have a greater understanding of children's perspectives and practices as sexual subjects in order to understand how we can more effectively support children and young people to build their agency, competencies and resilience in this area. We need to know more about how children construct their own sexual subjectivities in the early years of their lives and how they regulate the sexual identities of their peers, as this process does not just begin at puberty but is a part of the everyday lives of very young children. This information is important in providing children with knowledge and support about what they consider is important and relevant to them, as well as providing a greater awareness of how sexuality is experienced in the lives of children.

Chapter 3

Childhood innocence, moral panic and censorship
Constructing the vulnerable child

Introduction

The hegemonic discourse of childhood is intimately linked with the concept of innocence, which is equated with purity, naivety, selflessness, irrationality, and a state of unknowingness, or of being less worldly – all of which characterize the child as vulnerable. The discourse of childhood innocence plays a critical social function in defining and regulating differences between the adult and the child, of which sexual innocence is central. This chapter examines the connection between childhood innocence and children's sexual subjectivities, providing a brief historical overview of the development of this relationship. Sexuality has come to signify danger in the lives of children through discourses of innocence and protection, which have largely dismissed children's sexual subjectivities (Bhana 2008; Davies and Robinson 2010; Egan and Hawkes 2007, 2009, 2010; Renold 2005; Robinson 2008, 2012a). Childhood as emotional capital is infused with sentimentality, romanticism and nostalgia, largely built on this idea of innocence, which is forever lost to adults. The social insistence on maintaining, protecting and prolonging childhood innocence – especially children's sexual innocence – in Western societies has been supported by broad socio-cultural, legal and political practices. This insistence has also been reinforced by discourses of developmentalism, in which understandings of children's physical, emotional and cognitive capabilities are influenced by social values and perceptions of childhood and innocence. The *innocent child* (imbued with race, class and gender) has become a figurehead for the ideals of Western civilization – almost becoming 'a substitute for religion', according to Hugh Cunningham (1991: 152).

It is within this context that transgressions from the cultural norms associated with childhood – particularly those practices contravening childhood innocence – foster broad public and private anxieties in society. Such anxieties often manifest into moral panic as a result of media frenzies that perpetuate community stereotypes, myths and misconceptions about children's vulnerabilities, so increasing community fears. Social conservatives have mobilized the discourse of childhood innocence as a powerful political tool to instil moral panic for political gain. This chapter investigates this moral panic, which has primarily focused on children's relationships with sexuality, and the current international debates on the sexualization of childhood, which have resulted in government and community calls for greater censorship, increased surveillance and regulation of both children's and adult's lives. It is ironic that the increasing regulation and censorship of childhood, in the name of protection, has rendered the child *more* vulnerable.

The origins and transformations of childhood innocence and childhood sexuality: a brief historical overview

The sacred and innocent child in the seventeenth century

The historical representations of children's sexuality can be seen to parallel the changing discourses of childhood and of childhood innocence. However, it is important to note that historical records relating to child sexuality overwhelmingly represent adult and official institutional perspectives, rather than children's accounts of their own experiences. Although the concept of childhood innocence can be traced back to Greek ideas on human perfection, Christian narratives and representations of the sacred child – as epitomized by the baby Jesus – have significantly influenced the discursive constitution of childhood innocence. Within Christian religious discourse, the child is constituted in opposition to the adult, who is positioned as the bearer of original sin in the biblical book of *Genesis*. This narrative of Adam and Eve's fall from grace as a result of giving into temptation and eating the forbidden fruit of knowledge in the Garden of Eden constructs the binary of the exalted and fallen, which is paralleled by the binary of the fallen and knowing adult and the innocent unknowing child. In this religious narrative, the child is viewed as representative of the purity, goodness and innocence that existed prior to the fall of Adam and Eve – a potentially redeemable space made possible through the inherent virtues of the innocent child and the repenting adult (Faulkner 2011).

Childhood innocence has historically been central to Western Christian religious discourse, especially through its significance in Renaissance art during the fourteenth to seventeenth centuries, and in the Romantic literature of the eighteenth century. Jean-Jacques Rousseau's *Emile* (1992 [1762]), an essay on education and on *man*, praised the *natural* innocence and goodness of the child – lost through the process of becoming adult. The linkage of innocence with whiteness has also prevailed, as reflected in *L'Innocence*, a painting by the nineteenth-century French artist, William-Adolphe Bouguereau (1825–1905). The painting features a child – Jesus – who is generally represented as white, angelic and protected from potential evil or harm. In Bouguereau's painting, the Virgin Mary, dressed in a white robe, stands holding a white 'spotless' lamb and the white Christ Child in her arms. The image of the Christ Child with the lamb (the sacrificial lamb – also a religious symbol of innocence) links childhood innocence also with the natural and the nonhuman. In the poem, 'The Little Black Boy' in Romantic poet William Blake's *The Songs of Innocence* (1789), innocence is also linked to colour. Blake locates childhood innocence in the *weakness of whiteness*, which is a central signifier of innocence, as well as privilege and childhood (Bond Stockton 2009: 31). The little black boy narrating the poem remarks:

> My Mother bore me in the southern wild,
> And I am black but O! my soul is white;
> White as an angel is the English child:
> But I am black as if bereav'd of light.

The little black boy is a representation of strength and experience, in which he loses any links to innocence. Kathryn Bond Stockton maintains that in the late twentieth century, 'Experience is still hard to square with innocence, making depictions of streetwise children, who are often neither white nor middle-class, hard to square with "children"'(2009: 33). Children who are perceived as disorderly, disobedient, chaotic and uncontrollable not only lose their status as innocents, but their identity as children, is also questioned. The virtuous and innocent child, tempted by *evil*, has further to fall and is harshly judged. This point also echoes the loss of innocence perceived to be associated with the *knowing child* – the child who has the language to speak about sexuality, considered inappropriate for its age.

Prior to and in the seventeenth century, according to Sterling Fishman (1982), child sexuality seems to have been given little attention, even by religious moralists. However, the need to protect childhood innocence as a reflection of divine purity generally prevailed amongst religious conservatives. The overcrowding of living spaces, especially amongst poorer families, resulted in adults and children sleeping in close proximity in the same rooms. Privacy in relation to sexual activities would have been difficult and it was most likely that children would have viewed adults' sexual behaviours and/or were sexually abused by adults, and/or were engaged in and experimenting with their own sexual activities either alone or with other children (Fishman 1982). It seems that one of the most notable sexual references associated with children during this period was found in the early seventeenth-century diaries of the physician to the young Louis XIII, who showed his genitals at the French Court and invited members to touch his penis (Jackson 2006; Cunningham 1995). Phillipe Aries (1962) argued that adults' enjoyment and encouragement of children's displays of sexuality disappeared in the seventeenth century as the discourse of childhood innocence gained prominence, and religious moral entrepreneurs of the time began to argue for increased modesty and greater surveillance and control of children's behaviour.

Salvaging the child in the eighteenth century

With the changing social, political and economic landscapes arising from the Industrial Revolution in the eighteenth and nineteenth centuries – especially the rise of capitalism and of middle class ideologies – the nature and role of the family in Western societies began to change to meet the social and economic needs of the time. Along with changes in the family, understandings of childhood also began to transform to meet the requirements of these broad socio-cultural shifts. The discourse of childhood innocence took on additional meanings, and became imbued with the middle class morals, values and privileges of the time. The modern nuclear family emerged, as large extended working class families fragmented into more mobile units consisting of immediate family members, who could be relocated easily to smaller homes in industrial cities in the search for work. Whilst there was increasing poverty amongst the working classes, the middle classes prospered, moving into new suburbs, establishing larger and more comfortable homes, and experiencing more leisure time. With this prosperity, children from middle-class families became more protected as their roles became increasingly differentiated from those of the adult. They became increasingly relegated to the privacy of the home, under the expected care, surveillance and protection of parents and other family members. Patricia Holland (2006: 8) comments, '"Childhood" was part of a more comfortable lifestyle based on an ideal of domesticity and privacy'.

The introduction of compulsory public education provided a means to fulfil industrial capitalism's demand for a more literate population, but it was also a means to control and regulate working-class children – who were perceived as unruly – and to school them in Christian moral and middle-class values. With the creation of age-segregated schools came an intensification of the separation between children and adults, and an increased focus on protecting children. It was during this time that certain knowledge, such as sexuality, became designated as for adults only. Upper-class girls, schooled in Christian moral values so as to become genteel society women, were expected to represent female innocence and virtue. Upper-class boys, on the other hand, according to Stevi Jackson, were chosen for preferential treatment: they were trained as 'the first specialized entrepreneurs in a society more and more centred on trade and manufacture' (Jackson 1982: 39). Such practices strengthened gender differences and reinscribed male privilege and power, especially within public spaces.

During the Victorian era in the USA, the United Kingdom and Europe, ruling-class gentlemen, empowered through wealth and privilege, frequently exploited working-class girls for their sexual satisfaction – a practice which was viewed as a class right (Wood 2005). Childhood innocence, equated with compliance and virginity in pre-pubescent girls, was highly sought-after – there was also less chance of contracting sexually transmitted diseases and of girls falling pregnant (Wood 2005). Sharon Wood, a US historian, claims it was considered that 'girls who played in the streets and alleys or were not shocked by sexual overtures made themselves fair game' (2005: 136). This comment highlights how girls were often blamed for their sexual exploitation, and were seen as failing to adequately protect themselves by *appropriate* responses or by staying indoors. Although innocence was generally considered an innate trait in children – especially amongst conservative religious communities – some refused to acknowledge it as universal among children, based on the perceived natural immorality of working girls. Woods points out that 'Even some Evangelicals rejected the idea of innate childhood innocence, assuming little girls could be depraved and degraded by nature' (2005: 136). These traditional gender and class-based assumed rights to exploit children's sexuality gradually began to clash with a growing move to protect children from mistreatment of all kinds.

The exploitation of children from poor families or institutionalized backgrounds in the workforce – where they were often subjected to physical abuse and long working hours in unhealthy and dangerous conditions – was central to the establishment of child protection laws in the mid-nineteenth century in the USA, the UK and Europe. In the USA, severe abuse suffered by the young Mary Ellen Connolly in New York in 1874 at the hands of her foster parents resulted in media outcry and public outrage (Shelman and Lazoritz 2005). Mary's abuse came to the attention of a Methodist missionary who tried to have the child taken from the foster parents. It was only when Henry Bergh, the founder of the American Society for the Prevention of Cruelty to Animals (ASPCA, founded 1866), and Elbridge Gerry, the ASPCA's legal counsel (who were also leading the campaign against cruelty to children more generally), became major advocates for Mary Ellen's case that the child was successfully removed from her foster parents (Beatty and Grant 2010). The case resulted in social policy reforms associated with child protection and the formation of the New York Society for the Prevention of Cruelty to Children (NYSPCC). Prior to this case, cruelty to animals had attracted greater public concern and legal policy recognition than the cruelty experienced by children, demonstrating the increasing influence of social reformers focusing on the plight of children at this point in time. Modern child protection legislation is considered to have originated from laws instigated by the NYSPCC, which significantly shaped the regulation of child labour, censorship around children's access to drugs, alcohol, weapons and what was perceived as obscene material, and regulating what were considered inappropriate leisure and living spaces for children (e.g. children were prevented from living in houses of prostitution). This legislation not only constituted children as requiring special state intervention in order to protect them from cruelty, but it equally considered that children (especially working-class children) required special attention and protection for the sake of their moral development, a perspective influenced by Christian and conservative values. The construction of children as different from adults was strengthened, and the boundaries between what it meant to be an adult and a child were legally reinforced. Innocence was articulated as the distinguishing characteristic on which to ideologically build and maintain the differences between adults and children.

Childhood innocence and the regulation of children's sexuality in the nineteenth century

The introduction of age-of-consent laws in the USA and UK in the latter years of the nineteenth century aimed to not only protect young children's innocence through intervening in their sexual exploitation, but also to curb the perceived immorality associated with sexual relations between adults and children across all social classes. Censorship of sexuality more generally was both a public and private affair in the Victorian era. Foucault (1978) in the *History of Sexuality* argues that children became critical in the repression and regulation of sexuality in constructions of and the policing of sexual deviancy, and in morality more generally during this time – a role that is still attached to the child today. The history of sexuality in Western society since the seventeenth century, according to Foucault, has been a process of turning sex into discourse – a process of power in which sexuality in Victorian Puritanism became regulated and repressed, whilst simultaneously taking on an element of titillation and eroticism. During the eighteenth century, theological and medical moralists viewed child sexuality – epitomized largely through masturbation – as sinful, physically injurious and as a pathological problem (Fishman 1982). This belief intensified during the Victorian era; it was considered a social evil impacting not just on the individual but also on the wellbeing of society more generally, necessitating strict measures to eradicate the behaviour.

In secondary schooling during this period, the regulation of sexuality amongst young people was a constant preoccupation of authorities who were on perpetual alert. As Foucault pointed out:

> [T]he space for classes, the shape of the tables, the planning of the recreation lessons, the distribution of the dormitories (with or without partitions, with or without curtains), the rules for monitoring bedtime and sleep periods – all this referred, in the most prolix manner, to sexuality of children.
>
> (Foucault 1978: 28)

The sexuality of the schoolboy became a public problem and was subjected to major surveillance and institutional intervention. Prolonged masturbation in childhood was believed by some medical professionals to lead to a weakening of the intellect of the individual over time, and to effeminacy and degeneracy in their offspring (Kociumbas 1997). Madness and suicide were also risks of spermatorrhoea, which is the involuntary discharge of semen without orgasm. Although there was a focus on boys' masturbation, girls were also warned not to engage in this risky behaviour, as it was believed to have critical medical consequences for them also, including nervous and uterine diseases, menstruation problems, sterility, headaches, flatulence and colic (Kociumbas 1997). Intervening in masturbation, particularly that of males, was central to medical campaigns, and restraining devices and surgical interventions were developed and utilized to curb this behaviour (Wolfenstein 1998). The medical theory of depleted nervous energy which emerged during the nineteenth century resulted in semen being considered a vital fluid of the nervous system, and many new physical and mental health conditions in males began to be attributed to self-abuse through the practice of masturbation (Kociumbas 1997). The perceived precocious interest in sexuality of some children was linked to mothers introducing learning through reading too early in childhood. Such solitary and sedentary behaviours were believed to prematurely excite the brain, leading to physical feebleness, stupidity, spinal damage and even death. Circumcision was advised if the child failed to stop its masturbatory habits, as it was perceived to inhibit excitability (Kociumbas 1997).

At the end of the nineteenth century and the beginning of the twentieth century, new specialized knowledge of childhood, framed within scientific discourses such as paediatrics and developmental psychology, constituted childhood as a particular state of being separate from adulthood. A range of new organizations and institutions were set up with children's welfare as the primary business, aligning with the discourse of ideal domesticity propagated through the middle classes (Zelizer 1985; Hendrick 1990; Thorne 2009). The medicalization of childhood resulted in the invention of many new childhood diseases, including premature sexuality (Kociumbas 1997). Defining and regulating what constituted normative sexuality in children and diverting non-normative forms became the focus of intervention. The construction of heterosexual monogamy sanctified through marriage became the norm through which all other sexualities were scrutinized and considered peripheral and perverse, including children's sexuality. Medico-sexual regimes defined and regulated normal sexuality. Foucault's (1978) history of this period highlights how the surveillance of children's masturbation led to its conceptualization and enforcement as a cultural taboo that required constant surveillance and policing by those in authority. The child's wellbeing was linked to the health of the nation and the construction of the good normative citizen-subject. Uncontrolled child sexuality was not only considered a threat to childhood and childhood innocence, but also to the social fabric of nineteenth-century middle-class society, constituted around family relationships and middle-class Christian morality.

During this time, childhood innocence became even more strongly equated with a denial of children's sexuality, with the good/bad child constituted in one's adherence to or rejection of Victorian Christian morality – those who did or did not engage in impure sexual thoughts or actions. The romantic image of childhood was reinforced to encompass white, Christian middle-class ideals, with children of the poor constructed as corrupted savages and heathens who were constituted as a threat to the welfare of the nation and as the imagined sexualized Other (Cunningham 1991; Jackson 2006). According to Foucault, the pedagogization of children's sexuality, in which children's sexual potential – considered precious and natural on the one hand, and contrary to nature, perilous and dangerous on the other – was viewed as requiring constant intervention from parents, families, educators, doctors and psychologists, in order to prevent the threat it was perceived to pose to the physical and moral development of the individual, as well as the 'collective dangers' it posed to society (Foucault 1978: 104). Continuing well into the twenty-first century, this pedagogization of children's sexuality has also involved the regulation and policing of children's access to knowledge of sex and sexuality.

Barrie Thorne (2009) argues that institutionally, childhood is formulated at the intersections of states, markets and family, and that throughout Western countries during this time these realms were being dramatically reconfigured. Viviana Zelizer (1985) has described this transformation as a movement from 'the economically useful child', who contributed to family labour and wages, to the 'economically useless, but emotionally priceless child', who has been made sacrosanct and removed from paid labour into the more protected worlds of families and schools. Harry Hendrick (1990) describes this process as children being removed from 'socially significant activity'. The process of consolidating and maintaining the differentiation between adults and children has continued at the forefront of public and private policy and practices to current times. The constitution of childhood innocence as the defining discourse of this differentiation has also prevailed and intensified. Ruth Benedict, an anthropologist during the 1930s in the USA, observed the extremities to which societies went to emphasize the differences between the child and the adult, noting that the child was to 'be protected from the ugly facts of life', including sexuality (Benedict 1938: 162).

The sexual/asexual child and discourses of protection in the twentieth and twenty-first century

During the twentieth century, the repression and denial of children's sexuality has continued alongside a new discourse of children's sexuality introduced primarily through the works of Sigmund Freud, particularly his *Three Essays on the Theory of Sexuality* (1976 [1905]). Sigmund Freud challenged the comfortable ideas of childhood innocence, arguing that sexuality was not absent or dormant in childhood, but rather that children had an active sexuality that needed to be expressed. Freud claimed that children's initial feelings that connected them to the world (especially to the mother) were sexual in nature. For Freud, childhood was centrally constructed around a flexible sexuality, a polymorphous perversity (Freud 1976 [1905]). That is, before understanding social norms, children find erotic pleasure and sexual gratification in any part of the body – behaviours which are considered perverse in adults. Once children learn social norms, they suppress these behaviours, which then become repressed (Freud 1976 [1905]). Freud argued that the suppression of childhood sexuality was the *cause* of adult neurosis, including sexual deviancy. A healthy mature heterosexual adult, according to Freud, experienced a *normal* – that is, unsuppressed – psycho-sexual development in infancy.

In the post-Freudian period of the 1970s and 1980s, in Western countries such as Australia, the Unuited Kingdom, Canada and the USA, there has been a re-evaluation of children's sexuality. This has largely resulted in the erasure of children's sexual subjectivities and sexual agency, and the constitution of sexuality as a danger to children (Angelides 2004; Robinson 2005a). Steven Angelides (2004) maintains that this re-evaluation was largely a result of the recognition of child sexual abuse as a widespread social phenomenon, and its reconceptualization from a practice in which the victims were often blamed for the behaviour, to a practice that is now largely viewed as an abuse of powerless children by powerful male adults or youth. In this context, children's vulnerability is linked to their lack of knowledge of sexual behaviours and to their limited access to power. All children's sexual encounters, even those with other children, have consequently been largely constituted as non-consensual. Angelides argues:

> [A]lthough reinterpreting the issue of power and its relationship to knowledge was a critical way for feminists to challenge our society's tendency to blame the child victim, the question and the discourse of child sexuality were unfortunate casualties of this process.
>
> (Angelides 2004: 153)

The discourse of childhood innocence regulates children's sexuality through its desexualization of the child subject, and the discourse of protection has largely supported this process (Angelides 2004; Renold 2005; Robinson 2005a; Egan and Hawkes 2009).

The discourse of protection has become increasingly powerful since the mid-nineteenth century (Egan and Hawkes 2009). Today, the discourses of childhood innocence and protection play a mutually reinforcing role in constituting and regulating political and legal policies, adult/child relationships, parenting practices, broader socio-cultural practices, censorship and children's access to knowledge in Western countries – and all of this under the perception of this being in the best interests of the child. It is critical that there are broad social and community policies and practices which operate to protect children from harm and vulnerability – particularly abuse, neglect and exploitation. How a society achieves this without disempowering children or negating their agency and sexual subjectivity, or using children to demonize and regulate others, must be the central aim of protective policies and practices (Egan and Hawkes 2009). The very methods often used in the name of protection contribute to children's despair, lack of competency and, ultimately, to their increased vulnerability (Corteen and Scraton 1997; Kitzinger 1990; Plummer 1990). The critical irony for children is that 'To be agents in one's own life one must cast off innocence' (Faulkner 2011: 8).

Stranger danger and moral panic

The relationship between childhood and sexuality has become increasingly constructed as one inherently fraught with danger. Since the 1960s in Western countries, based on an increasing awareness of the prevalence of child sexual abuse, public and private anxieties have intensified into moral panic about 'stranger danger' and children's public safety from the paedophile (Riggs 2011). Angela McRobbie and Sarah Thornton point out that moral panics act on behalf of the dominant social order, arguing:

> They are a means of orchestrating consent by actively intervening in the space of public opinion and social consciousness through the use of highly emotive and rhetorical language which has the effect of requiring that 'something be done about it'.
>
> (McRobbie and Thornton 1995: 562)

Public and private anxieties and moral panic around stranger danger have been fuelled by highly emotive and rhetorical language, primarily through mythical representations of the paedophile as an ever-present threat to children's safety and by political rhetoric that calls for parents to be ever-vigilant in watching and protecting their children, especially in public spaces (Levine 2002). The emotional capital invested in the child provides fertile ground in which to manifest social anxiety and moral panic (Irvine 2006).

These fears and anxieties often result in calls for greater regulation and surveillance, not just of children but also of parents. An Australian Research Council for Educational Research study conducted with 500 parents in the southern-eastern state of Victoria found that only 40 per cent of city parents thought it safe for their primary-school-aged children to go to school alone, with stranger danger and road safety cited as the main deterrents for the remainder (Arlington and Stevenson 2012). Despite parents' mixed opinions on this issue, those who do not adhere to dominant socially-sanctioned parenting conventions can find themselves targets of official surveillance. In Australia, for example, there have been incidents where parents have been cautioned by police, have had police reports filed against their names, and have been threatened to be reported to the Department of Community Services for allowing their school-aged children to walk to the local shops (exemplified by the case of a seven-year-old Sydney boy walking on a familiar route to the shops, which were 400 metres from his home) or to take public transport to music lessons alone (in this case, a 10-year-old girl) (Arlington and Stevenson 2012). The parents in these incidents believed that their children were mature enough to have this independence, but were also concerned about being labelled *irresponsible* parents (Arlington and Stevenson 2012) not just by authorities, but also by other parents.

Judith Levine points out that cases of molestation, abduction and murder of children by strangers are rare and are not increasing (Levine 2002: 24). The Australian Institute of Family Studies' Australian Centre for the Study of Sexual Assault conducted a study in 2002–3 with 6,677 women aged 18–69 years (Fergus and Keel 2005). The study found that 18 per cent had experienced sexual violence before the age of 16. Of these women, 2 per cent had experienced abuse by a parent (most frequently by the father) and 16 per cent by someone other than a parent. Of the abuse experienced by those other than a parent: 20 per cent was by a friend or friend of the family; 17 per cent by acquaintances or neighbours; 13 per cent was by someone else known; uncles, brothers, grandfathers, cousins, other relatives and other children/students comprised the greatest percentage at 37 per cent (with less than 10 per cent for each); and 13 per cent were strangers (Mouzos and Makkai 2004, cited in Fergus and Keel 2005). In this research, just under 80 per cent of the children who were abused knew the perpetrator. This reflects the findings of earlier studies, which state that relatives were the abusers in almost half of the child sexual abuse cases examined (Fleming 1997). The National Children's Home (1992, cited in Masson 1995) has estimated between one-quarter and one-third of child sexual abuse cases in the UK are perpetrated by a child or young person (Vizard *et al.* 1995). These figures reinforce and support Levine's (2002) findings that the stark reality is that paedophile strangers are not the main threat to children's wellbeing and safety. Seen in this light, the motivations behind the vigour with which the discourse of stranger danger has been taken up need to be publicly scrutinized. Ironically, stranger danger is a more comfortable discourse for many adults than acknowledging that children are more frequently abused by someone they know and trust, such as a parent or other close relative, neighbour, teacher or family friend. The stranger/paedophile (as constituted through the media) becomes the political scapegoat for all child sexual abuse, taking the focus off the abuse perpetrated by the average person (including the parent) in the family home or local neighbourhood. The family is critical to the foundation of social organization and of children's socialization – the paedophile stranger becomes a useful political tool to shift public sentiment away from scrutinizing the family unit and society more generally.

In recent years, anxieties have extended into fears associated with children's perceived vulnerabilities to strangers in the *safety* of the family home, who target children through chat rooms and social networking sites. Also, children's access to knowledge through television, the Internet, and other mobile communication technologies has resulted in an increased state of anxiety about the type of information that children are now privy to through these means. Parents fear children accessing pornography or other information about sexuality which has been deemed age-inappropriate. This anxiety is also related to the lack of control felt by many parents, as part of a generation who seem to be being left behind in terms of the technological advancements and new media that are so much part of the everyday lives of their children. Children's access to new media technologies has also raised additional anxieties about children's increased vulnerabilities to harassment and about their welfare more generally, in the face of an increasing use of popular social networking sites and mobile phones by children and youth as a means to sexually harass peers and others.

Official and unofficial regulation of the Internet, exemplified by the introduction of commercial Internet filters such as *Net Nanny*, aim to control children's time on the Internet, to limit their access to age-inappropriate knowledge (e.g. blocking pornography, *profane* words and information associated with hate speech and other particular words, such as 'adult', 'alcohol', 'tobacco', 'gambling', 'sex', 'sexuality' and many more) and to reveal children's online activities by alerting parents, providing them with reports on children's instant messaging and chat room activities, and allowing them easy access to their children's networking activities on sites such as Facebook, Twitter, Flickr, YouTube and Bebo. Similar Internet filters have been placed on computers in schools to control and limit children's access to certain knowledge in those contexts. This is often much to the frustration of many children and young people, who perceive that their education and research is generally curbed by extreme interpretations of inappropriate knowledge by school authorities, whom they consider overly cautious and untrusting of students (Robinson and Davies 2008b). This censorship and regulation, perceived by parents and authorities as critical to children's and young people's safety, often leads to conflicts between parents and children, and school authorities and students. Children and young people often seek information on the Internet that they cannot get from other sources, including from talking with their parents. Sexuality education is a good example of this, especially with regards to sexual orientation. Many young people who are dealing with uncertainties about their sexual orientation often only have the Internet for support. There are some parents who feel uncomfortable at *prying* into their children's personal communications (often done without their child's consent or awareness) but feel that they have no choice – these actions often cause further rifts between the parent and the child or young person.

Childhood innocence and moral panic as political strategy

In Western countries, moral panic is used as a political strategy by conservative governments and social moralists for maintaining the hegemony of the values and practices of dominant groups in society. Sean Hier's (2003) work on moral panic provides a useful framework for understanding this phenomenon as a political strategy of social ordering in societies that are being challenged and changed through processes of globalization, and through increasing awareness and articulation of identity politics. In his discussion of the heightened sense of moral panic in a risk-conscious society – commonly associated with the uncertainties of late modernity – Hier points out that there has been a 'process of convergence, whereby discourses of risk have conjoined with discourses containing a strong moral dimension' (2003: 4). 'Throughout modernity', he argues, 'the quest to establish a sense of existential security – such as community – has come at the expense of the de-legitimation of the Other: the criminalized, gendered or stigmatized' (2003: 15). Innocence and childhood innocence have been utilized in conjunction with protectionist racist discourses, as well as sexist, classist and homophobic discourses, to define and regulate Others – for example, women, Aboriginal peoples, refugees and queer subjects (Kincaid 1992; Faulkner 2011). An example of public and private anxieties manifesting in moral panic can be seen in reactions to the increasing number of refugees arriving by boat to Australia. Racist sentiment has underpinned the representation of refugees, who are perceived as 'selfish' and 'immoral' parents who risk the lives of 'innocent' and 'helpless' children for their own benefit. Tapping into this emotional capital has never been more effective than when it was used in the 'children overboard' *Tampa* affair by the conservative Howard government prior to the 2001 Australian federal election, in order to win a third term in office. Racist rhetoric was captured in altered images that depicted asylum seekers supposedly throwing their children overboard from their decrepit and leaking boat into the sea. Despite the fact that the public became aware that the images had been altered by some unknown entity to give a distorted view of the facts, media and political spin-doctoring had already constituted the refugees as immoral, inhumane 'queue jumpers' – a discourse of asylum seekers that has remained solid for more than a decade, as a result of continued moral panic fed by the media and current government policy and rhetoric.

Non-heternormative or queer subjects also fit into the context of the stigmatized Other in Hier's framework, through their mythical constitution as a threat to security and the community – especially to the child. These 'enemy stereotypes' or 'folk devils' (Cohen 1972) originate from 'everyday cultural stereotypes of the stranger' (Hier 2003: 17). The queer subject is readily couched in stereotypical understandings of the stranger, often historically centralized in public and private anxieties associated with *stranger danger*, as pointed out earlier. Myths serve to distance the queer subject from normative life narratives, instilling fears of their aims to undermine the *natural* moral and social order inherent in heterosexual relationships. With regards to the heightened sense of risk-consciousness, insecurity and moral judgment aligned with the process of othering the stranger, Hier concludes that 'as anxieties endemic to the risk society converge with anxieties contained at the level of community, we should expect a proliferation of moral panics as *an ordering practice in late modernity*' (2003: 19).

A proliferation of social anxiety and moral panic has historically been associated with children and sexuality, which has carried through to contemporary times (Egan and Hawkes 2008; Evans 1993). Janice Irvine (2006: 82), viewing moral panic as 'recursive conflicts over sexual issues', highlights the importance of emotions associated with panics. Irvine argues that it is critical to understand how moral entrepreneurs utilize panic to strategically manipulate community emotions in order to 'erode sexual rights' (2006: 86). The homosexual or queer subject has traditionally been at the centre of moral panic in relation to children through the mythical constitution of these subjects as either the paedophile, or recruiters of young children into a perceived lifestyle of hyper-sexuality, sexual abnormality and depravity. This social anxiety has impacted early childhood education in particular, with widespread suspicion of male workers as potential peadophiles, regardless of their sexual orientation. Very few men consider training or employment as early childhood teachers due to these myths, and those already employed in the field often encounter the suspicion of parents and other colleagues (Silin 1997; King 1997).

In 2007, moral panic arose in Poland in association with the BBC children's television program *Teletubbies*, sparked by comments made by Ewa Sowinska, the conservative Polish government-appointed children's rights watchdog (Robinson 2008). Sowinska, after viewing the program, remarked: 'I noticed that [Tinky Winky] has a lady's purse, but he's a boy ... At first I thought the purse would be a burden for this Teletubby ... Later I learned that this may have a homosexual undertone' (Reuters and Jensen 2007). Sowinska's reaction to the 'burden' of carrying a handbag soon escalated into homophobic fear when Tinky Winky was perceived to be a boy carrying a red handbag. National concern erupted in Poland in line with the perception that the program promoted the homosexual lifestyle to children. In this incident, the government instigated moral panic, primarily to try and gain widespread acceptance for the government's political agenda of sexual cleansing through a series of initiatives aimed at outlawing the promotion of homosexuality amongst Polish children and the dismissal of gays' and lesbians' civil liberties. The Polish Education Minister at the time, Roman Giertych, proposed legislation enabling the sacking of teachers who promoted the homosexual lifestyle in schools. This was not the first time that the Teletubby Tinky Winky had become the target of conservative, right-wing political and religious attacks. In the USA, the late Reverend Jerry Falwell also attacked the Teletubby character. Tinky Winky has been accused of being a gay icon, represented by his purple colour, and the fact that he carries a red purse and has a triangle shaped antenna, which are all viewed as codes for signifying gay pride or gay subjectivity. Public outcry associated with children's television characters is not new. Bert and Ernie from *Sesame Street*, and their famous late-1940s predecessors, *Noddy and Big Ears*, were also denounced as being gay and viewed as potentially influencing young children's future sexualities (Evans 1993). Nachman Ben-Yahuda (2009) states that 'moral panics are about struggles for moral hegemony over interpretation of the legitimacy (or not) of prevailing social arrangements and material interests. And, as well as being local, today they may also be cross-national or even global' (2009: 3).

Similar moral panics erupted in Australia during the period 2004–6 in relation to children's television and early education (Taylor 2007; Robinson 2008). The first incident was the airing of an episode of *Play School*, a long-time popular Australian Broadcasting Commission (ABC) children's television program, which momentarily (approximately 30 seconds) featured two mothers taking their child and her friend to an amusement park. This was in fact the second time that this particular episode went to air; the first airing received minimal public comment. The momentary segment, known as 'Through the window', consisted of the dialogue: 'I'm Brenna. That's me in the blue. My mums are taking me and my friend Merryn to an amusement park'. This statement, said by the young girl, was played over images of her two mums smiling and waving. This segment of the show usually explores families from different ethnic, social and religious backgrounds. The Australian Prime Minister at the time, John Howard, criticized the ABC for 'running an agenda in a children's program'. The second and third incidents were associated with conservative politicians and the media questioning the use of certain educational resources that were being used with young children in local-government-funded early childhood centres, and in some cases, the use of taxpayers' money to fund the development of the resources. The resources in question included *Learn to Include* (Harding 2006) and *We're Here: A Resource For Child Care Workers* (The Lesbian Parents' Play Group 2001), which incorporated representations of same-sex families developed to increase young children's awareness of family diversity and to counteract the homophobia and heteronormativity that begins early in children's lives (see Chapter 5). These particular moral panics were politically instigated, not just to reassert the hegemony of childhood innocence, but to also reaffirm the social order and conservative heteronormative morals and values as the foundations for citizenship and marriage, at a time when they were perceived to be under threat. In this and the other examples discussed above, discourses of childhood innocence and the homosexual as 'folk devil' were mobilized by conservative, right-wing politicians and moral entrepreneurs to strategically activate a moral panic to counteract the growing support in and outside the queer community for legislative reforms and equal citizenship rights, especially in relation to legal recognition of same-sex marriage (Irvine 2006; Robinson, 2008; Taylor 2007).

In 2012, the Malaysian Home Ministry banned the selling of the classic sex education book, *Where Did I Come From?* by Peter Mayle, first published in 1973 (Chong 2012). This heteronormative book teaches children about love, relationships, sex and pregnancy. The ban came in response to a public outcry by conservatives about the book's graphic description of sex, the pictures of nude male and female bodies, and the use of proper names for anatomical parts. Malaysian officials expressed concerns that the book could harm the morals of the community, ultimately agreeing with the complaints that the 'degree of obscenity inside the book was too much' (cited in Chong 2012). They also stated that the book may be considered suitable for children in Mayle's homeland, but it was not suitable in Malaysia. The book was considered to be in violation of Malaysian penal codes dealing with the distribution and sales of pornographic materials (Chong 2012). In this case, the book depicts only the very basic mechanics of heterosexual intercourse and reproduction, ostensibly posing far less threat to established social orders than representations of queer relationships. Nonetheless, the fact that even this bare minimum of information has so recently been deemed subversive and developmentally inappropriate for children provides a clear example of the increasing regulation surrounding children's sexuality education, not just in the West but globally.

Children are used as the prime instigators and beneficiaries of the social, political and economic policies and reforms that politicians and conservatives espouse. Henry Giroux (2000: 41) points out that 'Lacking opportunities to vote, mobilize, or register their opinions, young children become an easy target and referent in discussions of moral uplift and social legitimation. They also become pawns and victims'. Strategically, politicians and moral entrepreneurs position themselves as protectors of childhood innocence through the rhetoric of a disappearing childhood to ignite moral panic. Innocence erases the complexities of childhood as well as the differences that children experience in childhood, but also 'offers an excuse for adults to evade responsibility for how children are firmly connected to and shaped by the social and cultural institutions run largely by adults' (Giroux 2000: 40). Giroux makes the point that welfare reforms and policies in the USA have impacted severely on poor families and their children. This has included cuts to support for unemployment and children with disabilities, harsh compliance measures, low wages and inadequate child care. Giroux argues:

> The language of innocence suggests a concern for all children but often ignores or disparages the conditions under which many of them are forced to live, especially those who are generally excluded because of race or class for the privileging and protective invocation of innocence.
>
> (Giroux 2000: 41)

This is a point reiterated in Deevia Bhana's (2008, 2009) research into HIV and AIDS education in South Africa. This research focuses on how discourses of childhood innocence impact on HIV and AIDS education in primary schools, highlighting the political nature of this type of education in South Africa. Bhana argues that childhood innocence is constituted as white and middle-class through teacher attitudes and pedagogical practices. As HIV and AIDS is most prevalent amongst black communities in South Africa (as a result of structural and material inequalities stemming from years of colonialist rule and apartheid), HIV and AIDS takes on a racialized and class-based dimension, and is perceived by the dominant class as the disease of the Other. This perception has influenced the pedagogical practices of some teachers in South Africa, who perceive HIV and AIDS education to be more appropriate for black children. Bhana (2008) argues that this discourse of HIV and AIDS legitimizes the lack of education about sexuality and HIV and AIDS with white children, and reinforces the constitution of childhood innocence as white and middle-class.

The sexualization of childhood: the disappearance of childhood?

Public and private anxieties about children in Western countries such as the USA, the UK and Australia in recent years have increasingly focused on concerns around the 'disappearance of childhood' (Postman 1982). These anxieties are reflected in current international debates about the sexualization of children through different mediums such as advertising and television (e.g. music video programmes), and children's unregulated and accidental access to knowledge considered age-inappropriate on the Internet (Rush and La Nauze 2006; Bailey 2011; Papadopoulous 2011). As argued by Danielle Egan and Gail Hawkes (2008: 293), such debates are not new, but are reflective of the anxieties and panic of earlier social movements associated with 'potentially corrupting forces' in the lives and sexuality of children. They provide the examples of urbanization, immorality, immigration and fiction (e.g. comic books) to illustrate their point. The 'epistemological assumptions guiding the debate on sexualization in Australia', they argue, 'parallels the alarm that spurred the social purity movement at the turn of the century in the Anglophone west' (Egan and Hawkes 2008: 293). Fears, particularly in these contemporary debates, have been generally equated with what is perceived by some as an erosion of the socio-cultural *differences* between adults and children (Rush and La Nauze 2006). Childhood innocence, especially children's sexual innocence, is the central socio-culturally-constituted difference between adults and children, and it is fears of childhood sexuality and the loss of innocence that are paramount in these anxieties (Egan and Hawkes 2008; Lumby and Albury 2010; Taylor 2010; Renold and Ringrose 2011). Central to many of these narratives is a dismissal of children's sexual subjectivities, desires and agency, and a reiteration of gendered discourses that echo patriarchal and moralistic values, and double standards associated with young girls' sexualities in particular (Egan and Hawkes 2008; Tolman 2002; Hartley and Lumby 2003; Lumby and Albury 2008; Albury and Lumby 2010). As pointed out by Emma Renold and Jessica Ringrose, much that is written about these issues that

> draw attention to the problematic corporate practices that sexualize girlhood, [and] do so in ways that enable commentators to draw moral boundaries around (hetero)normative and age-appropriate notions of girlhood sexuality, isolating and regulating what is acceptable and unacceptable desire and practice.
>
> (Renold and Ringrose 2011: 390)

This point is reiterated by Catharine Lumby and Kath Albury (2008) who argue that these debates on the sexualization of children in the media tend to see the impacts on children – girls in particular – in a monolithic manner, dismissing the pleasures they 'take from media which are consciously irreverent and subversive of adult ideas of what they should be doing and thinking' (2008: 82).

Childhood innocence is used to foster social anxieties and moral panic, which in turn are aimed at reinstating a particular discourse of childhood, of the girl child, and of adult/child relationships which are being challenged by socio-cultural changes in post-feminist and neo-liberalist societies (Currie *et al.* 2009; Jackson and Westrupp 2010; Ringrose 2011). This international moral panic perpetuates the fears that young girls' sexual subjectivities are fixed in one of either two binary categories – the knowing-hypersexual-inappropriate child and the innocent-asexual-developmentally-appropriate child (Renold and Ringrose 2011). The moral panic is intensified when three, four and five-year-olds are viewed to be also playing out the knowing-hypersexual-inappropriate child of this culturally constructed binary, through their interaction with and consumption of popular culture and media. Adult-centric (and often moralistic and classist) readings and dismissal of children and young people's pleasure and desire, based on hegemonic discourses of childhood, undermine the complexities of childhood, especially children's gendered and sexual subjectivities, cultures and agency.

Numerous official reports and other literature on the sexualization of childhood (Rush and La Nauze 2006; Levin and Kilbourne 2008; Olfman 2009; American Psychological Association 2010; Bailey 2011; Papadopoulous 2011) predominantly conceptualize the sexualization of children in the media, advertising and popular culture as an abuse of children, a source of children's premature sexualization, and a contravention of public norms and morality. Much of this literature (e.g. Rush and La Nauze 2006; Papadopoulous 2011) makes direct cause-and-effect links between the sexualization of children and phenomena such as: children's engagement in violence; eating disorders arising from unrealistic body images deemed as sexy; engagement in unethical sexual behaviours (e.g. boys' engagement in sexual harassment); potential psychological disorders in children (though a recognition of the lack of research in this latter area is acknowledged in some cases); sexual behaviour at an earlier age; and the 'grooming' of children by paedophiles. These claims are problematic as they are based on limited research, make broad generalizations about all children, and do not include an analysis of the positive and pleasurable relationship that children have with popular culture and media. Children's views and voices are rarely included, if at all, in these current debates, despite being their central focus of concern. This omission perpetuates the misconception that children do not have something to offer, that they are unable to provide insights into their experiences and how they feel – especially about sexuality – and that children are passive victims, duped by media, advertising and popular culture. Research conducted by David Buckingham and Sarah Bragg (2004) in the UK, which focused on the impact of viewing sexual imagery in the media on young people (9–17 years old), whether intentional or not, found that this experience was not perceived by children or young people as encouraging them to have sex prematurely. Young people also indicated that the media was an important alternative source of information about sexuality, often considered more useful than other sources in their lives, such as schooling, or even parents.

The majority of the literature examining the sexualization of children does not offer an analysis of the complexities that exist in relation to children's peer groups, cultures, or in terms of children's sexual and gendered subjectivities (Lumby 1998; Taylor 2010; Renold and Ringrose 2011). As Buckingham and Bragg's (2004) research suggests, what children view as sexualizing images, how they read them, and the impact of these images may be very different from how adults' perceive children experience these images. I have conducted research with young children in which popular cultural images have been used to initiate discussions about relationships and love. Although the images often depict children engaging in adult-like practices, such as kissing and children dressed in wedding outfits as bride and groom (see Chapter 5) children clearly understand these images are portraying adult behaviours, and make distinctions between children's fantasy and play, and real life practices that they view as differentiating children from adults. Emma Rush and Andrea La Nauze raise concerns about the way that children's 'slowly developing sexuality' is 'moulded' into stereotypical forms of adult sexuality (Rush and La Nauze 2006: 1). They argue that the problem with the sexualization of children is 'that the precocious and unhealthy leaps towards the end of this development process are encouraged by advertising and marketing' (2006: 3). There is no discussion by Rush and La Nauze (2006) of how heteronormativity and the heterosexualization of children's gendered and sexual subjectivities (in or out of advertising and marketing contexts) – or even of class, ethnicity or race – impact on children's location in discourses that propagate 'stereotypical forms of adult sexuality'. Research with young children, including the research on which much of this book is based, clearly demonstrates that children have desires, actively engage in constructing their sexual subjectivities (as well as regulating the sexual and gendered subjectivities of their peers and of adults) at early ages, and find pleasure in the process (Thorne 1993; Renold 2005; Blaise 2010; also see Chapter 5). Sexuality is generally constituted in children's lives through adult (hetero)normative narratives that have sources well beyond marketing and advertising.

The fetishization of childhood innocence

Writing about childhood, the sociologist Zach Meyers (2007: 58) states: 'why sexuality is perceived to be inherently harmful is difficult to identify'. Or is it? As previously discussed, sexuality has become increasingly perceived as dangerous to children, primarily through discourses of stranger danger, child sexual abuse and child protection. It has also been constituted as dangerous because it serves a larger political agenda – one that is about the state of the future, according to Lee Edelman. Edelman (2004) argues that politics is practiced in the name and sake of 'our children's future': no child, no future (Bond Stockton 2009). Edelman points out that 'the cult of the child ... permits no shrines to the queerness of boys and girls, since queerness, for contemporary culture at large ... is understood as bringing children and childhood to an end' (Edelman 2004: 19). The repression of children's sexuality and the significance placed on childhood innocence has resulted in their fetishization and eroticism (Kincaid 1998; Bruhm and Hurley 2004; Walkerdine 1997, 2001). James Kincaid (1992: 4), taking up a Foucauldian position, argues that by 'insisting so loudly on the innocence, purity and asexuality of the child, we have created a subversive echo: experience, corruption, eroticism'. This has resulted in *the child* being constituted as a regulatory measure for normative sexual practices more generally (Kincaid 1998; Berlant 2004; Edelman 2004). Through the inscription of innocence on children's bodies, childhood and children have become increasingly fetishized (Bruhm and Hurley 2004; Faulkner 2010, 2011; Kincaid 1998, 2004; Walkerdine 1997, 1999), as epitomized by Vladimir Nabokov's novel *Lolita* (1955), a narrative about a middle-aged man's obsession with a teenage girl, and Stanley Kubrick's 1962 screen adaptation with the same name. The fetishization of innocence is also exemplified through the practice of children's beauty pageants and through Western consumer marketing and advertising campaigns in which childhood innocence is exploited (Robinson and Davies 2008b). However, the fetishization of innocence has not solely been related to childhood: it has also been associated with innocence or child-like characteristics in women, as illustrated by the Hollywood icon Marilyn Monroe. Part of the public representation of Monroe was a child-like innocence and vulnerability that was sexualized through her female body.

Affrica Taylor, utilizing Judith Butler's concept of performativity, argues that the sexualization of children in the media functions as performative adult projections, stating that

> the risky unintended consequences of repeatedly referring to more and more images of children as pornographic, of continually interpreting them in 'the eyes of the paedophile' and of speaking about them as a-priori sexual images, we can see that the performative effects of all these repetitive speech acts is to actively produce, enact and embody a sexualized way of looking at children.
>
> (Taylor 2010: 51)

Such a process was played out in Australia in 2008 in relation to photographs of young nude children, aged 12–13 years old, which were being exhibited by the Australian photographer Bill Henson. This resulted in moral panic, bringing to the fore heated and highly emotional debates about the line between pornography and art. The Henson photographs had previously been shown publicly in Australia without any controversy, but on this occasion it was the nude photograph of a young girl used for the invitation to the private opening of Henson's exhibition that sparked a national controversy, initiated by the media, which quickly turned into a 'tabloid frenzy' (Marr 2008). The controversy sparked violent public reactions, which led to the closure of the exhibition out of fear that the photographs would be vandalized and out of fear for the safety of the gallery's personnel, who had received numerous threatening emails and telephone calls about the pictures, some of which were on the gallery's website. The gallery was eventually raided, the photographs were confiscated, and Henson was threatened with possible charges related to child pornography. The controversy fed into more general social anxieties about the sexualization of children in the media, childhood innocence, paedophiles, the Internet, decency and censorship. However, any potential legal action against Henson was dropped when the Australian Classification Board found that the photographs were fit for 'G' classification – that is, fit to be viewed by all ages (Marr 2008: 117). The photographs were considered by authorities to be in a different league to images considered to be child pornography. As with any artwork, the photographs will continue to provoke many differing personal opinions, and the line between art and pornography will continue to be hotly debated (Bray 2009). For instance, Abigail Bray (2009: 174) puts forward the view that 'in the debates over Henson's photographs, narratives about *private* harm to children were put in competition with narratives about *public* harm to future of Australian Democracy'. It is extremely important to be vigilant in society around child abuse and children's sexual exploitation, but how this is done in some cases may need to be reconsidered in terms of how it impacts upon children and the potential perpetuation of abuse. In many respects, the incident can be seen as having perpetuated the fetishization of childhood and childhood innocence. The manner in which media censored the photographs of the children which were used in the reporting of the case – by placing black bars across the children's bodies to hide body parts – in fact made the images more confronting, and seemingly sullied or dirty (Marr 2008). Foucault (1978) argues in his repressive hypothesis that censorship intensifies the fetishization of the forbidden object, increasing the curiosity, the gaze, and the desire for that which is censored. As Taylor reminds us, censorship reinforces the power of the performative effects of speech acts: repeated public debates 'prolong and proliferate the reiteration of the unspeakable' (Taylor 2010: 51).

Key points in this chapter

This chapter has outlined the centrality of the discourse of childhood innocence in the regulation of both children's sexual subjectivities and those of adults, as well as its use as an effective regulator of broader norms associated with childhood and socio-cultural practices. Around the world, discourses of childhood and childhood innocence have been successfully employed to foster moral panic for political gains by social and moral conservatives. Moral panic operates to maintain the social order in societies and, in the context of childhood, it has especially been mobilized to perpetuate the hegemony of heternormative narratives. Instigated through media and political discourses, moral panic focused on stranger danger reinforces myths and stereotypes about children's public vulnerabilities, often eclipsing children's private vulnerabilities in the privileged white middle-class nuclear family. Discourses of childhood innocence and protection, which have largely rendered children's sexual subjectivities invisible, have often been the rationale for denying children access to relevant and important knowledge about sexuality and relationships.

Chapter 4

Schooling the vulnerable child

Power/knowledge and the regulation of the adult normative citizen-subject

Introduction

Children's education is foundational to the development of future citizen-subjects. It is also about the production of a particular kind of citizen-subject – one that conforms to cultural norms, upholds moral values, is monogamous, family-oriented and, above all, heteronormative (as discussed in Chapter 2). Further, the production of this heteronormative citizen is linked to the regulation of children's sexual subjectivities, especially through their access to knowledge. Incorporating Foucault's power/knowledge framework, this chapter explores the production and regulation of the heteronormative citizen-subject through everyday mechanisms of power operating in primary schooling and early childhood educational contexts (i.e. non-compulsory schooling prior to primary school). This discussion highlights the dominant discourses that operate in sexuality education in selected Western countries, with a focus on Australia. These discourses are also perpetuated through policies and practices operating in other fields, such as the family and law, all of which reinforce *regimes of truth* (Foucault 1980) constituting the normative citizen-subject. Through this process of becoming a citizen, children learn what it means to be a good future citizen and sexual citizen-subject. In educational contexts, when the boundaries of what is perceived to be normal gender subjectivity and appropriate knowledge for children are transgressed, external mechanisms of power are mobilized to strategically realign the child's or teacher's practices with dominant cultural norms. This has been particularly so when some children are perceived to be potentially queer sexual subjects through their gender non-conformance, and when children are given access to knowledge of queer subjects (Robinson 2008; Wallis and Van Every 2000).

Power/knowledge: schooling and the regulation of subjectivity

Education is a discursive field contributing to a particular regime of truth that works to normalize particular knowledge and socio-cultural practices that construct particular types of subjects. This process of normalization, operating through everyday mechanisms of power, works in conjunction with the othering of minority groups that are located outside dominant cultures, often deemed abnormal, deviant and problematic. Foucault argues that 'We are subjected to the production of truth through power and we cannot exercise power except through the production of truth' (Foucault 1980: 93). For Foucault, truths are constituted in discourse:

> There are manifold relations of power which permeate, characterize and constitute the social body, and these relations of power cannot themselves be established, consolidated nor implemented without the production, accumulation, circulation and functioning of a discourse.
>
> (Foucault 1980: 93)

In schools, multiple discourses circulate to provide competing versions of knowledge. Schools as a social apparatus are critical in perpetuating dominant relations of power and maintaining the status quo, producing and supporting certain knowledge over other truths. Everyday mechanisms of power in schools and in early childhood education act to classify, discipline, normalize and produce what it means to be a good child or student, a good teacher and a good adult citizen (Foucault 1977, 1978, 1980). Curricula, policies, organizational practices, teachers' pedagogies and interactions between children are effective instruments of power which, by privileging certain knowledge, propagate and perpetuate particular truths and representations of the Other. The knowledge that is excluded from curricula can be equally as powerful as that which is included. Regulative and repetitive practices in schooling become part of children's habitus as they tap into the cultural and social capital valued in schooling and society generally (Bourdieu 1991). Children who resist cultural norms and take up counter-narratives in their lives are often subjected to regulatory practices from adults and peers to realign their behaviours. Some children who do not conform to gender norms, for example, become targets of sexist, homophobic and heterosexist marginalization and harassment. These practices are a powerful means through which the behaviours of children (and adults) are policed and regulated. Homophobic and heterosexist discourses prevailing in schools construct particular 'truths' or knowledge about non-heterosexual and gender non-conforming subjects that underpin this behaviour.

Schools as microcosms of society tend to perpetuate conservative discourses around children's sexuality education, and are especially sensitive to the transgression of the community's dominant moral values in this area. Sexuality education has become one of the most controversial and regulated bodies of knowledge in schooling curricula – an area where cultural norms and moral values are highly influential. In most Western countries, parents are generally supportive of sexuality education in primary and secondary schools, but they play a critical role in the regulation around what, how and when this knowledge is taught. Parents' perspectives on sexuality education are not homogeneous: some take more conservative stances, believing that families should be responsible for teaching their children this knowledge, while others with more liberal ideas consider that schools – along with families – have an important role to play in educating children around sexuality (parents' perspectives and practices around sexuality education are discussed in Chapter 6). Parents who are more active in schooling politics and have strong opinions on sexuality education can be highly influential in determining sexuality education curricula. The research I have conducted in early childhood education in Australia highlights that parents – or more specifically, educators' fears of parents' objections based on cultural and religious values or conservative worldviews – are one of the main regulators of how sexuality is addressed with children, if it is at all (Robinson and Jones Díaz 2000, 2006). In most countries, parents have the right to withdraw their children from sexuality education if they so wish. In this way, parents – and schools, in a role of *loco parentis* – are positioned to determine what is in the best interests of the child, potentially disregarding the agency of the child herself or himself. This discourse of adults knowing what is best for children, especially those with parental responsibilities, is infused with relations of power that reinforce the adult/child binary, diminishing children's agency and voices. Law and policy work to legitimate this social arrangement, reinforcing the perception that it is natural due to children's age and status differences, and making this arrangement resistant to challenge and critique (James and James 2004). As I have pointed out previously, the hegemony of developmentalist discourses in children's early schooling is a major technology of power that operates to regulate and police the construction of the child.

Discourses of the knowing child and Developmentally Appropriate Practice (DAP)

Children's sexual subjectivities are primarily regulated through dominant discourses of developmentalism (Piaget 1973 [1929]). Developmentalist theory underpins the philosophies and practices that are foundational to teaching and learning in children's early lives. Developmentally Appropriate Practice (DAP), a concept stemming from psychological developmentalist theorists such as Piaget, has dominated early childhood education and the early years of schooling since the 1960s. This discourse defines the child and how children are expected to develop physically, emotionally and cognitively into adolescence, and finally into adulthood. It regulates what knowledge is considered appropriate for children at what age, and has been particularly influential on the way that sexuality has or has not been addressed with young children in the early years of schooling, including early childhood education. It is a powerful discourse of surveillance and self-discipline effecting both teachers and parents, and underpinning practices that aim to teach or raise children *correctly*. Both teachers and parents often want to be reassured that their practices are developmentally appropriate (Burrows 2000).

Developmentalist discourses reinforce the hegemony of childhood innocence, impacting the way that children are viewed and treated both in schools and generally in Western societies. Developmentalism has not just been utilized to normalize certain linear milestones in children's development, but it has also been employed as a discourse to regulate normative life markers across human development from childhood to adulthood (Halberstam 2005). These normative markers include schooling, sexual maturity, starting work, voting, monogamous marriage, reproduction and retirement – all of which are framed within heteronormative family structures, behaviours, morals and values, and are critical to the production of the heteronormative citizen-subject (Berlant 1997; Buckingham 2000; Jackson 2006; Kincaid 2004; Robinson 2012a; Richardson 1998; Silin 1995; Tobin 1997). These norms in children's expected life trajectories are all essential to the dominant narratives that are perpetuated as truths in schooling, and that work to regulate broad socio-cultural and political practices. Children have ultimately become markers of the heteronormative status quo (Berlant 1997; Berlant and Warner 1998; Halberstam 2005; Jackson 2006; Warner 1999). Steven Bruhm and Natasha Hurley argue that adult utopianism and nostalgia plague the constitution of the child, with the result that children are represented as the preferred form of the future:

> Caught between these two worlds, one dead, the other powerless to be born, the child becomes the bearer of heteronormativity, appearing to render ideology invisible by cloaking it in simple stories, euphemisms, and platitudes. The child is the product of physical reproduction, but functions just as surely as a figure of cultural reproduction.
>
> (Bruhm and Hurley 2004: xiii)

Karen Corteen and Phil Scraton point out that 'the infantilizing of children, sustaining childhood as a prolonged denial of personhood or citizenship, is particularly marked with regards to their developing sexualities' (Corteen and Scraton 1997: 99). Developmentalist discourses underpin perceptions that sexuality is irrelevant and inappropriate knowledge for children (James and Prout 1990; Alderson 1999, 2000; Hultqvist and Dahlberg 2001). It is in the context of sexuality that the state, parents and educators frequently curb children's knowledge, agency, independence, responsibilities and resilience (Curran *et al.* 2009). The child who is perceived to know too much about sexuality (i.e. has the knowledge and language to speak about sexuality beyond what is considered to be age-appropriate for children) is constituted as the non-innocent or corrupted child. Such knowledge in children is deemed a possible indicator of abuse in child protection discourse. It is deemed that young children who have this knowledge possibly gained it from an adult under suspicious circumstances, as most parents are considered to adhere to social norms that view this knowledge as inappropriate for children.

Researchers have begun to challenge the hegemonic position of developmental theory in determining children's capabilities for understanding and building competencies around complex concepts (Jenkins 1982; James and Prout 1990; Dunn 1995; Alderson 1999, 2000; Burrows 2000; Hultqvist and Dahlberg 2001). Goldman and Goldman (1982), based on research conducted with children aged five to fifteen which investigated their sexual thinking, critiques the unquestioned acceptance of Piaget's theory of knowledge in determining children's abilities to comprehend and critically think about their bodies and sexuality. Despite discourses that dismiss the relevance of sexuality to children's lives, my research with young children corroborates other research in this field which demonstrates that children are engaging with sexuality in their daily lives at very young ages, and are aware and think critically about their bodies and relationships with others (Blaise 2010; Davies and Robinson 2010; Goldman and Goldman 1982; Jackson 1982; Robinson and Davies 2010; Robinson 2012a; Tobin 1997). What is obvious from the results of this research is that formal sexuality education in schools is generally out of sync with the lives and experiences of children and young people.

Sexuality education in the early years of schooling: an international glimpse

Globally, sexuality education has continued to be a controversial subject that has been significantly regulated by cultural values and norms. Political, conservative and religious discourses have significantly influenced the philosophies behind, pedagogy of, and content in sexuality education curricula in elementary schools, as well as what is addressed – if anything – with children in early childhood education. Sexuality education is virtually non-existent in early childhood education, as it is generally perceived as irrelevant and developmentally inappropriate. The only context in which it is considered potentially relevant is in relation to family diversity. Sexuality education curricula in schools has historically been highly censored and regulated, and often framed within discourses that view teenage sexuality as dangerous, and sexuality as non-existent in, and a danger to, younger children.

Since the 1970s, in most Western countries, schools have taken an increasingly active role in sex education – a role that has continued to be strictly regulated and fraught with political tensions (Elliott 2010; Corteen and Scraton 1997; Haydon 2002; Mayo 2006; Robinson and Davies 2008b; Connell and Elliott 2009). There has been an ongoing debate amongst educators, parents, community members and politicians around whose responsibility it is to provide children with sexual knowledge at what age, and what information should or should not be a component of this education (Levine 2002; Allen 2004; Davies and Robinson 2010). As high-lighted by Sinikka Elliott (2010: 194), these debates 'are about far more than the sex education curriculum – they are fueled by and reproduce deep anxieties about childhood, sexuality, gender, marriage, and the institution of the family'. The introduction of sexuality education in the USA, stem-ming from high levels of teenage pregnancy, immediately became a central focus of the culture wars between conservative and liberal interests (Elliott 2010; Connell and Elliott 2009). However, as Catherine Connell and Sinikka Elliott (2009) point out, growing concerns about HIV and AIDS in the late 1980s led conservatives to push for abstinence-only sex education in US schools. The current dominance of abstinence-only sex education in the USA is a result of its promotion since the 1990s through policies and legislation such as the Adolescent and Family Life Act (AFLA), which states that the ideal sexuality education program 'teaches that a mutually faithful monogamous relationship in the context of marriage is the expected stand-ard of human sexual activity' (Connell and Elliott 2009: 85). Connell and Elliott point out that 'an increasing number of American youth are now receiving instructions in school on how to "just say no" to sex without learn-ing what to do if they decide to say yes' (Connell and Elliott 2009: 85). The abstinence-only sex education program offers medically and scientifically 'age-appropriate' sexual information to students framed within gender-normative and heteronormative discourses, and has limited relevance to young people's lives in the USA (Levine 2002; Connell and Elliott 2009; Elliott 2010). In fact, as Connell and Elliott argue, sexuality education in the USA is far more about the maintenance of social inequality. They con-clude that the process of implementing inclusive sexuality education in the USA (including gender diversity and sexual orientation) is problematic, largely due to the facts that federal funding is tied to abstinence-only man-dates; that comprehensive sexuality education models are embedded in rac-ist, sexist, classist and homophobic assumptions; and that private schools, which do provide inclusive sexuality curricula, are cost-prohibitive for most children from economically disadvantaged backgrounds.

Despite the critical importance of sexuality education to the health and wellbeing of children and young people, it is not a compulsory part of chil-dren's primary schooling in many countries (e.g. Scotland, Australia, South Africa and the USA). This is a reflection of the controversial nature of sexu-ality education and the differing socio-cultural values associated with this education for children. New Zealand introduced mandated classes at all levels of schooling in 2001, believing it to be critical to the health and welfare of the nation (Sinkinson 2009). This action was prompted by a 2001 UNICEF report on global sexual health statistics, which showed that New Zealand had a higher incidence of sexually transmitted infections

(STIs) and unplanned youth pregnancies than most Organization for Economic Cooperation and Development (OECD) countries (Sinkinson 2009). Similar concerns about high rates of teenage pregnancy in the UK (the highest in Europe) have led the government to consider the introduction of compulsory Sex and Relationships Education (SRE) in all government-maintained schools in the UK (Mason 2010). As of January 2011, legislation and government policy around SRE was still framed within the Education Act 1996, in which sex education elements of the National Curriculum Science Order are mandated for all primary and secondary-school-aged students. This curriculum includes anatomy, puberty, biological aspects of sexual reproduction, and the use of hormones to control and promote fertility. Secondary schools are additionally required to include discussion on STIs and HIV and AIDS. All other components of SRE (e.g. relationships and sexual orientation) are not compulsory (Family Planning Association 2011). Some primary schools may provide a wider SRE curriculum that includes human reproduction, contraception and STIs (Mason 2010). Parents in the UK have the right to withdraw their child from all or part of the SRE components, which lie outside the National Curriculum Science Order mandate. Although most sexuality education has been introduced into schooling as a result of strategic public health reforms, not all countries have been so responsive in making sexuality education compulsory at all levels of schooling. In South Africa, demands for compulsory childhood sexuality education to counteract the increasing number of children contracting HIV, AIDS and STIs have had limited success, due to cultural norms and discourses of childhood innocence (Bhana 2009).

Sexuality education in schools is often constituted within discourses of health, as shown by its location in health, physical education and personal development curricula in countries such as Australia, the UK, Northern Ireland and New Zealand. Sexuality education in schools is an important source of information for children, and young people often view it as their most useful and trusted source of sexual health information (Rosenthal and Smith 1995; Smith *et al.* 2000; Sinkinson 2009). However, despite this, young people – particularly from same-sex-attracted backgrounds – have also pointed out that much of their sexuality education has minimal relevance to their lives and needs (Allen 2004; Hillier and Mitchell 2008; Carmody 2009; Family Planning Association 2011). Research in the UK that surveyed 20,000 young people under 18 years of age highlights that 40 per cent thought the SRE they received was either poor or very poor. Approximately 70 per cent reported not receiving any information about personal relationships, and 73 per cent felt that SRE should be taught before the age of 13 (UK Youth Parliament 2007). Lynne Hillier and Anne Mitchell (2008) highlight the importance of finding ways of delivering sexual health information to same-sex-attracted young people that is meaningful and relevant, considering that their research indicates that this group are sexually active earlier, that young women in this group are five times more likely to report having an STI, and are equally as likely as heterosexual young women to fall pregnant. However, Hillier and Mitchell also point out that meaningful sexuality education for same-sex-attracted young people may be a long time coming:

> Many school communities are still struggling against opposition to the inclusion of sex positive health information for heterosexual students, and are less likely to be able to accommodate the needs of same-sex-attracted students or willing to take on advocacy for the issue.
>
> (Hillier and Mitchell 2008: 222)

The discourses of desire and negotiating intimate relationships are rarely addressed in sexuality education, but are important issues for young people (Carmody 2010; Robinson and Davies 2008b; Dyson and Smith 2011; Goldman 2010). Since August 2011, schools in the south-eastern Australian state of Victoria are required by law (the Equal Opportunity Act 2010) to take steps in terms of policy development and practice to prevent discrimination, including sexual harassment and victimization. The Victorian Equal Opportunity and Human Rights Commission have developed programmes to help schools understand their legal obligations under the new law. Schools now have a 'positive duty' to take steps to eliminate discrimination and develop strategies on how to build inclusive environments in schools.

Comparative research between the USA and Europe conducted by Levine (2002) highlights that, in cultures with a more liberal and open approach to sexuality, providing sexual knowledge to children and young people does not lead to social problems – contrary to the opinions often voiced by social and political conservatives. For example, in the Netherlands, where abstinence is not taught, contraception is free through the national health service and condom vending machines are widely available, virtually eliminating teenage pregnancy as a health or social problem (Levine 2002). Other research demonstrates that sexuality education delays initiation of sex and decreases the number of sexual partners a young person may have (Baldo et al. 1993; Franklin et al. 1997; Kim et al. 1997; Kirby 2008; Jemmott and Jemmott 2000). However, despite this evidence, the fear that sexuality education leads to earlier and increased sexual activity continues to prevail.

Research conducted in Australia and the UK has indicated that, in both countries, similar issues have impacted the scope and quality of sexuality education in elementary schools (Walker 2001). Walker and Milton (2006) point out that cultural and social openness in relation to sexuality education in both countries is minimal. The curricula in both countries tend to be dominated by scientific discourses of the mechanics of reproduction, particularly in plants and animals, with minimal coverage given to issues of gender, contraception, STIs, and sexual identity and orientation, despite these issues being common in children's and young people's questions. This research also pointed out that parents' and teachers' comfort with their own sexuality impacts on the scope of sexuality education offered to children, and that many teachers and parents experience uncertainty and embarrassment in their respective roles as educators and advisors on matters of sexuality. Further, the non-compulsory nature of much sexuality education leads to a marginalization of this subject in the school curriculum, which can diminish its design, planning, quality, implementation and effectiveness. The support of school leadership is important in raising the profile of sexuality education, as a lack of financial support for resources and a lack of teacher commitment and preparation also undermines its effectiveness (Goldman 2010). The absence of a sexuality education programme that views sexuality as a vital aspect of the whole person, that encourages awareness of diversity and respectful, ethical relationships, and that encourages agency, responsibility and informed decision-making can put children and young people at risk and undermine their physical and mental health and wellbeing.

Research by Karen Corteen (2006) into sexuality education – or more specifically, Sex and Relationships Education (SRE) – in secondary schooling in the UK shows that low prioritization and unsystematic or *ad hoc* provision of SRE in schools continues to prevail. Corteen (2006) points out that an over-reliance on utilizing outside organizations to undertake aspects of sexuality education in the UK means that many students do not receive the non-statutory SRE for their entire secondary school career. Sacha Mason's (2010) research in two primary schools in the UK reinforced the issues raised by Corteen around the discrepancies in policies and practices associated with SRE. Mason (2010: 160) also points out that teachers often 'pared down' the content for the groups that they taught based on their perceptions of the maturity of the children, commenting that 'teachers and coordinators were possibly partially responsible for the immature social development of the children (by withholding information in their limited curricula)'. Mason (2010) concludes that 'bravery' is required on the part of teachers and schools to overcome reticence to delivering a sexuality curriculum that is relevant to children and addresses important issues such as sexual intercourse, sexuality and the pleasure of sex as part of a loving relationship. However, this approach to sexuality education is still positioned within a conservative and heteronormative framework, in that sex is constituted as intercourse only and sexual practices outside loving relationships are not acknowledged.

The following discussion highlights how conservative, political and religious discourses regulate philosophies, pedagogies and curricula content in relation to sexuality education in primary schooling and in early childhood. These discourses are essential to the construction and regulation of the heteronormative citizen-subject early in life.

The regulation of the heteronormative citizen-subject through sexuality education in primary schooling: an Australian example

In Australia, individual states and territories determine the content, policies and procedures included in sexuality curricula, which can vary considerably. Much of this education is outsourced to other organizations, such as the Family Planning Association. With Cristyn Davies (Robinson and Davies 2008b), I undertook a discursive analysis of sexuality education curricula in primary schooling in the Australian State of New South Wales (NSW) since the 1950s. This research pointed out that what has been historically incorporated in the curriculum has been significantly influenced by the hegemonic socio-cultural and political discourses about childhood, sexuality, marriage, family and citizenship at the time. These discourses also frame ideals of the good child, good parent and good citizen-subject, a point also highlighted by Lisette Burrows (2000) in a discussion of the Physical Education Curriculum in New Zealand. Sex education in NSW elementary schooling (children aged 5–11), as in most other Australian states and territories, is located in the Personal Development, Health and Physical Education syllabus. Within this context, sex education in the latter years of primary education is generally framed within scientific discourses of sexuality encompassing human biology and reproduction – what can be called the mechanics of heteronormative sex and sexuality. In the earlier primary years, this process of reproduction is often framed in terms of animal and insect reproduction. In the latter years, there is also a focus on healthy bodies, contraception and risks associated with being sexually active or having unprotected sex, such as STIs and AIDS. Young people are encouraged to consider abstinence as a serious choice with benefits (Robinson and Davies 2008b). As discussed above, it is interesting that in the USA also, where conservative right-wing religious discourses are highly influential in the politics of some states, abstinence-only sex education has become a popular choice in schools (Elliott 2010; Levine 2002). Michelle Fine and Sara McClelland (2006: 299) argue that abstinence-only sex education has begun 'to assert a kind of natural cultural authority' in and out of schools. In the latter years of the elementary school sex education curriculum in NSW, some discussion of same-sex relationships is included, but its focus is more on the problems associated with this perceived lifestyle choice, such as homophobia and its consequences (Robinson and Davies 2008b). Both the official sex education curriculum and the hidden curriculum (that is, what students learn at school outside the formal curriculum; for example, what they learn from every day interactions with peers and teachers) perpetuate heteronormativity and construct same-sex subjects as abnormal and problematic.

Robinson and Davies' (2008b) research highlights how heteronormative, conservative and Christian moralistic discourses have historically underpinned knowledge production in relation to sexuality and relationships education (see Board of Studies, New South Wales, 1992, 1999a, 1999b). Despite the lack of sexuality education in the primary schooling curriculum, particularly in the earlier years, the construction of the normative sexual subject is constituted within health discourses and constructions of the normative adult citizen. In the political, social and cultural climate of the post-war 1950s, the constitution of the ideal child in the Health syllabus (Department of Education, New South Wales 1952) was influenced by concerns with rebuilding heteronormative families and relationships, and moral and ethical subjects. Providing children with sexual knowledge was seen as a family responsibility, reflecting the perception of sexuality education as largely a private concern. Integral to the construction of the ideal child-subject during this time was an unquestioning adherence to the normalizing regulatory practices administered through schooling systems, which were steeped in Christian discourses (Robinson and Davies 2008b). This was depicted in the 'health pledge' children were encouraged to take in schools: 'I will work to make my body healthy, clean, and strong, so that I may be a good Australian and do my very best work in the world' (Department of Education, New South Wales 1952: 3). This pledge also reflects how children are constituted as patriotic, productive, neoliberal subjects.

The pledge exemplifies Foucault's concept of technologies of self, through which children are encouraged to self-manage their own bodies and to comply with state regulations of appropriate citizenship – that is, take responsibility for her/his own success and wellbeing as a neoliberal subject. Schools, as disciplinary state apparatuses, have a compulsory captive audience – docile bodies – through which to construct knowledge and heteronormative moral subjects. Foucault's concept of the power/knowledge nexus operates through hegemonic discourses that are perpetuated through curricula, rules and regulations, philosophies, policies, and pedagogical practices that prevail in schooling (Foucault 1977). Schools, aiming to produce ideal adult citizens, sought to shape students through dominant discourses that linked health and hygiene with good citizenship (Robinson and Davies 2010). Stephen Ball points out that from the nineteenth century, the school and the classroom 'emerged as particular organizations of space and persons experienced by virtually all people, at one and the same time totalizing the power of the state and producing and specifying particular individualities' (Ball 1990: 5). Michael Apple (1999, 2001) has argued that what is taught in the curriculum and regarded as official knowledge is bound up with struggles and history of class, race, ethnicity, gender, sexuality and religious relations. Schools reflect broader societal prejudices, and actively produce gendered and heterosexualized subjects (Epstein and Johnson 1998; Kehily 2001), despite their constructed image as sexless organizations (Britzman 1997; Epstein and Johnson 1994). Furthermore, gender and sexuality are closely monitored through the surveillance of mannerisms and actions to ensure the maintenance of heterosexuality (Mills 1999), and any deviation from constructed norms may result in both implicit and explicit harassment, or punishment in the Foucauldian sense, in an endeavour to reassert the dominant position of heterosexuality (Foucault 1977). This punishment is essentially corrective in nature, and is utilized within the 'double system: gratification-punishment', where sanctioned behaviours are socially rewarded and challenges to the norm are derided (Foucault 1977: 180).

Since the 1960s there has been an increased awareness of the prevalence of child sexual abuse and an emergence of 'stranger danger' campaigns in Australia, the UK, the USA and other Western countries. Communal anxieties about child sexual abuse have impacted sex education debates in these countries, with a number of different consequences. This anxiety has increased regulation and surveillance of children and adults; influenced sex education curricula and pedagogies; raised an awareness of the need for children's education in this area; and further undermined children's access to agency with regard to their sexual subjectivities (Angelides 2004). Child protection discourses, which include a focus on stranger danger, have re-inscribed children's bodies as powerless, innocent and vulnerable; instilled a sense of insecurity and suspicion in adult/child relationships; and re-emphasized the relationship between childhood and sexuality as dangerous. The discourse of stranger danger has continued to ignite a moral panic that constitutes children's vulnerability primarily to the paedophile, despite evidence that children are more likely to be abused by family members or those they know. This has fuelled fears around old folk devils, such as the predatory homosexual. In research on constructions of sexual subjectivity during the culture wars, Cristyn Davies (2012) points out the ways in which the image of the child and constructions of childhood innocence are often used to regulate adults – and especially queer citizens. Davies argues that the 'inscription of the child as [a] metaphor [for innocence], [acts as] a kind of ground zero for the edifice that is adult life and around which narratives of sexuality get organized' (Davies 2012).

In Australia, the inclusion of sexuality issues in primary schooling, especially those associated with same-sex relationships or gay and lesbian identities, has been discursively constituted as controversial, with the result that special permission is required to include them in classroom discussions or activities. The *Controversial Issues in Schools Policy* (Department of Education and Training, Office of Schools, New South Wales 2007), introduced in 1977 and revised in 2005, is related to issues such as sexuality, drug education and child protection. The policy provides principals with the power of vetoing or censoring the inclusion of these issues in the school's curricula. This regulatory power has also been written into the *Personal Development, Health and Physical Education K–6 Syllabus* (Board of Studies, New South Wales 1992). In the introduction of this syllabus, the New South Wales Board of Studies points out that the document was 'designed to give all schools the flexibility to treat sensitive and controversial issues in a manner reflective of their ethos' (1992: 1). Consequently, school leaders play a critical role in how and if controversial issues such as sexuality are addressed in children's schooling. Dominant discourses of childhood and sexuality may influence individual leaders' perceptions of relevance and 'risks' associated with these issues, and impact their decision-making around the inclusion of these issues in children's early education.

The construction of the heteronormative citizen-subject in early childhood contexts through teachers' perceptions and pedagogical practices

The perception of the irrelevancy of sexuality and sexual knowledge to young children prevails in early childhood education, primarily as a result of the hegemony of developmentalist discourses in these contexts (Robinson 2002, 2005c; Robinson and Jones Díaz 2006; Surtees 2006). However, as in the schooling of older children and youth, heteronormativity prevails in these early years through the curriculum, teachers' pedagogies, institutional policies, and through children's everyday interactions with their peers and with teachers (Surtees 2006). Chapter 5 explores the ways in which children actively engage in the constitution of their own sexual subjectivities and in the regulation of the sexual subjectivities of others. Here, I want to provide a focus on how educators take up a regulatory role in relation to children's access to sexual knowledge and the construction of children as heteronormative subjects. Paradoxically, despite the prevalent perception that children are innocent, asexual and too young to understand sexuality, the construction of heterosexual identities and desire in early childhood is a socially-sanctioned and integral part of children's everyday educational experiences. For example, children's engagement in mock weddings is encouraged and even celebrated in many early childhood educational contexts, with games such as 'Catch and Kiss' and 'Mummies and Daddies' generally considered a natural and normal aspect of children's everyday play (Cahill and Theilheimer 1999; Casper *et al.* 1998; Robinson 2005c; Surtees 2006; Taylor 2008). Mock weddings often turn into elaborate celebrations, with parents invited to attend and to bring along photos of their own weddings to share with the children. Children get dressed in wedding clothes and exchange makeshift rings, imitating real adult weddings. Many educators do not consider these celebrations problematic, but some mothers participating in my research were concerned about these activities indoctrinating their girls into heteronormative practices, which they had tried hard to counteract in their children's lives.

These pedagogical activities reflect a process of heterosexualization which is rendered invisible through heteronormative discourses and naturalized within hegemonic constructions of gender that occur daily in early childhood settings (Boldt 1997; MacNaughton 2000; Robinson 2005c; Grieshaber 2008). These everyday play practices are also rendered invisible – and simultaneously made more powerful – when they are viewed as markers of children's healthy and normal gender development, which is always assumed within the framework of heterosexuality. As Judith Butler (1990: 17) argues, gender norms are strengthened through naturalized connections to the sexed body and sexuality: '"Intelligible" genders are those which in some sense institute and maintain relations of coherence among sex, gender, sexual practice, and desire'. Increased calls for stricter regulations of children's early education result when children's access to knowledge of sexuality or their play practices are perceived to transgress the strict boundaries of heteronormativity – for example, when children are taught about having two mummies or two daddies; when the young boy chooses to dress in women's clothing in dress-ups; or when two boys or girls want to marry each other during mock weddings. Young children learn early from the policing encountered in communities, media, educators, parents and peers that these transgressive scenarios are not normal or acceptable in most public spaces (Robinson and Davies 2007). The anxiety that some educators and parents – especially fathers – express about their young boys' gender non-conformance, such as dressing in female clothing or dressing up as princesses, reflects the power of Butler's argument that gender is normalized and understood through its connection with the sexed body and sexuality. The young boy's masculinity is questioned in relation to his sexuality, instilling fears for some that this behaviour will either lead to, or is reflective of, being gay (Davies 2008b; Kilodavis 2010; McInnes 2008; McInnes and Davies 2008; Boldt 1997; Wallis and Van Every 2000).

Legal discourses and the normative citizen-subject in schooling

In Australia, the UK and the USA there have been legal regulations imposed on schooling policies and practices that operate to maintain educational regimes of truth (Foucault 1980). This process has been most obvious in terms of the regulation of children's learning associated with queer subjectivities (Robinson 2008). The extremism associated with the regulation of children's access to knowledge about sexuality is also particularly obvious in the USA and the UK. In the USA, sex education curricula have been strictly monitored through the Adolescent Family Life Act (1981) – the first federal law specifically written to fund sex education (Levine 2002). According to Levine (2002), the aim of this act, framed within discourses of the conservative political Right, is to eradicate teen sex, teen pregnancy and abortion. The discourse of abstinence has featured most prominently in these curricula since the late 1990s, perpetuated by the powerful lobbying of the Christian Right, who have a strong influence on education (Apple 2001; Levine 2002). This influence is further reflected in regulations, such as the prohibition of instruction about contraception or condoms unless discussed in regards to their failure, as well as the requirement that educators point out that non-marital sex 'is likely to have harmful psychological and physical effects' (Levine 2002: 92).

The recent success of Proposition 8 in the US state of California further reflects the powerful influence of the Christian Right in regulating the good citizen as a heterosexual subject, maintaining the heteronormative status quo, and defining what is appropriate education for young children. Brought before the courts in November 2008, Proposition 8 sought to ban same-sex unions, which had been legal in California since June 2008. The proposition was initially passed, changing the Californian Constitution to define and restrict marriage to couples of the opposite sex and eliminating same-sex marriage as a legally recognized union. One of the main arguments upheld by many proponents of the proposition was that the change was necessary in order to prevent public schools teaching children that non-heterosexual marriages were acceptable. However, in February 2012, a federal appeals court with a three-judge panel ruled the ban unconstitutional by a vote of 2–1. At that time, Judge Stephen Reinhardt commented that the ban 'serves no purpose, and has no effect, other than to lessen the status and human dignity of gays and lesbians in California, and to officially reclassify their relationships and families as inferior to those of opposite-sex couples' (Leff and AAP 2012). Meanwhile, Judge Randy Smith, who voted against over-ruling the ban, stated that Proposition 8 had a greater purpose than treating same-sex couples as second-rate citizens, and that it could serve to promote responsible parenting among opposite-sex couples (Leff and AAP 2012). This statement reinforces how this proposed legislation not only aims to regulate same-sex couples, but also operates to regulate the behaviours of heterosexual couples with children in the process. Anti-gay marriage activists are proposing to appeal this ruling in the Supreme Court.

This proposition is similar to legal and constitutional regulations that have prevailed in other countries. For example, Section 28 of the UK Local Government Act 1988 – repealed in 2003 – prohibited any local authority from intentionally promoting homosexuality or publishing any materials that promoted homosexuality, and also prohibited the teaching of homosexuality as an acceptable family relationship in schools (Moran 2001). Despite its repeal, the continued negative impact of Section 28 on Sex and Relationships Education (SRE) and the lack of inclusion of same-sex attraction and relationships in this curriculum continues to be seen in UK schools (Corteen 2006).

The subjugation of non-heteronormative subjects

Research I conducted in 2009 (with Cristyn Davies and Anthony Semann) with queer families in the Inner Western metropolitan regions of Sydney, Australia, highlighted the heteronormative regulating practices in their children's schooling. Currently, heteronormative policies and practices in schooling exclude meaningful discussions about same-sex relationships and the socio-cultural and political experiences of same-sex-attracted subjects and their families. Same-sex families pointed out that pedagogical and administrative practices in many of the early childhood settings and elementary schools their children attend continue to perpetuate heterosexual norms at the expense of their children's emotional wellbeing. The failure to acknowledge different family structures, especially same-sex families, in schooling practices and policies (such as Mothers' and Fathers' Day celebrations) was a particular concern raised by many same-sex parents in my research (Davies and Robinson in press 2013). These same concerns have also been voiced in the broader lesbian and gay communities in Sydney (Roy 2011). In a community forum held in 2011 in the same region in which I conducted my research, same-sex parents raised their concerns to an invited panel of Department of Education and Community officials about the heteronormative practices prevalent in the schools their children attended. One lesbian mother spoke about her embarrassment of being the only female at an annual Fathers' Day breakfast at her daughter's primary school. This mother continued to endure this embarrassment in order that her daughter was not excluded from events in which all her classmates were involved. Another lesbian mother, who has a four-year-old daughter and a six-year-old son, commented:

> My daughter will make a Fathers' Day card, and she asks, 'Who do I give it to?' It's just confusion, you know, it is just – everybody else has the answer, it is so self-evident for most kids, but they get really confused.

This mother also relayed how her daughter was prevented from purchasing two Mothers' Day presents for her parents at the Mothers' Day event at her school. Her daughter was distressed that she could only purchase one gift and did not know which mother to give it to. When the child told the volunteer behind the stall that she had two mothers so required two gifts, the volunteer was unable to comprehend the child's alternative family structure and refused to allow her to spend her money on two gifts, in order to uphold the school's policy. These events act as revenue-raising opportunities for primary schools and are perceived as critical to the ongoing support of school activities and for purchasing educational resources. The school's ethics around the politics of consumption came up against the politics of recognition, wherein there was a refusal to acknowledge the child's alternative family structure (Davies and Robinson in press 2013). These normative practices instil a sense of loss in children, who become more aware of the potential consequences of their non-normative family structure as a result. This is not just a problem faced by same-sex couples that encounter the additional force of heteronormativity; single-parent families also have to endure the normative discourses that legitimate the nuclear family and exclude others.

A lesbian mother with a five-year-old son gave an example of the way that her son's life experiences were dismissed through the pedagogical practices of his teacher. During a lesson on transport, the classroom teacher asked those children who were taught how to ride a bicycle by their fathers to raise their hands. The majority of the class put up their hands. The teacher asked children to raise their hands if their grandfathers taught them. This process continued, with the teacher asking the same question with regards to brothers, uncles or a male friend of the family. There were only a few children left who had not put up their hands at the end of this process. The young boy, eager to contribute to the discussion by offering that one of his two mothers had taught him, was not invited to participate so felt dejected and marginalized by the teacher. He remained silent, pulled his cap over his face and began to cry. At this point, the teacher noticed that there was something wrong with the boy, stopped the class discussion and asked him what was the matter. Obviously upset, the young boy told the class that he had wanted to share his story of being taught how to ride his bike by 'Mumma H', the name he had given to this particular mother. Curious about the name the boy had mentioned, another boy began to question who 'Mumma H' was and why he called her that. Once he had confessed to having two mothers several children began to speak loudly all at once, pointing out that it was not possible to have two mothers. As the boy continued to defend his family composition, the other children's dismissal of the story became louder. The teacher did not intervene in the discussion, but gained the full attention of the class as the recess bell rang. When the boy got home, for the first time he told his mothers that he did not want to go to school anymore. What this narrative highlights is the way that the child's knowledge and practices were dismissed and disqualified by the pedagogical practices of the classroom teacher. In fact, the gender stereotyping in this practice would also have been dismissive for other children, regardless of their family structure, who were taught how to ride a bicycle by a female. Further, the lack of intervention by the teacher in the discussion that ensued left the five-year-old to defend the legitimacy of his family experience alone against his peers.

Dangerous knowledge and the perception of risk: regulating teachers' practices

The perception of risk can operate as a powerful means of social control, maintaining the status quo and dominant power relations underpinning societal inequalities. There is generally an element of risk involved in sexuality education and social justice education, regardless of the specific issues being addressed. This is mostly a result of challenging and disrupting the power of individuals as well as the broader socio-cultural, political and economic power relations that operate in society. Risk in this context is about the consequences of challenging what is often perceived as the natural order of things; that is, the colonizing practices where certain individuals and groups are viewed (or view themselves) as rightfully being in control, and as able to speak, define and decide for the Other (Cannella and Viruru 2004). Thus, generally, social justice pedagogy is about teaching and learning that deals with challenging and disrupting discourses (or common-sense or taken-for-granted truths) that underpin the inequities experienced by minority cultures (including non-heteronormative subjects), and focusing primarily on identifying and understanding the everyday relations of power, at both the micro and macro levels in society, that constitute and maintain these inequalities. The perceived risks in engaging in social justice education may be intensified when there is a move beyond simplistic and more comfortable touristic representations of cultural diversity (that is, those activities that view cultures as homogeneous, and which focus on foods, festivities, artefacts and so on – similar to a travel brochure) to practices that challenge the power relations that underpin social inequalities. Therefore, social justice pedagogy is not easy work, but rather involves dealing with the complexities of identity and teaching difficult knowledge or controversial issues – especially those related to counteracting homophobia and heterosexism with children.

Transgressing cultural norms carries a level of personal and professional risk on the part of educators working with young children. Anthony Giddens (1999: 31) refers to risk as 'hazards that are actively assessed in relation to future possibilities'. Discussing sexuality, especially lesbian and gay subjectivities and gender non-conformance, with young children is always constituted as a hazard that frequently ends in controversy (see Chapter 7 for a discussion of moral panic). Risks are constructed regulators; they are the potential consequences of the normalizing judgments, which are inherent in the societal gaze, and which discourage people from stepping outside the boundaries of socially-sanctioned values and practices. Foucault (1977: 177) points out that disciplinary power is 'everywhere and always alert, since by its very principle it leaves no zone of shade and constantly supervises ...'. Taking his concept of power further, Foucault says it 'is exercised through its invisibility; at the same time it imposes on those whom it subjects a principle of compulsory visibility' (1977: 187). This perception of power is reflected in the comment made by an early childhood teacher in my research:

> I can't do it [challenging homophobia and working for the inclusion of gay and lesbian subjectivities in early childhood education] anymore; the personal harassment and ostracism is not worth it at this stage of my life; it's way too stressful to be the only one that goes out on a limb.

Fear of anticipated resistance from families, managers, colleagues or community members results in the exclusion of critical discussions about these issues with young children, allowing particular discourses, myths and behaviours to go unchallenged, with often severe consequences. For example, homophobic harassment can result in young people (mainly boys) taking their own lives as early as 11 years of age. It is also depicted in youth hate crimes, such as the case of a 14-year-old shooting a fellow classmate because he openly identified as gay (GLSEN 2009; GLSEN and Harris Interactive 2012). Risk acts as a powerful social control, maintaining dominant relations of power constituted through cultural binaries, including adult/child, parent/educator, and heterosexual/homosexual. Resistance, to varying degrees, stems from those individuals and institutions that find it difficult to shift their worldviews to accommodate a different, more inclusive and equitable perspective of difference and non-heterosexual subjectivities. Resistance is also encountered from those who perceive and fear they have most to lose from a shift in this power, seeing their position and status as threatened in these changes.

Homophobia and heterosexist resistance, often rooted in values inherent in religion and seen across diverse cultures, prevails in many early childhood educational settings. This resistance is experienced in a number of ways: as a lack of support from colleagues or managers; as a questioning of the validity of the inclusion of these perspectives; as a refusal to incorporate anti-homophobia policy into practice; as overt and covert hostility; and as harassment and/or ostracism within the workplace, which can result in educators choosing to leave their employment, or being forced to leave in severe cases (Robinson 2002; Robinson and Jones Díaz 2000). The following comments by educators are indicative of the issues, experiences and perceptions of these issues that have arisen in my research:

> We have some gay staff and some positive images but some heterosexual staff still have a problem with it and there is some tension there.
>
> > (Early childhood teacher)

> I have discussed it but have often been met with very hostile responses.
>
> > (Director, early childhood education setting)

> I can see many barriers but they are all people. So many people are homophobic and show this bias openly that I feel we would have a real problem in introducing these issues into our program.
>
> > (Director, early childhood education setting)

> The service has a strong number of conservative families – as a lesbian director I am quite open about my lifestyle and family. However, I am concerned that incorporating a more proactive approach could be perceived by some as pushing my political views too much; sadly I think I am trying to dodge potential bullets.
>
> > (Director, early childhood education setting)

These comments are a reflection of the deep-seated hostility that still exists about non-heterosexual subjects – hostilities often passed on to young children.

Individual and community fears are often associated with powerful myths that connect gay and lesbian identities to paedophilia, child abuse or recruiting children. Myths that link gays and lesbians to paedophilic behaviour can marginalize and silence individuals (Khayatt 1992; Epstein and Johnson 1998; Riggs 2011; Davies 2012), keeping this form of discrimination off the anti-bias agenda in early childhood education contexts for fear of family and community reprisals. However, it is critical that early childhood educators continue to advocate for more inclusive pedagogies; and reinforce that research overwhelmingly indicates most child sexual abuse is perpetrated by individuals who identify as heterosexual and are family members or well known to children (Breckenridge and Carmody 1992; Easteal 1994).

For many early childhood educators, the personal risks involved in addressing sexuality education can prove to be difficult barriers to negotiate. Foucault's (1977) concept of surveillance as a form of disciplinary power and social control is critical to an understanding of the ways in which some individuals personally constrain themselves from taking risks or stepping outside societal norms. Notions of risk can be socially constructed and operate as a means of social control in order to maintain the status quo and the inequitable power relations that exist in society. Most are aware of the risks of either taking on or supporting a non-heterosexual identity. Consequently, some people choose not to take on the risks, perceiving the possible consequences to be too high; some negotiate the risks across their public and private lives; while others challenge the boundaries head on, as a matter of principle.

Audrey Kobayashi and Brian Ray (2000) highlight that institutions responsible for setting public policy and providing public services, such as health care, social services and education, 'represent a network that also functions ideologically to determine what kinds of risk are more or less acceptable and what levels of risk will be publicly tolerated' (2000: 402). This point is echoed in the research I conducted with Criss Jones Díaz (Robinson and Jones Díaz 2000), which investigated the perceptions, practices and policies of a group of early childhood educators in relation to dealing with diversity and difference in their services (see Chapter 2, *A hierarchy of difference,* this text). Kobayashi and Ray speak of 'a hierarchy of rights', pointing out that many rights are controversial, that not all receive the same support, recognition or priority, and that in fact a 'spectrum of political ideologies' results in 'varying degrees of commitment to equity provision' (2000: 406). Some early childhood educators who have strong commitments to social justice or anti-bias values across such issues as race, ethnicity, gender or (dis)ability can ironically also uphold homophobic and heterosexist values and practices (Robinson and Jones Díaz 2000). Consequently, early childhood education is part of the network that operates ideologically to determine what kinds of risk are more or less acceptable and what levels of social injustice will be tolerated publicly.

Difficult knowledge and power: sexism and homophobia/heterosexism

Building ethical values and practices early in children's lives is critical, and this is particularly so in the context of gendered relationships and sexuality. In recent years there have been a number of controversial incidents associated with the enculturation of violence perpetrated against women and girls, as exposed by and debated in the Australian media. Although many of the more public incidents have largely involved unethical and violent sexual behaviour toward women in the military, in the police force, and by some Australian elite sportsmen and college students, they are indicative of a much broader social problem (Pollard 2009; Braithwaite 2006; Knaus 2012). Further, homophobic violence continues to be rife in schools and in the broader community (Mason and Tomsen 1997; Ferfolja 2009; Davies and McInnes in press 2012; GLSEN and Harris Interactive 2012), while social networking sites such as Facebook and MySpace, in conjunction with mobile communication technologies, are becoming effective sites for harassing girls, women and queer subjects. These homophobic, sexist and often racist incidents are not just isolated to Australia, but are also relevant to other Western developed countries such as the USA, the UK and Canada (GLSEN and Harris Interactive 2012). These incidents and debates highlight an increasingly urgent need for greater community education about children's sexuality, sexual ethics and respectful relationships. As pointed out in Chapter 2, young children are also engaging in unethical and violent gendered behaviours, such as harassment and sexual assault (Australian Associated Press 2009) which inclusive education from an early age has the potential to prevent.

The socially sanctioned marginalization of non-heterosexual relationships and families is not just part of the formal sex education curriculum, but operates across both the formal and hidden curriculum as a whole in school settings on all levels, including early childhood educational contexts (Surtees 2005). Homophobia and heterosexism are everyday experiences encountered by many young people in schools, not just those who identify as LGBTQ or are those perceived to be queer, primarily through the different ways they embody their gender (McClean 1996; Britzman 1997). A recent national online survey of 1,065 elementary school students in 3rd to 6th grade and 1,099 teachers of kindergarten to 6th grade highlighted the prevalence of school bullying, including homophobic harassment, in elementary schools in the USA (GLSEN and Harris Interactive 2012). This survey indicated that 45 per cent of the children reported hearing 'that's so gay' or 'you're so gay' from other children at school often or all the time. Half of the teachers indicated that they hear children use the word 'gay' in a negative way sometimes, often or very often. A quarter of the children reported also hearing other comments like 'fag' and 'leso'. Sexist remarks associated with girls' and boys' gender non-conformance were also frequent (2012: xvi). The most common reason for being bullied or called names reported by the children was associated with a person's appearance, body size and perceived gender non-conformity – that is, a boy looks or acts 'too much like a girl' and a girl looks and acts 'too much like a boy' (2012: xvii). Almost one in ten children indicated that they do not conform to traditional gender norms; and of these children, more than half (56 per cent) indicated they had been called names, made fun of, bullied, or had been the centre of mean rumours, including those posted on the Internet. The report highlights that children who do not conform to gender norms are less likely than other children to feel safe at school, and sometimes do not want to go to school as a consequence (2012: xviii). These experiences are not dissimilar to those found in other Western countries, including the UK, Australia and Canada (Hillier *et al.* 2005; Hunt and Jensen 2007; Wolfe and Chiodo 2008).

Contrary to the right of students to feel safe in schools, homophobic slurs often go unchallenged by school authorities (Robinson and Ferfolja 2001; Davies 2008b; Robinson 2012a; Davies and McInnes in press 2012; GLSEN and Harris Interactive 2012). This harassment and alienation begins early in life, with young children learning that there are normalized performances of gender, and that they are required to conform, with critical consequences if they do not. The stark reality of homophobic and heterosexist violence, hate crime murders, and gay and lesbian adult and youth suicides, clearly supports the need to work with children early around these issues (Denborough 1996; Hillier and Walsh 1999; Mac An Ghaill 1994). Nothing makes this point more strongly than the fact that it is adolescent boys and young men who enact the largest percentage of hate crimes based on sexual identities (Chasnoff and Cohen 1997; Tomsen and Mason 2001).

Young children's gendered subjectivities are intimately linked to their constitution as sexualized subjects. Homophobic and heterosexist discursive practices are prevalent within their daily lives, policing their positioning within heterosexuality (Butler 1990; Epstein 1995; Robinson 2012a). Within the discourse of hegemonic masculinity, the aggressive rejection of different forms of masculinities, particularly those perceived to be non-heterosexual, is often played out in forms of harassment and violence (Connell 1995; Kimmel 1994; Mac An Ghaill 1994; Mills 2001; Martino and Pallotta-Chiarolli 2003, 2005; Robinson in press 2012b). Anti-homophobia and anti-heterosexist education needs to be included in sexuality education curricula from an early stage, as processes of prejudice, hatred and discrimination are already well under way in the early years of children's lives.

Key points in this chapter

I have argued throughout this chapter that the regulation of children's access to sexual knowledge plays a critical role in the production of children as heteronormative sexual subjects, assuring the perpetuation of the heteronormative adult citizen-subject. This regulation has serious implications for both the immediate and long-term health and wellbeing of children throughout their lives. It is critical that children have access to open, well-informed, honest discussions about sexuality education that takes account of children's agency, in order to build resilience and competencies in this area. A review and reconceptualization of current sex education curricula and pedagogies in schooling is especially important in this process (Robinson and Davies 2008b). In a society where children are increasingly required to negotiate and make decisions about a broad range of options in their lives represented through media, popular culture, consumer advertising and the Internet, it is essential to provide them with the critical skills to do this in a competent and confident manner.

Chapter 5

Children's sexual subjectivities

Introduction

This chapter focuses on children's sexual subjectivities – how children have been constructed as sexual subjects, how children construct themselves as sexual subjects, and how children regulate the sexual subjectivities of their peers. The discussion is largely based on research (Davies and Robinson 2010; Robinson 2012a) conducted with a group of four and five-year-old children and their parents, which explored children's understandings of relationships, love, marriage and intimacy, as well as how their parents viewed their understandings of these issues. This research reinforces other work in this area that highlights that, from an early age, children have a strong sense of desire, wish to act on that desire, and are actively engaged in constructing their sexual subjectivities (Boldt 1997; Goldman and Goldman 1982; Jackson 1982; Plummer 1995; Tobin 1997; Ryan 2000; Chrisman and Couchenour 2002; Renold 2006; Blaise 2010; Davies and Robinson 2010). Young children try to critically make sense of and sort through the bits and pieces of information they receive about sexuality. Children actively engage in making meanings about sexuality in their early lives based on this limited information (which is often misinformation, stereotypes or myths). They receive this information from families, peers, television, the Internet and through their daily experiences, especially of observing others – older children, young people or adults, and pets and other animals.

Life markers, such as being in love, boyfriends and girlfriends, marriage and having babies, are integral to the narratives of many young children's early lives and their perceptions of their destinies. Children's desires and love for a special friend are often played out in the context of fantasies of marriage. In fact, children can have an obsessive interest in marriage and they often rehearse the act of getting married in their play. This play-acting is frequently encouraged and celebrated in family and early childhood educational settings. Children's perceptions of marriage often frame their understandings of gender and of sexuality, and inform how these aspects of their subjectivities are played out in children's lives. Children generally take up the hegemonic discourse of marriage as being between a man and a woman, viewing this narrative as the *normal* social arrangement in which physical intimacy, love and having babies is legitimized. Children consider this as representative of the natural and normal progression of their lives into adulthood. The constitution of children as heteronormative subjects is not only inherent in schooling philosophies, curricula and practices, as discussed in the previous chapter, but is also part of the everyday practices in families and in children's interaction with each other. When children take up different narratives of gender and sexuality, they often meet resistance from their peers (as well as from many adults) who work to police their relocation in heteronormative discourses (Renold 2008; Gerouki 2010).

The young children and parents who participated in the research on which this discussion is largely based were recruited through several early childhood educational centres and playgroups in Sydney, in the Australian state of New South Wales (NSW). Information was sent out about the research to parents via these avenues, and those interested in being involved came to an information session I held to explain the project further and to answer any questions. Focus groups were held with several groups of parents who volunteered to be involved and separately with several groups of their young children. Parents initially gave their consent for their children to participate, but children were also asked to give their consent for their involvement. To initiate the discussions with both parents and children about issues of sexuality, relationships, love and marriage, a number of images were used from popular cultural texts and from media sources. There was an image from *Anastasia* (Krulik 1997) in which Anastasia was being held by her male suitor in a garden setting; a magazine advertisement for a coffee lounge, which depicted a young girl and boy around seven years of age drinking coffee and eating ice-cream in what looked to be a date between the two; a common postcard found in gift shops depicting a boy and a girl, around seven years of age, arm-in-arm in mock wedding outfits (see Figure 5.1); and a photograph which had appeared in a mainstream Australian weekend newspaper of a young boy and girl spontaneously embracing in an exaggerated Hollywood-style kiss (see Figure 5.4) (Hooton 2001). These images were used to begin conversations with young children in a similar way to the kinds of story-telling activities that they experience daily in their educational lives (Brody 1984; Fabian 1996; Jasman 1998; Pink 2005). This is a familiar process for young children, and is an effective means through which to talk with children about their ideas on the issues that the images reflect or other concepts that have relevance to the image. The same images were used with parents to prompt discussions about their perceptions of their children's knowledge around love, relationships, marriage and sexuality; how they themselves had gained knowledge of these issues when they were growing up; and what their practices were in regard to talking with their children about these issues.

The images included in the book (of which Figures 5.1 and 5.4 were used with parents and children) are interesting, in that all except Figure 5.4

highlight how representations of children kissing and children in wedding outfits have been historically popular images amongst adults, and have been often used for commercial advertising or postcards internationally.

Dominant discourses on children as sexual subjects

In Western societies, the construction of children as sexual subjects has been steeped in contradictions and constituted within a behaviouralist dualistic framework that views the sexual child as either natural or normal, or perverse and contrary to nature. From within this context, several discourses of children's sexuality have emerged, impacting the way that children as sexual subjects are viewed. First, the child has been discursively constituted as naturally innocent, immature and asexual – with the child's sexuality lying dormant until puberty and adolescence. Diana Gittins (1998: 167) makes the point that 'respectable' Victorian women were idealized as 'asexual, domestic and pure', and that these same values were applied to children. The precariousness of the child's innocence is acknowledged through the belief that it warrants protection from parents and the state. This discourse is reinforced by developmentalism – not only is the child believed to be physically or sexually immature, but also emotionally and cognitively undeveloped and incapable of comprehending adult concepts such as sexuality and desire.

Second, the child has at the same time been constructed as inherently perverse and sexually precocious, and as such is perceived as not only a danger to itself but also to the social and moral order in society (Jackson 2006). This discourse is oppositional to the asexual and innocent child, and produces a contradiction, which reflects the Madonna/whore binary. This binary has been mobilized to define and regulate the sexual subjectivities of both women and children, especially the girl child. Madonna/whore stereotypes have culturally constituted girls as either 'little angels' ('sugar and spice and all things nice') or as little 'vixens, Lolitas and flirts' (Gittins 1998: 167). Sigmund Freud's notion of the 'seductive child' in his earlier accounts of child sexual abuse reflect this binary, which has often been mobilized to blame the victim in such cases. Historically, this Freudian perspective impacted medical approaches to young women's claims of sexual abuse, in that young women were often believed to have been complicit in initiating the sexual encounter.

Third, other schools of thought have viewed children's sexuality as normal, natural and critical to children's intellectual development and healthy adulthood. This Freudian perspective of children's sexuality was popularized in the USA, Britain and Australia during the mid-1950s, largely through the works of Benjamin Spock. Spock's views on child-rearing prevailed through the 1960s and 1970s, which came to be known as the progressive era in terms of sexuality. Freud believed there were identifiable natural stages in psychosexual development during infancy, and considered these to be integral to a mature heterosexual adulthood. Unlike previous eras, where children's sexuality was perceived to be dangerous, parents were encouraged to accommodate children's erotic impulses and curiosities (e.g. masturbation) as much as possible, as they were perceived to be how children learnt about the world. It was considered important that children's minds were free to develop without inhibitions, fears and anxieties. Children's sex-play was seen as wholesome. Freud claimed that neurosis in adulthood, including sexual deviancy, was a result of repression of sexuality in childhood and childhood trauma. However, despite progressive values during this time, children's sexuality was viewed as needing to be contained within the privacy of the family home and not displayed publicly (Jenkins 1998). Henry Jenkins (1998: 211) points out that 'children display an inconvenient degree of sexual curiosity and pleasure'. This is an issue that is continually raised in my research and discussions with parents and educators of young children. They often find children's public (and private) sexual behaviour embarrassing and difficult to control. Young children soon learn the social taboos surrounding this behaviour.

A fourth discourse assumes the child's sexual subjectivity to be naturally heterosexual. This discourse dismisses the social construction of sexuality and desire that operates through broad socio-cultural practices in society. The discourse of compulsory heterosexuality underpins the constitution and regulation of the child as a heteronormative subject. Even though children are predominantly viewed as asexual or as having a dormant sexuality that emerges at puberty, children's sexuality is considered inherently to be heterosexual – heterosexuality is considered a given in the human subject in this discourse. This fixed understanding of sexuality is linked to gender and the sexed body, as argued by Butler in relation to the concept of the 'heterosexual matrix' (Butler 1990). This matrix is a framework of meaning through which understandings of sex, gender and desire (sexuality) are signified and constituted within natural and ideal relationships with each other. That is, gender is believed to stem from one's sex, and sexuality or desire is considered to come naturally from gender: femininity is naturally embodied in female bodies, masculinity is naturally embodied in male bodies, and 'modalities of desire and pleasure' (Butler 1989: 259) are constituted in these oppositional bodies – males desire females and vice versa. Gender and sexuality are considered stemming from the sexed body. However, this relationship is not natural, but rather is socially sanctioned through the effects of gender norms.

The construction of gender in children's lives is inextricably constituted within and normalized through the heterosexual matrix in which the process of heterosexualization is founded. Through the processes of gendering, children are constructed as heterosexual beings. Despite the prevalence of the dominant discourse of childhood, which constructs children as innocent, asexual and too young to understand sexuality, the construction of heterosexual desire and identities in early childhood is an integral part of children's everyday experiences (Thorne and Luria 1986; Davies 1989, 1993; Thorne 1993; Epstein 1995). Steven Bruhm and Natasha Hurley (2004) argue that 'People panic when sexuality takes on a life outside the sanctioned scripts of child's play'. Within all these discourses children's agency and voices are missing. Danielle Egan and Gail Hawkes (2009: 393) aptly point out that 'children's sexuality within dominant discourse is still ideologically dependent on what adults deem to be socially acceptable'. Young children's and adolescents' sexuality and sexual agency have traditionally been understood as a challenge to adult power and authority. Children and young people who demonstrate sexual agency are often perceived to be inappropriately crossing the boundaries of the adult/child divide. Adolescent power and autonomy is frequently expressed through active sexuality, and is often viewed by others as emanating from a lack of parental control and discipline (Gittins 1998). Children's agency is about being in control of their own bodies, being supported in understanding and exploring different ways of expressing gender and sexuality, being confident in challenging peer pressure, having an awareness and understanding of their rights, and learning to take responsibility for making their own decisions (McKee et al. 2010). The following discussion provides a glimpse of the perspectives of young children about relationships, love, and who they see themselves to be as gendered and sexual subjects. Children are subjected to similarly broad socio-cultural practices that aim to construct normative gendered and sexual subjects, but childhood is also a space where different ways of being are made possible (Robinson and Davies 2008a).

The discourse of marriage framing children's understandings of sexuality and relationships

The family is one of the most critical discursive fields in which the subjectification of children is enacted. Subjectification is the process by which individuals position themselves in and through discourse at the same time as they are subjected to the constitutive effects of those discourses (Davies 1994). Children negotiate the various socio-cultural and political discourses made available to them in their lives, locating themselves in particular discourses in order to make meanings of their experiences, feelings and everyday encounters. The beliefs about marriage held by the children in this research were complex and contradictory, as well as being fragmentary and partial. Children do not passively take up the discourses of their families, but rather are active agents negotiating the discourses available to them from various sources, sometimes finding investments in counter-narratives to those of their parents and other family members.

Still, discourses of heteronormativity largely constituted and regulated children's understandings of marriage, which were not only perpetuated through their experiences of attending weddings and of family values and practices (for example, wedding photos on display in homes is a common practice), but also through their peers, media, children's literature, popular culture and schooling, which all constitute marriage as a heteronormative practice. Children in this research generally had a preoccupation with marriage, which was reflected in their engagement in mock weddings in their play activities and in their everyday discussions with their peers about who they intended to marry. Children frequently questioned their parents about when they got married and often asked other adults they met if they were married or intended to marry. Marriage was considered a rite of passage and an expected part of children becoming adults. Children primarily connected marriage to adults having children, and their understandings of sexual relationships were framed within this context. This was highlighted in the following conversation with a group of four and five-year-old girls:

Researcher:	Can kids get married?
Rita:	No way.
Researcher:	Why not?
Rita:	Because they won't get children.
Researcher:	Because they won't get children?
Belinda:	They are children.
Sara:	Because they are too young.
Researcher:	Why do people get married?
Mel:	They are in love with somebody.
Belinda:	Children can't get married, yeah because the Dad has the stuff that makes the kids.
Sophie:	I know what it is called, sperm.
Researcher:	Yes.
Belinda:	And the wife has the egg.
Researcher:	Yes.
Sophie:	When the sperm meets the egg that turns it to an egg, the egg hatches and the baby comes out.

The children were not asked any questions about how babies were made by the researcher, but they made a strong connection between marriage, reproduction and sexuality more generally. Children's narratives of having babies are often pieced together from what they already know, from bits of information they receive from adults, other children, television or from watching animals reproducing. Belinda has some of the language to convey her understandings of the process of fertilization and reproduction, but her notion of an egg is based on what she is familiar with, a chicken egg, and her experience of watching a chicken hatch from an egg.

The discourse that marriage was for having babies was so strong amongst these children that it eclipsed the personal circumstances of some of the children whose parents were not married. The discussion brought out this contradiction for Sophie in particular, who suddenly realized that having babies was not necessarily linked to marriage. Sophie sat quietly in deep thought until she exclaimed:

Sophie: My mum and dad aren't married, [pausing deep in thought] but ... [pausing again to think about it] ... they aren't married!
Researcher: They have children.
Sophie: Yes, but they aren't married.
Researcher: Why else might someone get married?
Sophie: Mmm ... [pausing and thinking] ... because if they are lonely they want someone to live with.
Belinda: [In a loud voice, looking surprised] They aren't married!

Sophie's review of her understanding of marriage and its links to having children led to a broader perspective of marriage as possibly being more about relationships between adults. In this case, Sophie could imagine that loneliness could bring two people together in order to consider marrying. Belinda followed the conversation intently, coming to a similar surprised revelation as Sophie as she realized the significance of Sophie's parents not being married for her own understandings of marriage and its role in producing children. The children soon moved on to the next point of discussion about their own plans to marry:

Cindy: I have already decided who I'm going to marry.
Researcher: Have you? Who is it?
Cindy: It is at my big school. Well I have got two so I don't know which one.
Researcher: And what are their names?
Cindy: Billy and Nash.
Researcher: Are you going to get married Sara?
Sara: Yes.
Researcher: Why do you want to get married?
Sara: I don't know.
Christy: I've got a boyfriend.
Researcher: You have one do you? What's his name?
Belinda: [Quickly answering for Christy] William. He is at my school.
Researcher: What makes him special?
Christy: He's my cousin.
Researcher: He's your cousin?
Belinda: You can't marry a cousin, that's what my Dad and Mum said.
Christy: Well, he's too old – he's 12. But I think he is very kind and silly.

Having a boyfriend provided some status for the young girls amongst their peers in the group – it was aligned with being older or more adult-like (Renold 2005). Belinda, taking up a normalizing and regulating position, reminds Christy that she cannot marry William because he is her cousin. Christy and Belinda were close friends but they were often competing for the dominant position in the group, speaking more than the other children and often challenging each other's comments. After being challenged by Belinda, Christy tries to salvage her suddenly more precarious position of power in the group by quickly dismissing her interest in William, indicating that he was actually too old for her. Being interested in an older boy, regardless of his cousin-status, had some positive kudos for Christy and she was not willing to forgo that completely, quickly reaffirming her interest in William and stating why she liked him. Belinda's comment also highlights how boyfriends are viewed in terms of potential marriage partners; she is quick to undermine any kudos that Christy gained by having a boyfriend, especially an older boyfriend. Belinda's comment is even more powerful as she takes up the authoritative voice of her parents.

Marriage was considered an expectation amongst all of the children. Although one of the girls, Angelina, who was just about to turn six, commented, 'You don't have to get married'; but she went on to point out that marriage was a central part of her plans. Children were very much aware of marriage as symbolic of becoming an adult – a process that some children were eager to engage in, as indicated in the following conversation with four-year-old Rita and three-year-old Toby:

Researcher: When does someone get married?
Rita: When they are bigger. And one boy and girl get married.
Researcher: When they are bigger. Are you going to get married?
Rita: When I'm bigger.
Researcher: What about you Toby? Do you think you will get married when you are bigger?
Toby: I'm already bigger!
Researcher: You are already bigger? And you have already gotten married – you told us didn't you? [A mock wedding during dress-up play in preschool]
Toby: Yeah.
Researcher: Will you get married again when you are bigger?
Toby: Yes. I will be a grown-up soon.

These conversations highlight several issues about marriage for these children. Young children are engaging in the discourse of marriage early in their lives, and are fantasizing about people they wish to marry and are enacting these fantasies in their play. All the children unquestioningly believed that they would naturally get married when they were older, but for Sara, the

Figure 5.1 United States, circa 1920s: *Boy and Girl Dressed up as Bride and Groom, Outdoors on Steps*, H. Armstrong Roberts.

reason why she would get married was not yet part of her processing. The children's understandings of marriage reflected broader social norms, which constitute marriage in heterormorative frameworks, as reflected in this instance by Rita, who added that marriage is between a boy and a girl. Getting married is representative of becoming an adult and encompasses a level of power and authority that children are eager to possess. Toby is keen to be recognized as an adult and to take on some of the power and status that this represents. Throughout the focus group, Toby and Rita were in a constant battle for recognition and power, with each trying to assert their authority over the other (a point that I discuss further below). In this case, Toby, being the youngest, smallest, and the only boy in this group, tries to assert his power and authority by claiming that he is already bigger and has already been married. Although this was a pretend marriage during dress-ups at his preschool, he tries to use the symbolic and emotional capital of marriage as currency to gain some status in the group.

Wedding celebrations take on a carnivalesque atmosphere (Bakhtin 1994), and it is this aspect in particular that heightens young children's interest in and attention to marriage. The spectacle of the wedding ceremony – the dressing up of the bride and groom, the bridal gown casting the woman in the fantastical role of princess, the wedding cake, the presents, the food, music, dancing and laughter – captures not only children's pleasure and imagination, but also their desire as they become witnesses to a rite of passage that awaits them in adulthood. The marriage ceremony becomes a spectacle that is continually played out in children's everyday lives through fantasies, such as being princes and princesses for a day. This kind of play becomes a rehearsal or a parody of pseudo-adult intimate relations, maturity and power. In some cases, children become central to the adult wedding pageant in the roles of flower girls or pageboys. In the Bakhtian sense, the carnivalesque nature of weddings provides a context in which the power distinctions between adult and child can be momentarily blurred and levelled, especially for young children, as both engage in a ritual which involves a love of dressing up, romantic fantasy, dancing, cake, and having fun. This all becomes a critical and powerful discursive point of the enculturation of children into normative discourses of adult relations and practices, and a point in which children actively make meanings of marriage.

Children and kissing

Kissing for some children is a symbolic gesture through which they express their desire and feelings for someone special they 'really, really' like or love. On another level, the game of Catch and Kiss is part of young children's play culture that is reflective of an awareness of their own gendered and sexual subjectivities. It can be viewed as a flirting game in which children usually chase, catch and kiss their target – generally someone of the opposite sex that they are interested in. It is part of the process of heterosexualization in young children's lives – a process in which children's desires are constituted within gender norms (Butler 1990). The expression of this desire is integral to their intelligibility as heteronormative gendered subjects. Not all children enjoy the thrill of the chase, as pointed out during my research by a mother of one four-year-old boy, who relayed her son's trauma around being the target of this behaviour from two enthusiastic young girls who professed that they liked him. When caught, her son was pinned to the ground as they attempted to kiss him. The mother was particularly concerned at the lack of intervention in this behaviour from his teachers. Mindy Blaise's (2009) discussion with a group of five and six-year-olds in an early childhood classroom highlights the significance of heteronormative discourses of gender in the lives of those young girls in her group. Perceptions that girls have to be sexy to get a boyfriend, or that they have to be pretty, dominated amongst the girls, undermining the counter-discourse that girls did not have to be pretty to get a boyfriend and that other factors such as being smart are important.

Marriage was not just linked to having babies for the children in this research but, outside the play context of Catch and Kiss, it was viewed as another legitimate context in which kissing others was acceptable. The discourse that sexual intimacy is acceptable and appropriate between married couples underpinned many of the children's perspectives, often to the

Figure 5.2 France, circa 1938: *Children Kissing in Paris*, Lucien Aigner.

surprise of their parents. This is reflected in Louisa's comment on her son Luka's wish to marry his girlfriend. Luka, who was in Kindergarten (the entry year for students in the Australian primary school system), viewed marriage as a rite of passage to being able to kiss his girlfriend. Louisa comments:

> Luka links marriage to kissing. He says you can only kiss someone if you are married. I don't know where that comes from, I just don't know. I think he can't wait to marry, I think it might be like a wow factor and then they are going to kiss. Because he has just realized that you can only kiss girls when you are married. He is going to marry Bridget.

Annette, mother of four-year-old Thomas, echoes this in a similar comment:

> Children have this thing that when you get married you can kiss. And I guess that's what he watches at home on the Wednesday, with my mum and dad, they watch the *Bold and the Beautiful*.

What is highlighted in these comments is not just that the marriage process gives one access to kissing, but it is sometimes considered by children to be the only means through which kissing is made possible, as in Luka's eyes.

For Luka, marriage is perceived as the means through which intimate physical relations, such as kissing, are socially and morally sanctioned – a discourse that is obviously not necessarily perpetuated by his parents. Louisa's comment that Luka has only just 'realized' that you can 'only' kiss girls if you are married highlights a particular discourse of marriage that is conservative and moralistic. This demonstrates the way in which children are influenced by the discourses of marriage and relationships that prevail in other contexts beyond those in the family, particularly those perpetuated through popular culture and media. Children's familiarity with the narrative of marriage no doubt impacts on their perceptions of kissing between adults, as shown in the comments made by this four-year-old:

Researcher: What happens when you get married?
Rebecca: Um, the girl dresses up pretty and the man he dresses up too.
Researcher: Oh right. And then what happens?
Rebecca: Um, they kiss each other.

The end of the traditional marriage ceremony and the beginning of new married life is signified through the following announcement, or some variation of it: 'I now pronounce you man and wife. You can now kiss the bride'. The kiss becomes part of the spectacle of the marriage ceremony, which links marriage with sexual/romantic expression. Children's perception of marriage as regulating sexual and romantic expression (e.g. kissing) is a cultural ritual in which all of the children in this study wished to partake, particularly the boys. Marriage was representative of adult power and status, and seen as the avenue through which one's desire could be fulfilled. Luka was especially keen to be married to his girlfriend, as conveyed by his mother Louisa in the following comment:

> Luka has been talking about marrying so and so from school, from Kindy [Kindergarten]. And you know, my husband is trying to say, or was talking the other night that, you know, you just don't know who you are going to marry Luka. You just don't know who you are going to marry when you grow up, because you might not love so and so, you might fall in love with other people. He goes, No! I'm marrying Bridget and that is it. So I mean I know he is only little but like, and he goes I am going to marry that person and that is it, and he stormed off, and he was really upset.

Luka is emphatic about his desire to marry Bridget, who is in his class, despite his father's attempts to relay the notion that marriage is an adults' practice and that by the time Luka is old enough to marry, his feelings for this girl will have changed. Luka is not willing to concede that he has no access to the privilege of marriage associated with adulthood, and claims that his desire to marry his girlfriend is legitimate regardless of what his parents think. Luka's anger at his parents dismissal of his feelings also reflects the strong emotions he has for Bridget – which he calls love.

Children and being in love

Being in love is often considered to be a prerogative of adults, with children's and young people's claims of being in love often dismissed as childish, naïve, cute and fantastical. In a recent article, Diana K. Sugg (2012), a Pulitzer Prize-winning journalist and now a freelance writer and a mother of two sons, wrote about her five-year-old son Sam, who proclaimed that he had fallen in love with his classmate Emma. Sugg tells how her son had been bringing his friend Emma home for weeks, and that they had been having a 'grand time' playing and hugging, which Sugg and her husband had found humorous and 'adorable'. Her son's announcement of falling in love had left them surprised and unsure of how best to deal with the situation. In the article, Sugg interviews the director of preschool psychiatry programs at Johns Hopkins Children's Center in the USA, who points out that romantic love is often experienced early in a child's life, generally around five or six, and that this love is genuine and should be respected, accepted and not be trivialized by adults. Sugg concludes the article by summing up the everyday experiences of her son's relationship with his girlfriend:

> Emma and Sam have decided they're going to get married. They've practiced their wedding dance. They've named their five children. More importantly, they have fun, and they watch out for each other. She makes him cards; he brings her the water bottle she left behind.

The children's future plans reflect an unquestioning normality and naturalness that is inherent in romanticized heteronormative narratives of life, and this is reinforced by the mother's tone of voice and acceptance of the children's relationship. The article ends with Sugg noticing Sam's happiness as he holds Emma's hand in the back seat of the car. There are two interesting points arising from this article. First, that young children's claims of love are real and parents need to find ways of supporting these feelings rather than dismissing them as childish: the consequences of doing this were obviously what Luka's parents were dealing with in the discussion above on children's understandings of kissing. Second, it begs the question of how Sugg, her husband, the director of preschool psychiatry programs, as well as the many readers of this article, would react if this narrative was not framed in heteronormative terms – that is, if Sam claimed to be in love with James, and they had practiced their wedding and wedding dance, named their five children, and were holding hands in the back seat of the car. This narrative is also reflective of the lives of other young children, but does not in many cases elicit the same reactions from parents and professionals.

The following discussions highlight young children's perspectives of being in love:

Researcher: What does being in love mean?
Sophie: Their hearts are together.
Researcher: Can children be in love?
Sophie: They can be in love but they can't get married.
Researcher: What do you think Sara? Can children be in love?
Sara: Yes.
Researcher: Have you been in love?
Sara: Yes.
Researcher: How do you know that you were in love?
Sara: It is a hard question.
Researcher: Yes it can be. [Turning to the others] How do you know when someone is in love?
Sophie: Because they are best friends and they love each other. They look and smile at each other.
Researcher: Have you been in love, Sophie?
Sophie: Yes, in love with my boyfriend.
Researcher: What does that mean?
Sophie: I love Ben.
Researcher: What does it mean when you love someone?
Angelina: You feel like marrying them.
Researcher: Can children be in love?
Angelina: Yes.
Researcher: What does 'in love' mean?
Angelina: They really, really, really, really love each other.
Researcher: Have you been in love?
Angelina: Um, yeah.
Researcher: Who have you been in love with?
Angelina: My best friend, Lauren, a girl.
Researcher: What makes her special?
Angelina: Um, because when we are at school she always lets me go first to be in games.

For some children, being in love does not necessarily fall into heteronormative frameworks, as in Angelina's case. What is interesting in these comments is, for Angelina, being in love means 'really, really, really, really' loving someone that you feel you want to marry – once again highlighting the significance of marriage in symbolically demonstrating how much you love someone. Angelina indicates that she has experienced being in love with her best friend – someone who is kind and takes care of you in some way. Being in love with your best friend is not an uncommon scenario amongst young children. What is interesting is that Angelina makes the point that Lauren is a girl, perhaps reinforcing this important point just in case it was not recognized from Lauren's name. Angelina may have wanted to emphasize the transgression in her choice before the researcher potentially made it. How young children's desires are regulated by adults and their peers to fit gender norms and how they resist or conform to these norms is an every day interaction negotiated by young children, as we can see in the following section.

Children's regulation of the heteronormative gendered subject

The relationship between knowledge and power amongst children in this research was evident through children's interactions with each other. Children mobilized discourses of age, heteronormativity and social agency to increase their power and positioning amongst siblings and peers. Discourses operate through language and constitute the different knowledge that we have available to us; often these discourses appear invisible, or are not a part of our everyday conscious awareness (Foucault 1974). In the early years, children's knowledge is frequently constructed through the framework of 'procedures' (Davies and Robinson 2010). These procedures – that is, set steps followed in the learning process – might include learning to cross the

Figure 5.3 Location unknown, 1965: *Children Bride Groom Wedding,* H. Armstrong Roberts.

road, toilet training, or helping to bake a cake, where children follow the set stages to reach their goal. Young children often engaged this mode of learning to process information of which they have limited knowledge (Davies and Robinson 2010). Children's understandings of relationships, marriage and sexuality followed procedures that were located in moral and heteronormative discourses, even if their own reality was different. Children often make assumptions about sexuality based on gendered relations represented in popular culture and in their everyday lives.

An interesting discussion and power struggle occurred between Rita (four years old) and Toby (three years old) around Toby's eager assertion that he had married his best friend, Patrick. Rita rebuked Toby's experience, stating that children could not get married, and that two boys could not get married. Her critique of Toby's experience was largely based on her own experience of never having seen two children or two boys get married. Rita eventually mobilizes her age, size and discourses of heteronormativity to make her point – which is confirmed by Petra, a four-year-old, who has the final say:

Researcher:	Can children get married?
Rita:	No.
Researcher:	Do you think children can get married, Toby?
Toby:	Yeah ... I already got married.
Researcher:	Did you? Whereabouts did you get married?
Toby:	We were wearing dress ups. My Nan has this dress that I had on.
Researcher:	What were you wearing?
Toby:	We were wearing it in dress-ups. And it had flowers on it.
Researcher:	Flowers all over it? That's good. Who did you marry?
Toby:	My best friend. With him ... Patrick.
Researcher:	Can two boys get married?
Toby:	Yeah.
Rita:	They can't. I've never seen that.
Researcher:	You don't think two boys can get married?
Rita:	No ... because I am bigger than him [referring to Toby].
Researcher:	[To Rita] Can you tell me why you don't think children can get married?
Rita:	Because I have seen grown-ups get married ... [pausing to think]. Kids can.
Researcher:	Kids can too? You have changed your mind. Can you tell me why kids can?
Rita:	Cause they can have little dress-ups.
Researcher:	What about two girls, can they get married?
Rita:	No. It's the same as the boys.
Toby:	I don't know ... [thinking]. No.

Researcher:	No. Why can't two girls get married?
Toby:	Because I have never seen one.
Petra:	No.
Researcher:	Can you tell me why?
Petra:	Because two girls or boys can't be with each other ... only girls and boys can be with each other.

On the question of whether children can get married, Rita reassesses her initial position based on Toby's experience of being in a mock wedding. Rita, asserting her status as an older, more knowledgeable member of the group, distinguishes between children, who can get married through play (dress-ups), and adults, whose marriage is perceived as real. As reflected in the children's comments, strong heteronormative discourses prevailed amongst the children's understandings of love and marriage. Drawing on her experience of heteronormative conventions of marriage, Rita regulates Toby's experience by insisting that two boys cannot get married. In this case, Rita mobilizes her substantial size difference to try and make her point of view prevail over that of Toby's, who remains silent after Rita's challenge. Despite the momentary challenge by Toby with a personal counter-narrative about the potential of two boys marrying and providing an account of different performance of gender, he succumbs to Rita's position of power and follows her logic around the question of two girls marrying. Toby points out that two girls could not marry because he has never seen it happen. Petra has the final say and is adamant that marriage is solely a heteronormative practice.

In another group, some children again challenged the heteronormative conventions of marriage, reflecting the authority and trust that children placed in their personal experiences and in their parents' knowledge:

Researcher:	Can two girls get married?
Belinda:	Well, that's called ... um ... you have a girlfriend but they can't get married to the girlfriend.
Sophie:	Girls can get married, because what happens if you have two mums.
Researcher:	That's a good point.
Sophie:	At school there was a girl and she had two mums.
Researcher:	And were her mums married?
Sophie:	Yes ... I am not real sure.
Researcher:	Can two boys get married?
Sophie:	Yes, because I have seen somebody who has two dads. Because they can have two mums, that's what my dad says. And two dads.
Researcher:	And were the dads married?
Sophie:	Yeah.

Sophie challenges Belinda's assertion that two girls cannot get married through her understanding and experience of same-sex families. Having no demonstrated awareness that same-sex marriage is not legal in Australia, Sophie mobilizes the discourse that links and normalizes having children with marriage. Her logic is that if you are a mother or father, then you must have had children and you therefore must be married – a logic that she has already found lacking in her own case as her parents are not married, as discussed earlier in this chapter. What this conversation highlights is that many children experience and engage with difference in their lives, including same-sex families, and develop an awareness of same-sex relationships more generally. Some children challenge normative discourses based on this awareness and experience, introducing counter-discourses into other children's lives for consideration.

Children's sexual agency

As mentioned earlier, in my research with the young children that has been the foundation for much of this chapter, I utilized several pictures to start conversations with both the children and their parents around relevant issues addressed in the study. One of the images used was a photograph titled 'The Kiss', which captures the uncensored performance of a young boy and girl (approximately seven years old) embracing in a Hollywood-style French kiss (see Figure 5.4). After watching the failed attempts of adult actors to engage in a meaningful kiss as required by the photographer, who was taking pictures for an advertisement for denim jeans, the boy and girl unabashedly declared that they had what it took to do the job properly, and quickly engaged in their interpretation of the kiss required. This photograph appeared in a weekend magazine supplement to a major Australian newspaper in a regular segment called 'The Moment', which invites readers to send in photographs with a brief background story. In this photograph, both children are bare foot, standing on an old jetty. The boy is bending over holding the girl around the neck and waist, and kissing her on the mouth. The girl's back is arched and she is in a lunging position in order to keep her balance. Her hand is grasping the boy's arm, which in turn is clutching on to the waist of her skirt. The skirt is hitched up slightly, and her mid-riff area is exposed due to the riding up of her shirt. This photograph challenges the hegemonic reading of childhood and children as innocent, naïve and unknowing in terms of sexual expression, and destabilizes the boundary between adulthood and childhood. In the background brief to the picture, the photographer, Anthony Browell, comments:

> There was so much energy in them – it really showed what the models were lacking. We continued with the shoot, and we did get something in the end, but it didn't have anything on those kids. No spark, no magic.
>
> (Browell 2001)

Figure 5.4 Australia, 2001: *The Kiss*, Anthony Browell.

The children's sexual agency, confidence, and knowledge of how to perform such a kiss confronted many adults viewing the photograph. Many felt surprised and troubled, whilst some considered it fascinating and cute. In the photograph, the children represent themselves as knowing, passionate, sexual, adult-like, uninhibited and in control. The photograph captures a rawness and brashness in the children's sexual subjectivities that leaves uneasiness in some viewers, as it destabilizes 'the normative practices that make everyone else feel safe and secure' (Halberstam 2005: 10). One of the mothers, Margot, commented that it was the children's engagement in 'passion' that she found most disturbing:

> I think there is something about the pose, because it is so grown-up, it is a passionate pose, it is a passionate kiss and the passion therefore leads to a sort of sexualization and that's what, if they were standing straight, kind of giving one another a kiss even with arms wrapped around one another would be, to me, just far, far less offensive. It is the pose, because it is depicting passion, and passion equals sex, and they are just too young for that pose and I think that is what it is about ... it is all very disturbing.

Showing this photograph to parents participating in my research led to a questioning of how children know about sexuality and how to behave in such a manner. This led to some considering their own childhoods, as demonstrated in the following discussion, which arose in one of the adult focus groups:

Martin: Shocking!

Jenny: Well I think – I don't know how it actually makes me feel, but I think it is really interesting that children that young are able to play up that narrative so successfully, in fact almost more successfully than adults in a particular kind of way because it is so familiar to them, that they know precisely what to do.

Martin: How do they know?

Jenny: Well, exactly, I don't know – it is all around them all the time, so it is not, it is kind of – it is not shocking. I mean it is sexualizing in that sense that there is something shocking about it, but then it is also so familiar that it is not shocking at all. I think that if I saw that as a young person I would have wanted to be that girl in a narrative that I felt that I could never get. But I would have to be quite honest about it, it is absolutely true, that is probably what I would have wanted – not necessarily the level of sexualization but what seems to be inside a narrative that I didn't have access to for whatever reasons.

Children's responses to the photograph reflected a similar uneasiness in that it also troubled their understandings of the adult/child binary. The children examined the photograph intently:

Belinda: The last one ... what is that?

Researcher: What is happening in that one?

Christy: They are kissing each other.

Belinda: It looks like married but it can't be. It looks like ... because they are kids.

Christy: The first one [a picture of two children in a mock wedding] was married.

Researcher: Do kids kiss like that?

Belinda: I am not really sure. No that looks – they must be grown-ups. Grown-ups dressed like kids.

Researcher: They are grown-ups dressed like kids?

Belinda: Yeah.

Belinda and Christy's responses to the photograph are fascinating. First, Belinda's comment that 'it looks like married' reinforces how powerful the discourse of marriage is in children's lives, particularly in relation to how they tend to view and legitimate sexual expression and intimacy between adults. The fact that children are kissing in this fashion confuses Belinda: since she is aware that children cannot marry each other, she dismisses the possibility of it being two children kissing. To make sense of the narrative, Belinda repositions the children in the image as adults dressed as children.

Childhood as queer time and space

As reflected in some of the children's comments discussed above, childhood can be viewed and experienced as a potential counter-public, or a queer time and space, in which alternative imaginings about gender, sexuality and life markers are possible. Robinson and Davies (2007) argue that childhood becomes a counter-public or a queer space when children subvert dominant discourses of childhood and gender, doing childhood and gender differently. They point out that 'queer space refers to the place-making practices in which queer identities engage, as well as new spaces constructed by queer counter-publics' (2007: 21). Counter-publics are 'parallel discursive arenas where members of subordinated social groups invent and circulate counter discourses to formulate oppositional interpretations of their identities, inter-ests, and needs' (Fraser 1992: 123). Children, like adults, are shifting and contradictory subjects; they negotiate the different discourses of gender they encounter in their lives and the relations of power that are perpetuated through these discourses. Most children take up normative performances of gender and strictly regulate not just their own performances, but also those of other children (and of adults). However, some children engage in counter-hegemonic performances of gender – sometimes in public, but often in pri-vate spaces away from the regulating gazes of others (Robinson and Davies 2007; Davies 2008a). Robinson and Davies (2007), in a discussion of young girls' negotiation of masculinity and femininity, highlight the ways that young girls challenge normalizing gender discourses through enacting their desires to perform their genders differently – for example, wearing male clothing. They point out that children are aware of the restrictions that regulatory norms impose on their practices and much of their transgressive behaviours are *closeted*, a mechanism imposed through children's self-surveillance of their own gender performances.

The recently-published children's storybook *My Princess Boy* is written by Cheryl Kilodavis (2010), who is a mother of a young boy who loves to dress up as a princess. Kilodavis devised the story to open up new conversations about doing gender differently, as well as to counteract the largely negative responses that her son was experiencing from other children (and some adults) as a result of his gender non-conforming behaviours. Supportive of their son's wishes to transgress normative discourses of gender, the Kilodavis family are contributing to the development of a counter-public in childhood, in which alternative gender identities can be renegotiated and reconceptual-ized. Children's early educational experiences can contribute to the formation of a space in which children can do gender differently, through providing a safe and supported environment in which children can explore and experiment with gender. But most often, early childhood educational settings and schools are institutions that regulate and police normalizing performances of gender and sexuality (Blaise 2005; MacNaughton 2000; Robinson and Jones Díaz 2006; Surtees and Gunn 2010). One of the major concerns encountered by many early childhood educators is the issue of parents not wishing to have their young boys dressing up in female clothing whilst in their care. This concern stems from parental fears, particularly from fathers, that this practice will result in their boys growing up to be gay in later life (Robinson and Jones Díaz 2006). Interestingly, there is not the same degree of fear expressed about young girls dressing up in male clothing. Girls' tomboyish behaviour is not necessarily considered problematic unless it continues into later adolescence and early adulthood – when the young woman does not seem to be growing out of the behaviour (Robinson and Davies 2007). Children's desire to cross-dress or to transgress the rigidity of gender-normative behaviours does not determine children's sexuality. However, some children who do this may indeed choose a non-heteronormative sexual identity, in the same way that some children who do not cross-dress or transgress normative gender behaviours may choose a non-heteronormative sexual identity.

The following excerpt is from an interview conducted with Peta, an early childhood educator who is frequently misread by children (and some adults) as male. Peta recounts the story of one particular young boy, Harry, who refused to believe that she was female:

> We were reading *Paperback Princess* and this young boy, Harry, said, 'Are you married?' I said no that I wasn't married and he looked at me and said, 'And you are a boy'. I said no I'm actually a girl you know and he said 'No!' I said that I really and truly am and he said, 'No!' I said that I really, really was a girl and some of the girls in the group said, 'Yes she is a girl'. I said Yeah, yeah I am a girl and that sometimes I joke but this wasn't a joke and that I really was a girl. I told him to go to another educator and ask if I was a girl and he goes and asks and she says, 'Yes, she is a girl' and he said 'No!' He went around all the educators and came back but he still wasn't convinced. The next day came and he came back and he said to me 'You know how you are a girl?' and I said yes, 'And I thought you were a boy' and I said yes, and he said, 'Do other big people ever think you are a boy?' I said what makes you think I'm a boy and he said 'Well your hair' and I said yes I have short hair but there are some girls who have short hair and pointed to one of the other educators, and he said 'Right, but you wear boys' clothes' and I said yes boys can wear these clothes and I pointed to another educator who was wearing jeans and I said sometimes boys can wear girls' clothes and girls can wear boys' clothes and that it was just like how he wore dresses and

swishy medallions in dress-ups and he said 'OK'. Then he said, 'Well your voice, your voice is really low' and I said yes it is low and he said, 'It is like a man's voice'. I said some boys have high voices, but he still found it difficult.

Harry's reading of Peta as male and his refusal to be corrected demonstrates the rigidity of some children's binary understandings of gender, despite engaging in transgressive gender behaviours themselves. In the early childhood centre that Harry attends, he is able to wear female clothing during the day if he so wishes, without being made to feel it is inappropriate by other children or adults. He chooses to wear a particular long silky dress, with a dangly necklace and a special hat, especially when he is feeling upset. Peta points out that the clothing soothes Harry's moods and fears. As seen throughout this chapter, children generally distinguish between dress-ups or play acting, so Harry may have seen his behaviour as different from Peta's everyday public performance of gender as an adult. Young children often rely on oppositional gendered readings of the physical body and physical appearance to determine whether someone is male or female. Judith Halberstam (2005) critiques the perpetuation of the binary man/woman gender system, pointing out that it fails to address the multiple performances of male and female that currently exists. Within this binary gender system, masculinity is rigidly associated with the male body, not a performance of gender that is also produced and sustained across female bodies. Peta's performance of female masculinity destabilizes the normative gender binary.

Key points in this chapter

In this chapter I have demonstrated how representations of childhood reinscribe normative narratives of life that are essential to the construction of the normative adult citizen-subject. Vital to this process are the ways in which these narratives and life markers of human development are constituted within heteronormative paradigms, and rendered invisible through processes such as the heterosexualization of gender in young children's lives. From very early ages, children learn to read and take up these normative everyday signifiers of what it means to become adults, and are both gatekeepers and resistors of these discourses. There seems to be minimal disruption of this process in their early lives – in fact, moral panic erupts when there is any transgression of these normative processes. The discourse of childhood innocence operates as a powerful regulator and protector of this process, especially in terms of regulating what knowledge is available to children around areas often considered adult issues. Children negotiate these hegemonic discourses of what it means to be a child, adolescent and adult, as well as what it means to be a normative gendered and sexual subject. However, despite childhood being a period of extreme regulation, it is also potentially a time in which doing childhood and identity differently is made possible through some children's search for more flexible ways of being and of expressing themselves. Childhood can be a queer time and space which allows for transformation and critique of the 'practices and structures that both oppose and sustain conventional forms of association, belonging, and identification' (Halberstam 2005: 4). In order to envisage alternative ways of being, it is critical that children have access to, or inherit, a broad range of knowledge that includes alternative subjective possibilities that are often found within the contexts of subjugated knowledges.

So that children can build their confidence, competence, resilience and understandings of ethical relationships and of themselves as sexual subjects, it is imperative that the way that children's sexual subjectivities are predominantly viewed is reconceptualized. Critical to this is a shift away from childhood sexuality being mobilized to produce and regulate the normative and the deviant subject (Berlant 2004; Egan and Hawkes 2009). Counter-discourses that accept children as sexual subjects in their own right, that have broad understandings of sexuality beyond heterosexual/heteronormative sex, that uphold children's sexual subjectivities as equally important as other aspects of their identities, and that provide children with agency are also essential to this reconceptualization. Within current discourses of children's sexuality, as discussed above, children's agency as sexual subjects has either been non-existent, dismissed or minimal. Freudian acknowledgement of children's sexuality provided some chance of sexual agency for children, but this was short-lived, the result of a conservative backlash against permissiveness, and the hegemony of protectionist discourses that emerged during the 1980s and continue today.

Chapter 6

Parents, children's sexual subjectivity and the transmission of sexual knowledge across generations

Introduction

This chapter explores parents' practices associated with fulfilling their role of raising sexually-literate children. This discussion investigates parents' recollections of their sexual subjectivities as children, their experiences of the sexuality education they received in the home, and how these experiences have impacted their practices and approaches to the sexuality education of their own children. The discussion is largely based on research conducted with the parents of the children whose comments were featured in the previous chapter on children's sexual subjectivities. The parents in this research were all heterosexual and mainly female (with the exception of one male, Robert), but representative of a broad range of socio-cultural and ethnic backgrounds. Their children were all in early childhood education or kindergarten, and ranged from three to six years of age. This research illustrated that social taboos associated with sexuality and hegemonic discourses of childhood (especially those reinforcing childhood innocence) had impacted their experiences of sexuality education in the home as children, and also influenced their practices of providing this information as parents. These social taboos operated in conjunction with child development and child protection discourses to regulate their practices in this area, particularly in terms of their performances of parenting in front of other parents. Parents' discussions of their experiences as sexual subjects in childhood highlighted agency and an active participation in building relationships with special friends, being in love, awareness of desires for others, and in constructing their lives primarily around heteronormative narratives. These experiences were similar to those expressed by their children. Children's involvement in constructing these narratives in their lives is generally not equated by parents and other adults with the idea of an active sexuality in childhood. Dominant discourses that constitute sexuality in adult-centric frameworks operate to dismiss children's sexual subjectivities by viewing activities of sexual expression more as normal aspects of children's play. Children continue to be viewed largely as asexual beings.

This chapter also explores the difficulties many of these parents encountered in talking with their children about sexuality and relationships. These parents expressed feeling immobilized through discomfort when they were asked questions about sexual matters. Their often hesitative, dismissive and silent responses reinforced children's awareness of the social taboos associated with sexuality, impacting their confidence in talking with parents about sexual matters, despite wishing to do so. Most parents indicated that they felt the need to begin addressing sexuality early with their children, as they perceive their children to be living in a society which is becoming more dangerous and saturated with sexual imagery and messages. However, the difficulties that many experienced in initiating and negotiating these discussions often meant that they never eventuated. Despite many parents' recollections of their inadequate education about sexuality as children in the home, certain practices were replicated in the parenting they engaged in with their own children.

Where did I come from? Talking to children about sexuality

Debates about whose responsibility it is to educate children about sexuality, relationships and ethical behaviours – either parents or schools or both – has continued to be a politically hot topic in many countries, as pointed out earlier. Most parents in this research considered sexuality education to be a dual responsibility between parents and schools. They believed that it is important that schools take an active role in sexuality education, knowing that many parents do not always provide children with sexual knowledge for various reasons. One mother argued that schools had an important role in particular in educating children and young people about peer pressures around engaging in relationships and sexuality – a topic that she felt schools were better equipped to handle effectively. Robert, the only father participating in this study, commented on the difficulty for parents in talking with their children about sexuality, and pointed out that there was always a need for an outsider to support the process:

> With something so loaded as sexuality, it is so emotional and it is hard to be objective, especially around intimacy, it is inevitable that there is conflict when we try and teach or instruct, or learn. So there is always a role outside the family, there has got to be. I think, anything, even learning to drive a car. Have you sat in a car and tried to teach a family member to change gears?

What is common across the differing opinions in these family/school debates is that parents are considered central in imparting this foundational knowledge to children (Walker 2004). As another mother upheld, 'it is the family's role to model a good relationship, whatever that happens to be'. Despite the importance of both families and schools contributing to children's sexuality education, it seems that in both areas, children often do not receive effective education about sexuality (see Chapter 4 for a discussion of sexuality education in schools). For the parents in this study, for example, neither schools nor parents were the main source of their knowledge about sexuality during childhood, as shown in the following discussion:

Researcher:	Where did you get your information about sexuality from when you were children?
Isabella:	Friends.
Rachel:	The book *Where did I come from?* It was fantastic.
Christina:	Surely your parents told you about it all?
Rachel:	They told us nothing.
Christina:	Really? I did get 'the talk' from my parents, well my mother.
Isabella:	Who gave you *Where did I come from?*
Rachel:	A friend gave it to me.
Tina:	I got my information from friends and then we also got the book *Where did I come from?* But I knew it all before then.
Researcher:	How?
Tina:	Friends. I remember friends telling me and then I told other friends.
Robert:	The funny thing with me is that my mother told us about sex but she did it the night before she left my father, and I couldn't work it out, she was actually distraught, she was crying, she came in and said, to all three kids – 'I've got something to tell you'. She told us about it, and for years I couldn't work out why she did it that way and at that time. She was such a strict Catholic, I think it was sub-conscious but she knew that she was never going to have sex again ... but I thought it was such a funny way to do it.

The main sources of information on sexual matters (which focused largely around reproduction and birth) for these parents as children were friends and books – especially what has become a rather iconic book about the 'facts of life' written by Peter Mayle (1973) titled, *Where did I come from?* Conversations between parents and their children were often fraught with tensions when they did occur. These conversations tended to be one-off talks – euphemized as 'the talk' by many parents – rather than a planned course of action discussed between parents (Walker 2004). However, these one-off talks tended to occur at significant times, primarily when changes occurring in children's and young people's bodies could no longer be ignored, such as a young girl's first menstrual period. Robert's comment above demonstrates that his 'talk', which occurred when he was eight years old, seemed to have been caught up in his mother's emotional trauma of leaving her husband. Talking to children about sexuality was linked to times when children and parents were in highly emotional states of anxiety. The fact that children's education around sexuality is often framed in one-off, highly emotionally-charged moments raises concerns about the effectiveness of this education.

Similar to other research in the area (Holland *et al.* 1996; Walker 2004; Dyson and Smith 2011; Martin and Luke 2010), this study also showed mothers to be the main providers of children's sexuality education. Despite some changes in parenting practices across the sexes, mothers are still the primary caregivers of young children, largely responsible for their early education in the home and their health and wellbeing. Most of the mothers in this study believed it to be their role, rather than their partners', to talk with their children about sexual matters. Most were even less confident about their partners' abilities to talk to their children about sexual matters than they were about their own. Given this established role, mothers pointed out that their children generally came to them if they had health issues or questions around sexuality (see also Dyson and Smith 2011). Some mothers commented that, on occasions, their partners discussed with them the kind of information they believed should be relayed to their children about sexual matters and relationships, but left it up to them as mothers to relay this information. In some instances, mothers with boys positioned their male partners to take up the responsibility of talking with their son(s) about sexuality. However, these cases appear to be exceptions to a prevailing trend (Holland *et al.* 1996; Walker 2004). There was also a tendency for the parents to be more concerned about the vulnerability of their female children to sexual danger. Robert expressed his concern about his daughter's vulnerability:

> Sometimes you focus on your own gender because you seem to be more aware of what your own gender can do and I wouldn't be worried about my daughter's behaviour, but I know, and I've seen the extremes to which even very young men can go, and that does worry me. Because I don't know what it is about the way men act things out, but when they get extreme they get very extreme, and it could be like a father protective thing.

Children's and young people's confidence about talking about sexuality can depend on how willing their parents are to discuss sexual matters openly in the family (Walker 2004; Ingham and Kirkland 1997). It has been found that no matter how unsure parents feel in talking with their children about sexuality, is important to keep talking openly about it (Holland *et al.* 1996; Walker 2004). In the following comment, Caroline points out that her mother delayed conversations with her to what was considered a more appropriate time, despite Caroline's curiosity for answers at an earlier age:

I remember always looking in my mum's drawers and asking what the tampons were and she said, oh you know, they are there for you in a few years' time, and you know, you are going to get your period and we will go through it then, but this is what you use when you get your period.

Poor communications between parents and their sons and daughters can generally exacerbate the difficulties of talking about sexuality, as pointed out by Kate in the following remark:

I gathered knowledge from older friends. I didn't want them [parents] to talk to me about it because they hadn't really talked to me about anything else and the idea of my mum then taking on a mother role and sitting down to say, oh this is what is going on, it just disgusted me. I just didn't want a bar of it. So I think the only reason I told my sister when I got my period was maybe because I needed a pad or something like that, or because I had some of my friends who had got free samples that you sent away for or whatever, so that's what I had. And I think I said it to her and said don't tell mum, because I just didn't feel close to mum. And then she did, she told her and mum came in and chucked a wobbly on my bed, and I was like eek, I know what I need to know, go away. So mine certainly didn't come from home and that type of thing. I gathered most of my information from other people. But we did have that book [*Where did I come from?*].

Kate's remarks demonstrate the difficulties of starting conversations about sexuality with one's children when open discussions about other issues are not generally part of the relationships that parents have with their children. However, the social taboos around sexuality and the cultural discourses that underpin the construction of binary relationships between parent/child and adult/child make it difficult to broach topics that are intimate and personal in nature, such as one's sexual subjectivity. This can be the case even in families where positive relationships exist. Isabella reinforces this point:

I have a very good relationship with my mother, I've always had a very good relationship with my mother ... I have lots of discussions with her now about all manner of things and probably always have, but I just never, and I know lots of people do, but I just would say, my mother is my mother, she is not my best friend. She never has been, and I think to me, I see those roles as separate ... where I have seen women where their mother is their best friend and they've had this very open relationship where they talk about sexuality and everything you know, yeah, I actually have viewed those relationships as quite unhealthy and that person the way they've gone about many of their life's relationships has been, from my perspective, unhealthy ... it would have been very awkward to

go to my parents about certain things, but I don't think I would have
ever felt that there were shutters. And my parents worked very hard at,
I think, having the door open so to speak.

Tensions between children or youth and their parents in regards to sexual
matters can be intensified in contexts where cultural and religious values are
more conservative around gender, sexuality and relationships. These tensions
can manifest into volatile encounters between parents (particularly fathers)
and their sons and daughters, especially in their teenage years. Lynne, who
was from a conservative traditional Chinese family, relayed her fear of
broaching any discussion of her having a boyfriend with her father. In her
early teens, Lynne's father had seen her holding hands with a boy in public
and had punished her severely when she returned home. Lynne remarked
that talking about sexuality with her parents was just not possible because of
their strong religious views and traditional values. Meanwhile, Penny, in the
following comment, highlights the tensions that existed between her, as a
young woman, and her parents:

My parents were pretty strict ... I mean for me to do anything I got to
the point where I knew I had to lie about it. Someone else's mum knew
where we were, and there would be someone else's parents if things
came down to it, that I would probably have been able to go to had
I been in trouble, but there was no way I would have done it with
my own family. And so if I had lied about being out and found myself
in a sticky situation, I would have been so ashamed, there was no way
I would have rung them, no way in hell. When I had kids I wanted to
be firm with them and wanted to protect them in some ways, but also
wanted to be open enough with them that they could trust me and to
talk to me about things, and also to know that if they were in trouble
that they could come to me.

For many parents (as the above comments testify), conversations with their
children about sexuality are complex, contradictory and are perceived to
pose risks of various kinds. These existing tensions can result in some parents avoiding talking to their children about sexuality: the right time for
the talk never arises. Many parents feel they lack the confidence and the
skills to negotiate these tensions and to talk effectively with their children
about sexual matters (McGuire et al. 1996; Hughes et al. 1999). The following point made by Isabella, a mother of two young girls and a boy,
demonstrates the difficulties she faced when her five-year-old daughter
started to ask about sex:

I was mortified when my daughter started to ask details about sex, which
I always thought I would be so cool about and then I just went bright

red and she kept asking for more and more details and it was really embarrassing for me. In the end I had to change the topic to something else to try and distract her.

In another instance around pregnancy, Cynthia relayed an experience in which she avoids addressing sex and childbirth with her first child, a daughter who was born by caesarean. Cynthia was extremely concerned that she might have to explain vaginal births to her daughter if her second child was to be delivered in that manner. Cynthia was anxious about having to explain how the baby 'came out from between her legs':

Cynthia: Because I'm pregnant my daughter keeps asking me, how did the baby get in my tummy, and my husband the other day said, maybe we should say the stork. How do you explain to a four-year-old? I didn't want that to happen at four. You know what I mean? I don't know what to say, other than, well, I'll explain it to you when you are five.

Researcher: What's the difference between four and five?

Cynthia: Oh they are so much more worldly at school I guess. It is me actually putting it off. She will be 27 before I will tell her. It is really hard.

As indicated by Isabella and Cynthia (and her husband), in the absence of effective strategies, parents often avoid openly and honestly answering children's questions about sexuality. They often resort to myths and stereotypes to 'make up' stories, or put off the conversations until the child is older.

Pivotal to opening up honest dialogue with children about sexuality is a parent's readiness to address the issues with children (Davies and Robinson 2010). Joy Walker (2004: 242) argues that parental provision of sex education is dependent upon 'parents' perceptions of whether their child is ready to know about a particular issue and whether they are ready to let their child know'. Parents' practices of talking with children about sexuality are generally regulated by discourses of child development. These discourses instil perceptions that children are too young to handle open and honest discussions about sexuality, often leaving parents with their own questions around what is considered to be too young. The notion of childhood innocence is enshrined in developmental theory, which increases parents' anxieties about negatively impacting children's emotional states if they broach the subject of sexuality *too early*. A mother, who was also an early childhood educator, epitomizes this perspective in the following comment:

I think children are really too young to deal with sexuality issues. They have no understandings of it; it isn't part of their experiences … Like they do get into playing house, mothers and fathers and getting married, that kind of thing, but that's normal everyday play that children like to get into. They see it all the time on television and in their lives. But beyond that, I don't think it's appropriate and it's not part of their experiences.

As Jessica Fields (2005: 550–551) asserts: 'Understandings of children as ideally sexually innocent help determine the content and course of a range of cultural conversations about young people's sexuality, including contemporary debates over sexuality education'. As a result of the social taboos and discourses that regulate parents' approaches to sexuality education with their children, sexuality is reinforced as difficult knowledge, and childhood innocence becomes a convenient excuse not to take these issues up with children.

Parents' practices of talking with their children about sexuality are significantly influenced by their own childhood experiences with their parents. Those who had negative experiences talking with their parents about these issues declared their aims of doing things differently with their own children. Isabella's comment typifies this attitude:

> My parents are my parents, and you know, I have lied on many occasions to do things, but I would just have to let them be and just learn from them and not repeat the same mistakes they did with me. So when it happens with my son I'll just, you know, recall what happened with me and do it better.

Rachel reiterates how personal childhood experiences can influence practices across generations. Her mother was very open and honest about sexuality with her and her sister, but her mother's own experiences were very different:

> My mother was like that with us because she had the complete opposite growing up – in an effort to protect her, her mother told her absolutely nothing. Literally she was giving birth when she found out – she realized her sex education was go to bed and do good things. That was literally it.

Other parents confessed that despite their aims to approach talking with their children about sexuality differently to their own childhood experiences, due to a lack of confidence and skills, many fell back on the practices they had learnt from their parents. Tina commented:

> I shocked myself when my daughter first asked me where do babies come from. It took me by surprise and I felt I wasn't prepared – I didn't know what to say. I found myself telling her exactly what my mother said to me 'one day you will find out and you don't have to worry about that now'. She has never asked me again and I don't know how to approach it with her now. I swore I was never going to be like my parents and there I was, being my mother! It was scary.

Many parents stated that their strategy around knowing when to approach talking with their children about sexuality education was determined by the perspective that, if children were ready to ask the question, then they were ready to hear the answers. However, as demonstrated by Tina and others throughout this discussion, many parents are often not ready or equipped to fulfil this strategy. This discourse, that if children are ready to ask the question then they are ready to hear the answers, echoes the philosophies articulated in child-centred pedagogies associated with children's learning. However, early childhood educators, like these parents, often have similar difficulties fulfilling this pedagogical strategy, especially around what is considered difficult knowledge, largely as a result of social taboos, discourses of childhood innocence, and normative conventions that see parents as being the primary educators of children in these areas (see Chapter 4 for a further discussion of this point). To this end, it is little wonder that many children rely on their friends, the media, and the Internet to answer their questions about sexuality.

The regulation of parents' practices around sexuality education: the influence of child protection discourses

Whilst parents were reluctant to talk generally or positively about sexual matters, they were less reluctant to talk about its negative aspects, especially in relation to 'stranger danger'. Parents were particularly concerned about protecting their children from sexual predators and other forms of abuse. This reflects the impact of child protection campaigns in recent decades and the media preoccupation with stranger danger and the paedophile. The discourse that sexuality is dangerous to children was paramount for some parents and influential for all. Parents spoke more easily and frequently with their children about stranger danger than about other aspects of sexuality education. As stated by Karin Martin and Katherine Luke (2010: 298) 'there is widespread cultural agreement that parents should protect their children from sexual abuse, but there is not nearly as much consensus about what parents *should* be saying to their young children about other sexual issues'. The discourse of stranger danger arose in the child protection campaigns of the 1960s and still prevails, despite the criticisms that it confuses children into believing that all people they *know* are safe. Stevi Jackson and Sue Scott (1999: 93) acknowledge that 'while it is well documented that sexual risk to children is most likely to be posed by intimates, it is "stranger danger" that hits the headlines, captures the popular imagination and informs education campaigns.' Protecting children from sexual abuse is considered a key role of being a good mother. In my research for this book, mothers generally articulated their anxieties around providing enough appropriate knowledge to enable their children to become competent sexual subjects without breaching the normative moral, social and developmental values inherent within child protection discourses (Davies and Robinson 2010). Some were concerned that other parents (particularly mothers) and professionals working with children, such as teachers, would judge their parenting if their young children displayed more knowledge of sexuality than what dominant socio-cultural discourses legitimate as appropriate. This anxiety is reinforced through official child protection discourse in which knowledge about sexuality is constituted as a key indicator in determining the possibility of a child having experienced sexual abuse (Government of Western Australia: Department of Child Protection n.d.).

At the completion of one of the information sessions I held for parents associated with this research, a mother approached me privately, acknowledging that she felt she could not speak publicly about the sexual knowledge she provided for her daughters. She feared that others would make judgements about her being a *bad mother* for transgressing normative boundaries of appropriate sexual knowledge assumed for children at certain ages. Foucault (1977) argues that recognizing surveillance as a form of disciplinary power is critical to an understanding of the ways in which some individuals or institutions self-regulate risk-taking behaviours or the stepping outside of societal norms. In this case, this mother felt strongly that providing her girls with sexual knowledge early in their lives was critical for their safety and wellbeing. Discourses of protection and being a good mother regulated this mother's performance of parenting, which was curtailed by the fear of being judged by other parents. The *knowing child* is often perceived with suspicion (Kitzinger 1990). The constitution of children's sexual knowledge within discourses of sexual abuse and danger, rather than as knowledge that might increase children's competency, is problematic.

Addressing children's education about child protection and supporting children's rights around their bodies in the home can raise challenges for parents and some family members. It disrupts the hegemonic discourse of the family being a safe-haven for children and the central place where children can implicitly trust that the practices of adults close to them have children's best interests at heart. The discourse of stranger danger locates children's sexual abuse outside the home and distances it from family relations, absolving parents of the need to recognize that children are most vulnerable to abuse by adults they know and trust (Breckenridge and Carmody 1992; Calvert *et al.* 1992; Easteal 1994; Mouzos and Makkai 2004; Richardson and Bromfield 2005).

Parents' recollections of becoming heteronormative subjects: learning through osmosis

Most of the parents in this research acknowledged the operation of heteronormative discourses of sexuality, relationships, marriage and family in their own childhoods, and see similar discourses expressed in the lives of their children.

Parents pointed out that, as children, their understandings of sexuality, gender norms and protocols, and relationships and marriage just seem to happen unconsciously, without question or resistance on their part. As one mother succinctly put it, 'somehow you just obtained your knowledge by osmosis'. On the subject of establishing relationships and getting married, Mary pointed out that 'there is that assumption that it will all happen and there is no question that it won't'. Cynthia, from the same focus group, quickly added, 'it just seemed like it was part of life's steps that, you know, you were going to get married and be the princess for the day'. Cynthia's comment highlights an unconscious conformity to pre-determined normative milestones, where life is viewed as progressing in a linear manner, and getting married is viewed as a significant event in this process. Despite lacking a strategy in childhood to make it all happen, Cynthia accrued a desire for marriage, believing it to be what everyone did:

> I always thought I would get married, I guess, doesn't everyone think that? I don't know how I was going to do it. It is just something that I always knew about and I can't recall or say how. I am sure from at least age, actually from even at preschool, I would have, I am pretty sure I would have understood the concept. I am pretty sure in fact, I am almost certain, I had a boy in mind. I still know who the boy was ... the lucky man ... I did have a gender concept of it being girl/boy ... It was a thing that you do when you are grown-up that is just sort of normal and you just kind of just cuddle up and that and got on with it.

Cynthia's narrative of her childhood beliefs reflects a similar discourse to that of her son, who she pointed out 'is so into marriage at the moment'. This comment surprised Valerie, another mother in the group, as she considered the 'obsession' with marriage was a 'girl thing' and that she would not have imagined a five-year-old boy would have been engaged with the subject of marriage in that same way. Reiterating the practices of children, Jennifer also recalled her own romantic fantasies and desires in childhood for a special boy, commenting that she would often rehearse her potential married name –'Mrs So and So' – out loud to herself in private and with certain friends. Christy echoes the experiences of other parents in that she learnt from a very early age that marriage was an expectation that was not questioned, but she points out that this perspective did not necessarily come from her family:

> I don't quite know where it came from because as far as TV and Disney movies and that type of thing, I didn't watch a great deal of that when I was little but I know I did have some of those like Golden Book adaptations of things, so maybe it might have been in there and I knew some pretty gaudy Christian Andersen fairytales, but I loved reading when

I was little too, so there was that thing, so that kind of got me into that fairytale stuff. I don't know if I ever thought about the girl/boy thing, I think in my head it was a boy generally, I think. When I think back and I think about pretend play I was into *Wham* and George Michael ... now my dreams are shattered, but I remember doing that with my sister and playing and being aware of you know, dancing for a reason, you know ... but as far as a wedding goes, yes certainly, I knew about it even though I had not been exposed to it from my family.

As a child, Christy (like fellow parent Monica, who appears below, as well as most of the children in this research) never really considered marriage a choice but rather conceived of it as a natural process that was integral to fulfilling one's role as a normative subject. It was also the means through which desires were fulfilled and one gained power and agency. As pointed out in the previous chapter, normative models of marriage and desire are generally viewed within a heterosexual framework by children. Ironically, as pointed out by Christy, heterosexual fantasies of desire were often built on assumptions of the heterosexuality of the one desired – assumptions made by both children and adults. The pop singer George Michael, the subject of Christy's desire as a young person, later came out as gay, shattering her fantasies and dreams. Christy's recognition of her embodied desires as a young person was articulated in her awareness that she was 'dancing for a reason'. This experience of becoming aware of one's desires is played out in the gender performances of many young girls, who often fulfil their fantasies through pop stars. The music and dance style may be different today, but the desires and fantasies have been similar across generations. Other parents also noted fairytales and the media as influential sources in their perceptions of the normative narrative of marriage and of gendered relations:

Researcher: Where did you get your understandings of marriage when you were children?
Isabella: From fairytales, I remember clearly wanting to get married and living happily ever after; yeah the prince thing.
Rachel: Yeah, fairytales. I remember getting upset because I didn't have blue eyes and blonde hair. I thought I couldn't be a princess and that I couldn't get married.
Robert: I remember vaguely on TV there was this movie, a bit like 'Bugsy Malone' where kids got married. I remember it had an effect on me to think that kids could do what adults were doing.

These comments raise some important issues. First, Rachel's point reflects her understandings as a child of the concept of the princess as physically represented by those with fair hair and blue eyes – ruling her out in her perspective as a child. Feminine beauty in Western fairytales and the media is often represented through hegemonic discourses of Western beauty, which are racialized. These representations of beauty convey powerful messages about who is considered beautiful, who is not, and which girl is most likely to succeed in marrying the powerful prince (Davies 1989). If a child does not fit the image, it can obviously leave an indelible imprint in one's mind, as in Rachel's case. Similarly, Robert's comment about the impact on him as a child of the representation of children doing what are considered to be adults' practices and behaviours demonstrates the power of the adult/child binary in young children's lives. The thought that it would be possible for children to engage in adult practices (perhaps made even more plausible from a child's perspective through representation in film), and to share in the power and agency equated with adulthood, can leave an equally lasting imprint.

Love and relationships: recollections of sexual subjectivity in childhood

In the previous chapter, children's understandings of relationships and being in love were explored. It was pointed out that parents and other adults often dismiss children's experiences and feelings as trivial and childish play. Yet, parents' recollections of their own experiences of being in love as children demonstrate strong feelings similar to those expressed by their children. Parents often forget their own experiences in childhood when dealing with their children around these issues. Concerns about love and relationships are part of many children's everyday lives, and are integral to the construction of their sexual subjectivities – as highlighted in the following discussion:

Researcher:	When did you first understand what love meant as a child?
Nida:	From very early, from at least four or probably even three.
Researcher:	Did you perceive love and being in love differently?
Nida:	I would have associated being in love with romantic feelings versus I love my mummy and my daddy. I understood that differentiation from very early, at least four, possibly three.
Monica:	I remember as a four-year-old always asking my mum if she was in love with my dad, I don't know why, maybe that was from fairytales, from reading those, and always asking, are you in love with dad? I loved Snow White. I loved those stories, so that would make sense that that's where it would have come from.
Researcher:	What did it mean to be in love? What did you perceive it to be as a child?
Monica:	Happy. Yeah, I guess an element of happiness.

Nida: I think it is a little bit like when you have a crush, it is that thrill of seeing, you know, when you are teenager, it is like oh, he spoke to me, or he didn't or whatever. And when you are little it is sort of a similar version of that. I remember being in line and having to hold hands in kindergarten, and just randomly being thrown together with the object of my affection and thought wow I got him. And I think it is that, you know, you get that, there is that excitement there and so there is that whole positive reinforcement about that internal thrill that you get. So the first time you experience that, there is a little bit of almost addiction to that feeling, and so if you get that feeling very young then you will sort of follow it.

Nida's comments point out that children know and feel the difference between love for their parents and love for another special person in their lives. Recalling a crush on a boy when she was a young child, Nida relays feeling an embodiment of her excitement – 'the internal thrill' – when she was 'randomly thrown together with the object of her affection'. This thrill is reinforced through its affect – through the embodied experiences of interest, surprise, and joy (Sedgwick and Frank 1995); and, as Nida points out, once you have felt it there is no turning back, 'you follow it'. A similar point was raised by Valerie, who stated:

I just always had crushes and it was like, you know, your day would be more exciting if you saw that boy at school, or you saw that guy at work, you know, it kind of made you want to go there. It motivated me really.

It is important to point out that silence tends to prevail around the pleasurable aspects of sexuality such as these in children's sexuality education at school and in the home (Fine 1988; Allen 2004; Angelides 2004; Martin and Luke 2010). Instead, children's sexuality education tends to be framed within discourses of danger and sexual abuse as pointed out previously.

In the following conversation, parents discuss their sexual subjectivities and recall the importance of having boyfriends or girlfriends in their childhoods. They also highlight the way that some children negotiate the social taboos and regulatory practices of adults:

Researcher: Do your children talk about having girlfriends and boyfriends?
Christy: My daughter definitely does, yes. She's got three boyfriends, she told us about two of them.
Isabella: Yeah, they all talk about boyfriends. They are always asking their friends do you have a boyfriend?

Researcher: When did you start to understand about boyfriends and girlfriends in your childhoods?

Christy: Well interestingly I had a boyfriend in kindergarten; it was a really intense relationship. When I was up at the school for my daughter's parent-teacher night – we actually had the same kindergarten teacher believe it or not – the teacher was telling me about my daughter's relationships with two boyfriends in her class, saying that it is quite intense and serious, you know, but she said that it is very unusual in kindergarten. And she said, funnily enough, I remember you had a very intense boyfriend-girlfriend relationship too; I remember it because it is unusual.

Researcher: How did others respond to this relationship?

Christy: I think everyone thought it was really sweet and we were encouraged I would say. They were always asking me about my boyfriend.

Isabella: Not in kindergarten I think, but later in primary school, the boyfriend-girlfriend thing is OK, like it became kind of cool to have one in primary school, but not in kindergarten.

Rachel: I was very young, I remember I started school at four and I remember having one boy and going, you are my boyfriend. And I remember always being obsessed with boys, and I have, my whole life.

Tina: I had boyfriends all through primary school, very early on. I remember one of the little boys came to my sixth birthday party and brought me a flower and that was made a big deal of. But that kid was like a womanizer from five years old. I swear to God, like he used to lay on the ground in the kindergarten class when girls had to go over and put your books in a tub, to see what undies everyone was wearing.

Researcher: Did the teacher intervene?

Tina: No, not really. The teacher said something to him but he kept doing it. Then she just said to keep away from him and ignore him; and that he would get sick of it one day.

Rachel: My dad wouldn't let me stay over at [boy's name]'s house one time. I was seven. It was because we were going to be sleeping in the same bed and I didn't get that at all – I mean we get what the problem was, but dad was really firm about it, he said no, you are not staying.

Isabella: I remember kissing this red-haired boy I liked on the back in assembly in, probably Year 2, and him looking at me with disgust and pretending it hadn't happened. But then somewhere between that year and the next, boys' interest in girls changed. I changed schools at the end of Year 3 and I remember within a couple of days of being there somebody coming up to me and asking if I wanted to go around with [boy's name] and I thought, what is he talking about? And I had no idea what they meant by going around with, perhaps it meant walking in circles and I thought what the hell is this about? Do you want to go around with him? What? Go where?

Robert: I didn't have girlfriends, or boyfriends, when I was young but I remember being conscious of the fact that other people did, and generally they were the people who had some kind of social status. So it was something to aspire to, like they were sort of on the other side of the fence and, to be honest, secretly I think a lot of other people were trying to get there.

Christy: Yes, with the kids behind the sheds.

Robert: Yes I wanted to get where they were, but one observation, I don't know, it has changed a bit, but I still find the pattern is still there. I think the level of fantasy about relationships is a hell of a lot higher than the level of participation. I still think that still applies today you know, even with teenagers.

This discussion highlights several important points – children's interpellation into compulsory heterosexuality, the regulation of children's relationships by parents, the sexual lives of some children that often escape the parental gaze, and the representation of having either a boyfriend or girlfriend as cultural capital in children's cultures. The repetitive questions to children around whether one has a boyfriend or girlfriend from both adults and their peers become moments in which children are interpellated into compulsory heterosexuality. The French philosopher Althusser (1971) argued that in the process of interpellation, individuals come to understand themselves as subjects through ideology. In this case, repetitive references to being a boyfriend or girlfriend in opposite-sex frameworks constitutes the child ideologically as heterosexual (Lloyd 2007). Children learn to see themselves as heterosexual subjects; for some, there is an awareness of a discomfort with this socially prescribed arrangement, but they soon learn that conformance is often the safer option. Sara Ahmed states that:

[S]exual orientation involves bodies that leak into worlds; it involves a certain way of orientating the body towards and away from others, which affects how one can enter different kinds of social spaces (which presumes certain bodies, certain directions, certain ways of loving and living).

(Ahmed 2004: 145)

Children learn to negotiate these spaces and orientations early in their lives.

Rachel's comment highlights how as a seven-year-old she becomes aware that her relationship with her boyfriend is regulated by strict socio-cultural taboos around childhood and sexuality, and that there are perceived risks of some kind associated with such relationships. Rachel and her boyfriend are aware of why her father says she cannot sleep over at her boyfriend's home, but they do not agree with his strict stance. This regulation is juxtaposed against the intimate relationships between children that occur in secret 'behind the back shed'. Aware of the social taboos about sexuality, some children learn to explore their sexuality with other children, away from the regulatory gaze of adults. Robert's comment indicates his curiosity and his wish to be involved in the 'behind the back shed' activities, which, along with his being someone's boyfriend, would have give him access to a certain cultural capital valued amongst his peers. However, as Robert also points out, the symbolic power associated with these subject positions is often utilized by children and young people who do not engage in some of the practices. Some children's unethical behaviours, as indicated by Tina, are often reinforced through a lack of effective intervention strategies on the part of teachers and other adults. These behaviours are not always grown out of, but rather individuals can become more skilled at engaging in unethical and sexually harassing behaviours throughout their lives (Alloway 1995; Robinson 1996, 2000, 2005d, 2012b).

The same group of parents talked about how they negotiated these relationships with their own children:

Researcher: How do you handle discussions with your children around relationships or having or not having boyfriends and girlfriends?

Rachel: I think it is really sweet, one of my daughter's boyfriends, who is six, has got a bit freaked out and asked his mum, does that mean I have to kiss her? He was a bit scared, but his mum told him, no you don't have to kiss her. I don't want his mother or father coming around knocking on my door so it is probably a good thing not to kiss her. He was a little bit spun out by it, but was happy to go along with my daughter. He is the most popular boy in the class and everyone wants to be his girlfriend.

Researcher: How are you handling it with her?

Rachel: I am quite happy about it. I think it is really sweet, because they are not playing at kissing or anything like that.

Robert: They are just special friends.

Rachel: They might get married, or they might not, she says.

Robert: When my daughter changed from a childcare to a pre-school there was a boy there. It wasn't that hard to work out that his parents had recently broken up. From the moment my daughter was there, he knew I was her father and he quite aggressively kept coming up to me whenever I came in telling me that my daughter was his girlfriend, and that she was to come over and stay at his house. And he was also telling me that she could do it at mummy's house, but not at daddy's house, and daddy was going away. My daughter didn't want it to happen. She wanted to ignore it completely but it was interesting how this boy whose parents had gone through relationship problems, was looking for a relationship himself, and almost too aggressively.

Isabella is confident in pointing out that boyfriend and girlfriend relationships were not part of her two girls' lives, but this was in contrast to the comments made by her daughter. Isabella's oldest daughter, who was four years old, spoke about playing Catch and Kiss with her boyfriend and other children at pre-school, which was verified by her friend who went to the same preschool. The issues highlighted in this last conversation above echo and reinforce some of those raised in the previous chapter focusing on children's sexual subjectivities. Children's connection of kissing to their understandings of boyfriend and girlfriend relationships is stressed in Rachel's comments. Her daughters' boyfriend was feeling anxious that his status of boyfriend meant that he would have to be involved in kissing a girl. It is interesting to point out younger children around three, four and five link kissing with marriage (see Chapter 5), while older children begin to associate it not just with its legitimization in marriage, but also in boyfriend and girlfriend relationships. Some boys in particular, as they get older, and before they rediscover kissing again in their later teens, express a dislike for engaging in this behaviour. An eight-year-old boy whom I interviewed told me he thought kissing on the lips was especially 'disgusting'. His mother had told him that it was appropriate to kiss his girlfriend on the cheek, but not on the lips, which suited his needs well. Kissing for Rachel is symbolic of going that step further in a relationship, which was not suitable for her daughter. Rachel was happy for her daughter to be in the relationship with her boyfriend, which she considered sweet, especially if it did not involve kissing.

The symbolic importance of playing out girlfriend and boyfriend relationships for some young children is demonstrated in Robert's story about the four-year-old boy who had claimed his daughter as his girlfriend, despite his daughter's active disinterest. Robert equated the young boys' overly aggressive behaviour with the fact that his parents' relationship had broken up. Normative family relationships are important to young children, as they are reflective of their status as normative subjects, considered important in children's peer groups. Family breakdowns are difficult for children to negotiate in this respect. The young boy's perceived overly aggressive eagerness to establish his own normative relationship may have been a way of restoring his own status, which he may have perceived as having been lost amongst his peers.

Subversive parents and conforming children

As pointed out above, it is important to children to be viewed as normative subjects by their peers. However, in some cases, children's wishes to be considered normative subjects by their peers can be in tension with the counter-narratives that some parents take up in their lives and those they wish to convey to their children. The following discussion outlines these parents' concerns around normative narratives of gender and relationships:

Researcher: How have your experiences in childhood impacted the way that you talk to your children about sexuality, relationships and marriage?

Rachel: I've tried to avoid the traditional fairytales with the kids.

Isabella: Yeah, same here for that whole idea of the Prince Charming coming to rescue you – a lot of girls from our generation were caught up in that, you just need the right man to save you, so the traditional-type story and fairytales I try to keep away from.

Rachel: Yeah, we don't have them at home. But the kids know something is subversive when you have Princess Smarty Pants who just wants to live with her pets and doesn't want to get married. They know something is wrong with the story. So they are the ones I like to read, but they don't like to listen to them.

Robert: I've noticed in terms of the way I talk to my kids, and it is something that we all have in common is that we all came from broken families, all our parents divorced, and yet we are not all married but we've all been in the same relationship with the same person for a long time. But I guess maybe in our generation the people you know, as adults, are a little bit more cynical about that ideal. We don't talk to the kids that much about romanticizing or I don't think so. People with different backgrounds might be different but I think particularly if you've been through that situation, which a lot more kids have these days. When the family laws came in in '75, a lot of kids went through divorce after that period and so you see that effect later on.

Isabella: I'd tell them that it is an institution and you have to be mad to go to an institution.

Despite Isabella's, Rachel's, and Robert's counter-narratives to romantic love and marriage which inform their parenting about these issues, their children's perspectives are still firmly invested in normative narratives of romantic love and marriage, as was demonstrated in Chapter 5. The children's dismissal of alternative narratives is reflected in Isabella's comment that her children were critical of her attempts to provide a subversive story line as represented in *Princess Smarty Pants* (Cole 1987). The children resisted the alternative narrative by refusing to listen to the story. Children's resistance to non-normative narratives of romantic love and marriage presented in alternative stories is also highlighted in Bronwyn Davies' (1989) research focusing on the construction of children's gendered subjectivities. Rachel's comments provide yet another example. When Rachel married she chose not to take her partners name, although her children have their fathers' surname. This alternative narrative of marriage, which relinquishes the traditional patriarchal practice of females taking the surname of their male partners, causes some distress for her daughter who shows her anger and resistance to this choice by threatening to 'eat' her mother if she does not change her name to that of her family name:

Rachel: Somebody [her daughter] is upset that I haven't changed my name.
Robert: Really?
Rachel: She gets occasionally really angry about that. She tells me that if I don't change my name she is going to eat me.
Robert: Oh really, wow.
Rachel: She gets really upset and says that she is not going to have me if I don't change my name.

Belonging, particularly with regards to family, is an important part of children's identities, and they often do not want to be considered as different from their peers in any way that could lead to their rejection. The previous chapter demonstrated the significance of marriage to children's normative subjectivities and indicated how contemplating marriage was a common practice amongst them. Girls in particular often engage in discussions about whom they intend to marry, voicing aloud to each other what their new names would be if they married certain boys. The fact that Rachel did not take her partner's name in marriage is problematic to her daughter as the difference in her and her mother's names signifies the marriage and family as being non-traditional and non-normative, and also potentially marks her daughter as being different. In another example, a nine-year-old boy who articulated that his greatest wish was that his mother and father would get married reiterated the concern that some children have around alternative approaches to marriage and family. His reasoning for wanting his parents to marry was, 'it would make me and my brothers and sister feel better'.

Key points in this chapter

In order to contribute to children's confidence, competence and resilience, it is critical that parents are supported and educated about how best to communicate information about sexual matters to their children. Social taboos associated with sexuality contribute to the silencing of such conversations, whether they are between adults or between adults and children. Parents' practices in this area are heavily influenced by dominant discourses of childhood and childhood innocence. In the study that formed the basis of this chapter, parents were often acutely aware that it was critical to begin educating their children early about sexual matters to build children's sexual literacy. However, many parents were concerned that they did not have the skills to talk effectively with their children about sexuality. As Cristyn Davies and I have pointed out previously (Davies and Robinson 2010), there is a disjuncture between parents' perceptions of their children's awareness and knowledge of sexuality and relationships, and the knowledge many children already have of these issues. It is little wonder that this is the case when conversations with children about sexual matters and relationships are avoided by many parents. Parents can underestimate their children's capacity to understand information about sexuality and relationships. There are important socio-political, cultural, economic and individual benefits in effectively communicating this information to children. Knowledge about sexuality and ethical relationships has crucial implications for children's health and well-being, and has critical benefits associated with sexual health that are carried into adolescence and adulthood. Building a society that is more critically reflective about gendered and sexual relationships, and that contributes to new cultural norms of non-violence and ethical relationships, needs to begin in early childhood.

Chapter 7

Critical conversations

Building a culture of sexual ethics early in life

Recapping the ideas and arguments around childhood, sexuality and sexuality education for children

This book has examined the connection between childhood, innocence and sexuality, and the ways in which hegemonic discourses impact on broad socio-cultural values and practices in Western countries. A central focus has been how innocence is foundational to the ways in which knowledge – especially sexual knowledge – is constituted and regulated in children's early lives. Discourses of childhood and innocence have been employed to perpetuate and regulate citizen-subjects largely through the hegemony of heteronormative narratives in children's early educational experiences. The nature of children's early education about sexuality in the home and in schools has been central to understanding the construction of children's gendered and sexual subjectivities throughout the chapters in this book. The inclusion of both children's and adults' voices has been pivotal to the book's discussion of childhood sexuality – an area that continues to be highly controversial, yet integral to the everyday lives and identities of both children and adults. Despite its relevance to children's lives, sexuality has been constituted as adults-only in Western society, and has continued to be simultaneously considered both irrelevant and dangerous to children: irrelevant, because young children are predominantly viewed as asexual or latent sexual subjects, and dangerous, because children's sexual subjectivity is predominantly viewed as the object of predatory adults.

Of particular significance in this research is that the children involved have shown themselves to be active participants in the construction of their sexual subjectivities and those of their peers. Children's understandings of themselves and others as sexual subjects are constituted in heteronormative narratives of gender, which construct children as particular types of boys and girls, perceived to have particular kinds of pre-determined futures (Renold 2005). These heteronormative narratives are rehearsed and played out in children's everyday lives. Those children who wish to express their gender and sexual subjectivities differently – that is, to transgress the boundaries of heteronormative narratives – often find themselves harassed, marginalized, ostracized, and humiliated by peers and some adults.

Children's comprehensive and inclusive sexuality education is important for their health and wellbeing, not just in childhood, but also throughout their lives. However, as demonstrated throughout this book, children often do not have access to quality comprehensive sexuality education programmes in schooling. Additionally, the sexuality education they receive at home is often sparse and haphazard, if they receive any at all. Sexuality is generally considered difficult knowledge, and talking with children about sexuality is a problem for many parents and educators (Walsh 2001). These difficulties stem from the socio-cultural taboos about sexuality that exist in many cultures and that often prevent adults from openly discussing these matters with children and young people. Childhood innocence is integral to the perpetuation of many of these taboos: it functions to regulate and define differences between adults and children, and maintain hegemonic relations of power between them. Childhood innocence is especially equated with sexual innocence, and it is the perception that adults must maintain that state of innocence in children for as long as possible which underpins the strict regulation of children's access to information about sexuality, both formally and informally. However, the benefits of maintaining this state of innocence, perceived to be in the best interests of the child, are questionable, as I have argued throughout this book.

Globally, research highlights the need for children's access to quality comprehensive sexuality education programmes in order to build their resilience, competencies and awareness of ethical practices early in life. In many countries, this is not happening and children are often left to try and educate themselves around these issues. The United Nations Educational Scientific and Cultural Organization (UNESCO) states:

> We have a choice to make: leave children to find their own way through the clouds of partial information, misinformation and outright exploitation that they will find from media, the Internet, peers and the unscrupulous, or instead face up to the challenge of providing clear, well informed, and scientifically-grounded sexuality education based in the universal values of respect and human rights.
>
> (UNESCO 2009: iii)

The organization also believes that effective sexuality education needs to include 'structured opportunities for young people to explore their attitudes and values, and to practise [*sic*] the decision-making and other life skills they will need to be able to make informed choices about their sexual lives' (UNESCO 2009: 2). The rest of this chapter focuses on key issues to be addressed in the area of children's sexuality education, and suggests strategies for how parents, educators and other professionals working with children might begin to provide effective, comprehensive and positive sexuality education in children's early lives. A critical component of this sexuality education is the inclusion of programmes that address sexual ethics and build children's awareness of ethical relationships, providing children with the critical thinking skills required in order to negotiate and engage in relationships in an ethical manner (Carmody 2009). It is also important that sexuality education programmes with children are framed in a context in which the pleasure of sexual relations is equally addressed. In order to develop the types of programmes that are required, it is essential that taboos and myths that currently constitute understandings of childhood and sexuality for many are acknowledged, challenged and deconstructed.

Sex education in schooling curricula needs to take up the principles of effective education embodied in the idea that 'the purpose of knowledge is not to affirm the order of things but to work against itself' (Britzman 1998: 73). Theorists such as Deborah Britzman (1998), Jonathan Silin (1995) and Eve Kosofsky Sedgwick (1990) remind us that it is critical to question normative narratives that perpetuate inequalities and socio-cultural practices that maintain hegemonic relations of power. In terms of children's access to sexuality education, it is important to question normative assumptions constituted in Western developmentalist frameworks that perceive children as not ready to engage in sexuality education early in their lives. The fact is that many young children are living in cultures in which public and private representations of sexuality are ever-present in their daily lives, both influencing and impacting the way children constitute themselves as sexual subjects.

Where do we go from here? Reconceptualizing the relationship between children and sexuality

How might we start to reconceptualize the relationship between children and sexuality, including children's sexuality education? I will begin by sharing a personal story of an encounter I had during the time I was writing this book. It was one of those unforgettable, totally unexpected moments that leave you with a great deal to think about. A friend bought me a ticket to see The Veronicas performing at a small theatre in Sydney's inner Western suburbs. The Veronicas are an internationally successful Australian girl band comprised of twin sisters Jessica and Lisa Origliasso, now in their late 20s, whose music is described as electrorock, pop punk and rock. At the time of the concert, The Veronicas hit single 'Untouched' was rocketing up the Australian and US music charts, experiencing similar success to several previous hit singles from their first album, which went platinum four times. The Veronicas present a performance of gender that is confident, hip and has attitude. Lisa challenges heteronormative conventions of sexuality in that she is publicly out about her lesbianism. The pair present as savvy and in control, with their style of music matching the personae they portray.

On the day of the concert, my friend who had bought me the ticket told me she could no longer attend, so I spent most of the day chasing up people who might want to go at short notice in her place, but in the end had no luck. I arrived at the theatre and queued with other concertgoers waiting to have our tickets checked before being let into the venue. When I was seated I scanned the room, noticing that the majority of the audience was between 7 and 14 years of age, and female. With a sense of surprise and increasing uneasiness, I quickly searched for anyone who looked over the age of 15, and thankfully noticed a few mothers scattered around the room that were obviously chaperoning groups of excited young girls, and the odd boy, waiting impatiently for the concert to start. Continuing to scan the room, I spotted two gay men in the front row of the mezzanine room where we were located, which overlooked the seating area below. With an almost empty row of seats beside me, I took the opportunity to dash to the balcony to check out the audience below. It was also filled with tweens. I quickly returned to my seat, weaving my way through a cacophony of screaming girls who had gathered close to the balcony to get a position that gave them a better view of the stage. I sat back down, linked my uneasiness to the fact that I was one of a very small number of adults in the room, also noting that I was an adult alone with no children. I tried to become inconspicuous – which was near impossible. I had unsuspectingly found myself smack bang in the middle of a tween event.

During the support act, an American male pop rock band – Metro Station, whose members appeared only slightly older than the tween audience members – arrived on stage. The all-boy band had come to notoriety through the release of their music on MySpace. As they performed, I observed the tweens who gathered and surrounded me, blocking any view I had of the stage once the music had started. For the next hour, the young girls, and the odd boy, bopped, gyrated, sang and screamed in their obviously carefully chosen outfits, with their styled hair, to songs with familiar lyrics. Even the interval became part of the tweens' performance, with a resoundingly loud communal rendition throughout the theatre of the hit song 'Sex on Fire' by the Kings of Leon, which was being played in the background. Even the five-year-old who was standing in front of me did not falter on the lyrics and her dance performance seemed carefully choreographed, no doubt from hours of practice in front of a mirror and with friends. I was reminded again of this scene by the YouTube hit featuring two young girls (one four and the other three years of age), dressed in pink costumes and dancing, with the four-year-old singing flawlessly to the Nicki Minaj hip-hop song 'Super Bass' on *The Ellen DeGeneres Show* (Ellen 2011).

When The Veronicas arrived on stage, the tween screaming was particularly loud, and the singing, gyrating and dancing were even more vigorous.

The tweens lapped up every lyric, dance move, word and joke made by the twins. I watched their chaperones, mainly mothers I suspect, enjoying their children's excitement. The mothers joined in the dancing and singing when their favourite songs came on, but returned to their seats when they were tired out from trying to keep up with their tweens. It was clear they enjoyed watching their children relishing the moment. Despite the inter-mittent screaming and the need to protect myself from the constant jos-tling by the girls beside me – dancing on their seats so they could get a better view – I also actually managed to enjoy the first half of The Veronicas as much as the tweens. Looking around, I noticed the two gay men again in the front row. I felt particularly sorry for them as they were imprisoned in the middle of it all; they sat like stone figures, daring not to move or to take their eyes off the stage and look sideways at the tweens. The security guard assigned to our section of the theatre carefully watched them throughout the whole concert. I could feel their tension and the impact of the gaze they encountered.

I did manage to escape at the beginning of the second half of the show and went to watch the rest of the concert standing at the back of the main theatre downstairs. I had a great sense of relief at having gotten away; this new position would allow me to make my exit quickly at the end of the con-cert. My new position was also a refuge for some of the other unsuspecting adults in the room, who looked equally traumatized by the social discomfort of being an adult surrounded by children who were screaming and dancing. As I left the theatre, I ran into a barrage of parents and carers waiting nerv-ously and eagerly at the door to spot their children as they emerged safe and sound from the crowds. As I walked home reflecting on the evening, I thought of my seven-year old niece, thinking how much she would have enjoyed my spare ticket!

This three-hour concert was not about The Veronicas for me; it became a sociological glimpse into tween culture and adult/child relationships. The event staged the anxieties of those who call for greater censorship around the sexualization of childhood in the media and popular culture. This tween event overwhelmingly showed these young children to be avid consumers of popular culture – especially popular rock music, a genre which is unapolo-getically upfront in its sexual lyrics and provides competing images of gen-dered relationships that move between misogyny and sexism, through to young women's assertion of a new found agency in which they 'call the shots' in a post-feminist world. The tweens in the audience were unashamedly tak-ing up the call of popular culture, with performances of gender and different narratives of childhood that challenged the cultural binary of adulthood/childhood and the hegemony of childhood innocence – just as others have done in previous generations. Whether it is the four-year-old singing the lyr-ics of 'Sex on Fire' or reciting the challenging hip-hop lyrics of Nicki Minaj, and knowing the provocative dance moves to go with it, this event provided a glimpse into the changing nature of childhood itself. At the concert these tweens were excited and having fun; they were confident and uninhibited, eager to be seen and to assert their agency, and to be 'in control' like their older role models – The Veronicas.

I walked away from this concert thinking about the dilemma inherent in moving the debates about the sexualization of childhood, protection, censorship, media and popular culture forward, and how we can negotiate the changing narratives of childhood effectively and the need to acknowledge and foster children's agency. I do not believe that a reliance on censorship and regulation – which continues to dismiss children's voices, needs and pleasures they find in media and popular culture – is the answer. A more nuanced approach that takes into consideration the complexities of children's lives is important. With changing narratives of childhood, I maintain that if we wish to ensure children's healthy sexual development, we need to work more collaboratively with them to construct counter-discourses and allow readings of childhood that are founded not in innocence, but in agency, competency and knowledge. I was heartened by the fact that some parents and carers/guardians (albeit perhaps reluctantly) had allowed their children to go to such an event, providing them with an opportunity to develop and demonstrate their agency and responsibilities within these contexts. This experience demonstrated that some parents had found a way to engage with their children in popular culture, by sharing it with them.

Counteracting the myths and contradictions of childhood, sexuality and sexuality education with children

It is important that children are provided with effective sexuality education that offers them the best chances of developing a healthy sexuality. In order to do so, it is equally important – as illustrated throughout earlier chapters – to acknowledge the myths and contradictions that exist in relation to childhood and sexuality. The following discussion highlights some of these myths and contradictions.

Myth: Children are asexual and sexuality is irrelevant to young children's lives

Children, like adults, are sexual beings and their relationship to sexuality is constituted early in their lives. Research overwhelmingly demonstrates that children from early ages are proactively trying to understand and construct themselves as gendered and sexual subjects – physically, emotionally and intellectually (Goldman and Goldman 1982; Chrisman and Couchenour 2002; Larsson and Svedin 2002; Sanderson 2004; UNESCO 2009; Brennan and

Graham 2012). Children engage in sexual behaviours, such as touching themselves and masturbation, which they find pleasurable (as they are to adults). This is healthy and normal behaviour, but some parents can become concerned that it may be a sign the child has been abused (Brennan and Graham 2012; Mitchell 2012). As a consequence of the prevalence of the discourse of sexuality as danger to children, all children's sexual behaviour has become suspicious; distinguishing the differences between children's normal healthy sexual development and indications of sexual abuse have become difficult for parents. Discourses of childhood innocence, abuse and exploitation overshadow the fact that sexuality – just like age, gender, ethnicity and social class – is a significant component of children's identities and is important to the way they see themselves and others in the world. As I have pointed out previously, a major contradiction that exists is that children are generally perceived as asexual beings and sexuality is perceived to be irrelevant to children's lives. However, the construction of children as heterosexual subjects through everyday heteronormative practices is a central component of children's early education, both in and out of the home.

Myth: Talking with children about sexuality is developmentally inappropriate

Starting sexuality education in the early years has multiple benefits for both children and parents, especially in terms of building the foundations of sexual literacy early in children's lives and making potentially challenging conversations easier to approach in the later years. Talking to children about sexuality, including using correct anatomical names for the body *is* developmentally appropriate, and is important for encouraging children's healthy sexual development. Adults often view sexuality through an adult-centric lens which focuses on sex acts, thus reinforcing the perception of sexuality as inappropriate for – and irrelevant to – children. Sexuality for children is generally about love, relationships, and emotional and physical pleasure. Children at very young ages are thinking about kissing and touching as a means of demonstrating their strong feelings for other children (or a parent or another adult). Openly discussing these issues with children is important in order to encourage children's ethical behaviour early around these issues, and to counteract the sexual taboos which undermine the development of open and positive relationships between parents and their children around these same issues later in children's lives. Talking to children about these matters sends an important message to children early, that sexuality and sexual pleasure are not shameful or wrong. Providing children with accurate information about their bodies and how they change is important for children's healthy sexual development. It also means that they do not have to piece together answers to their questions based on myths and misconceptions (Aggleton *et al.* 1998; Bickmore 1999; Brennan and Graham 2012; Carmody 2009; Goldman and

Goldman 1982; Haydon 2002; McKee *et al.* 2010; Robinson and Davies 2008b; Walker 2004; UNESCO 2009). Children need to learn the differences between private and public behaviours, and it is important to start early, when they are learning about the pleasures of touching their own bodies and the comfort they often gain from doing this (Brennan and Graham 2012; Walsh 2011).

Myth: Sexuality education encourages children to be sexually active earlier

Overwhelmingly, research indicates that sexuality education rarely, if ever, leads to early sexual initiation. In fact, evidence shows that it delays the commencement of young people's first sexual encounters. It also reduces unsafe sexual practices, which decreases the incidence of sexually transmitted diseases and unwanted pregnancies, and has benefits for overall health throughout one's life (Baldo *et al.* 1993; UNESCO 2009; Wellings *et al.* 1995). Introducing sexuality education early in young people's lives also decreases the chance of their experiencing child sexual abuse (Brennan and Graham 2012; Mitchell 2012).

Myth: Children who transgress normative gendered behaviours in childhood will turn out to be gay

It is common practice amongst children to cross-dress in different gender clothing during their play. Many children enjoy exploring their gender identities by transgressing the normative gender boundaries that are generally enforced on them. It is often parents' concerns (and sometimes those of educators) for the child's wellbeing amongst their peers that lead to negative reactions to the child who engages in these practices. As I have argued elsewhere (Robinson and Davies 2008b), boys dressing up in girls' clothing is often perceived as a major threat to dominant forms of masculinity, which are linked to heterosexuality. In transgressing the boundaries of acceptable masculine behaviours, these boys are also often viewed as proto-gay subjects. This behaviour elicits great fear in some adults as a result of the dominant discourses associated with homosexuality, which constitute gay males (and also lesbians) as abnormal and deviant. Young girls do not tend to inspire the same fears associated with their 'becoming gay' as young boys, especially through the process of dressing up. This is because when girls and women dress up in masculine clothing, they take up some of the authority and social value that is inherent in masculine subjects, which is seen as less challenging than when young boys divest themselves, through their dress, of the masculine authority which is perceived to be rightfully theirs. Generally, it is not until young girls continue this behaviour into adolescence that it begins to be seen as problematic by some parents (Davies 2008a; Halberstam 1998). But, while some children who do cross-dress may indeed identify as gay or lesbian adults, others will not; similarly, while some children who strictly conform to gender norms may also identify as gay or lesbian in adulthood, others will not.

Myth: Once I've done 'the talk' I've done my bit as a parent

Children's sexuality education (including sexual ethics education) at home or at school should not be viewed as a one-off talk. Sexuality education is not just about sex, pregnancy and birth, but is also about relationships, ethical behaviours and sexual orientation. Sexuality education needs to be normalized as a topic that is possible to broach in everyday conversations between parents and children. These conversations need to happen early, and they need to occur often. This will allow some of the taboos and anxieties associated with discussing sexuality to be counteracted. Fostering open and honest discussions with children generally sets a context in which children will be more willing to discuss any issues with parents. Sexuality education is difficult to negotiate for many, but having the knowledge and resources to help discuss this information with children can make parents more confident in answering questions honestly (Brennan and Graham 2012; Walsh 2011).

Building ethical relationships early in life

In 2011, the New South Wales government in Australia introduced legislation for primary schools to include a special ethics education course as an option for students whose parents have requested their exemption from religious education. The St James Ethics Centre has been designated as the official approved provider of these classes, and has established a separate organization called Primary Ethics, which is directly responsible for the development and delivery of these programmes. The classes are currently designed for Years 5–6, but will also become available to children in earlier grades at a later stage. The classes are run by volunteers, who undertake ethics training in the organization (New South Wales Department of Education and Communities 2012). The ethics programmes are philosophically and pedagogically based on 'communities of enquiry', where groups work collaboratively, engaging in facilitated critical discussions and reflections to construct personal meanings and confirm group understandings about certain issues. Issues dealt with in these programmes include: being left out, sharing and bullying, the feelings and interests of others, and being a good friend (St James Ethics Centre 2012). Unfortunately, these classes are not compulsory (similar to the sexuality education discussed in Chapter 4), nor are they taught by trained teachers with specialized training in the field of ethics who are part of the school's full-time teaching staff. Whilst ethics education, just like sexuality education, is of great value to children at an early age, the fact that ethics classes are currently positioned as a fill-in subject for religious education means they may be destined for marginalization and little financial support in Australian primary schools.

How sexuality and ethics education are taught in schools and whose normative values and morals are upheld in programmes needs to be examined when reviewing current sexuality and ethics education, or when new programmes are being developed (Rasmussen 2010). As school curricula tend to perpetuate the hegemony of dominant groups, these programmes have not addressed sexual ethics as part of their core business with children. Research shows that children can and do engage in unethical sexual practices with other children, including gendered and sexual harassment and homophobic-based harassment. This behaviour tends to increase as children get older, and is a widespread practice in secondary schooling (Keddie 2009; Hillier *et al.* 2005; Martino and Pallotta-Chiarolli 2005; Robinson 1996, 2000, 2005d). When children engage in this behaviour, it is often dismissed as cute and as 'children being playful' (Robinson and Davies 2008; Renold 2005). One parent in research that I undertook for this book raised concerns about her five-year-old son, who was feeling traumatized after being harassed by two girls at school. The child was forcefully pinned to the ground by the two girls, who then touched and kissed him. A teacher, present when the incident took place, did not intervene – believing it to be normal children's play.

How might we begin to think about ethics and sexuality with young children? Australian sociologist Moira Carmody (2009), whose research has focused on sexual ethics education for young people, has utilized a Foucauldian theoretical framework of ethics to develop a sexuality education programme with and for young people 16–25 years of age. I suggest that this approach might also be useful in working with younger children, or for thinking about what an ethical sexuality education programme might look like for younger children. Carmody's programme focuses on four main concepts: care of the self (that is, taking care of yourself in relationships); care of others; negotiation; and reflection (Carmody 2009: 89). These are important concepts which could also be utilized to help children review their experiences, relationships and interactions with others. Approaching sexual ethics (or ethical relationships generally) through these concepts early in childhood can encourage children to begin thinking and communicating in an ethical way about sexuality, and the skills they develop in this area will continue to become more sophisticated as they get older. Children are capable of reflecting critically on their own desires and wants, or on how behaviours and comments from others make them feel (*care of the self*). They are also able to reflect on the impact of their desires, wants and behaviours on others (*care of others*). The story of the five-year-old boy above who felt traumatized by being the target of the girls' Catch-and-Kiss game provides a good example for young children to begin reflecting on these issues. Healthy sexual development occurs in an environment free from unwanted activities, and developing children's understandings of ethical relationships early contributes to the creation of such environments (McKee *et al.* 2010). It also makes children more aware of unethical practices, whether engaged in by peers or adults.

In the example above, the issue of ethics and consent are central. The young boy has not consented to being involved in the girls' game, but they continue to harass him. Catch and Kiss is a common game that many children enjoy playing. It generally involves daring children to chase, catch and then kiss the boy or girl of their interest and desires. In some cases, all children consent and all find pleasure in being involved, but in other cases consent is not given, making this game – and others like it – a very different experience for some children. Developing children's critical awareness around these differences is important. Catch and Kiss for many girls and boys is an integral activity in the construction of their gendered and sexual subjectivities, particularly amongst peers, and to their developing understandings of heteronormative relationships. Building children's awareness of relationships, of relations of power, and of the importance of negotiating consent is critical in building ethical awareness and encouraging healthy sexual development and non-violent behaviour early in children's lives. In order to build children's understanding of the importance of caring for themselves in relationships and interactions, it is important for them to reflexively consider their behaviours. In the present example, the young girls need to consider how the Catch-and-Kiss game makes them feel (e.g. excitement, pleasure, nervousness), whether they can envisage an instance in which they could feel differently about engaging in the game as they played it (e.g. being persuaded by friends to be involved in something that they are not sure about), and identifying what the contributing factors to feeling differently might be (e.g. peer pressure). Engaging children in reflexive thinking about the boy's needs, the impact of the girls' behaviour and their use of aggression in this instance could contribute significantly to the process of building children's ethical awareness and caring for other people.

Negotiating and asking are also important skills to develop in building children's ethical practices (Carmody 2009). The mismatch between the boy's feelings and the young girls' desires to express their interest in him reflects the need for the girls to engage in different and more ethical strategies that are equally spontaneous and pleasurable for all. Carmody argues that not asking or negotiating 'may result in one person's needs dictating what happens, without regard for the other, but it may also mean opportunities for exploration of unimagined possibilities are lost' (Carmody 2009: 90). Building positive relationships is significantly linked to the development of communication and negotiation competencies, including assertiveness skills. Learning to ask permission, or finding out about what a person wants or needs, as well as being able to say what you want and do not want are critical skills for both children and adults. The concept of agency has been central to the discussions in this book. In healthy sexual development, children's sexual agency is about learning that 'they have control of their own sexuality and are in control of who can take sexual pleasure from their bodies' (McKee *et al.* 2010: 16). This agency is also about being able to assertively stand up for one's rights, confidently resist peer pressure, and take responsibility for the decisions one makes (Impett *et al.* 2006; McKee *et al.* 2010). All of these attributes are important to begin learning in early childhood.

Encouraging critical reflection about one's own and others' behaviours and practices is paramount in building ethical awareness. Learning to be reflexive includes understanding one's actions, how they impact on the other person, what one's feelings and intentions were at the time, what was good or bad about the experience, how one makes sense of one's actions and their consequences, and how might one do it better next time (Carmody 2009). It is important that children begin to learn to be reflexive in their lives and that adults support children to begin to think critically in this manner. Learning to think critically is also about developing children's political awareness, about how identity – e.g. age, gender, class, cultural backgrounds, sexual orientation, and religious faith – might lead people to think and approach situations differently.

Building children's abilities to understand and critique a broad range of media is also important to developing healthy sexuality and ethical relationships. This skill is essential for counteracting the sexualization of children in the media that children and young people encounter daily (Taylor 2010; Hartley and Lumby 2003; Buckingham and Bragg 2004; McKee *et al.* 2010). As pointed out previously, censorship is not the most effective way to counteract this problem; providing children with critical literacy skills and political awareness is paramount. Encouraging children to reflect on the pleasures of media, popular culture and gender performances – and when those pleasures may be compromised through various means – is an important distinction on which to focus children's awareness.

Building a programme of sexual ethics education suitable for young children provides them with essential skills and more positive, equitable and respectful discourses with which to understand difference, relationships, body image, sexuality, and their own sexual and gendered subjectivities. Developing programmes for parents to address these issues and other aspects of sexual ethics with children effectively is equally important. Educating parents about the processes involved in building children's ethical practices will give them support and confidence in handling these issues with their children, and encourage a home environment in which open and honest discussions are possible around these issues, which are often considered difficult. Essential to programmes for both children and parents is the inclusion of discourses that counteract the harassment and ostracism directed at young children who transgress normative gender performances, or at young people who do not wish to engage in heteronormative practices and who may or may not choose to live a heterosexual lifestyle. Self-acceptance and a positive attitude towards one's own sexual identity are imperative to healthy sexual development (Impett *et al.* 2006; McKee *et al.* 2010). Parents' initial reactions to their children's non-conforming gender behaviours or ambivalence about their sexual identities are critical in maintaining trust and open communications with their children throughout their early lives.

In the context of this discussion, the teacher's lack of intervention in the earlier example of the Catch-and-Kiss game raises some pedagogical concerns. Catch and Kiss is a common game amongst children, but it is not just neutral children's play as perceived by the teacher in this scenario. The game is infused with normative gender practices and is foundational to children's demonstrations of their heteronormative gendered and sexualized subjectivities amongst their peers. In this particular instance, there is an element of violence and coercion on the part of the girls and distress for the young boy. If a witness stands and watches unethical behaviour without intervening in some way, they directly condone the behaviour. Thus, if the teacher observed the boy's distress, they should have intervened. If the teacher did not register the boys' distress, it may have been due to the boy not publicly showing his stress amongst his peers, especially if his masculinity was challenged by the two girls. He may have kept his feelings private until he felt safe to talk about it. The teacher's perception that it was just children's play may have eclipsed an awareness of the boy's distress, but it may also have been due to a gendered perception that the boy could handle himself against two girls. As this example reflects a reversal of normative gendered practices, the teacher may have thought differently about the incident and intervened if it was two boys harassing a girl. There are multiple possibilities for the lack of intervention, but it does reinforce a strong message that there is nothing wrong with the girls' behaviour. To build a positive sexual ethics education programme for children, the ethical behaviours of others – children or adults – also need to be scrutinized by children. The training of teachers to administer sexual ethics programmes with children effectively is crucial to the programmes' overall effectiveness. This training needs to include a critical reflection on one's own values, beliefs and practices, especially in terms of what are considered normative performances of gender and sexuality for children and young people.

Final comment

Throughout this book I have argued that it is important to begin to reconceptualize our understandings of childhood innocence, in order to rethink the ways in which we educate children, particularly about knowledge considered to be difficult – such as sexuality. This is a critical shift in thinking that is about building children's resilience, competencies and agency as sexual citizens. I would like to give the concluding comment to Foucault, who aptly reminds us: 'There are times in life when the question of knowing if one can think differently than one thinks, and perceive differently than one sees, is absolutely necessary if one is to go on looking and reflecting at all' (Foucault 1985: 8).

References

Aggleton, P., Oliver, C. and Rivers, K. (1998) *Reducing the Rate of Teenage Conceptions: The implications of research into young people, sex, sexuality and relationships.* Abingdon, Oxon: Health Education Authority.

Ahmed, S. (2004) *The Cultural Politics of Emotion.* London: Routledge.

Albury, K. and Lumby, C. (2010) 'Too Much? Too Young? The Sexualisation of Children Debate in Australia'. *Media International Australia* 135: 141–52.

Alderson, P. (1999) 'Human rights and democracy in schools – do they mean more than picking up litter and not killing whales?'. *International Journal of Children's Rights*, 7: 85–205.

Alderson, P. (2000) *Young Children's Rights: Exploring beliefs, principles and practices.* London: Jessica Kingsley.

Allen, L. (2004) 'Beyond the birds and the bees: Constituting a discourse of erotics in sexuality education'. *Gender and Education*, 16(2): 151–67.

Alloway, N. (1995) *Foundation Stones: The construction of gender in early childhood.* Melbourne: Curriculum Corporation.

Althusser, L. (1971) *Ideology and Ideological State Apparatuses, in 'Lenin and Philosophy and Other Essays'*, trans. B. Brewster. London: New Left Books.

American Psychological Association (APA) (2007) *Report of the APA Task Force on the Sexualization of Girls.* Online. Available at: www.apa.org/pi/women/programs/girls/report.aspx (accessed August 2011).

American Psychological Association (APA) (2010) *Report of the APA Task Force on the Sexualization of Girls.* Washington, DC: American Psychological Association. Online. Available at: www.apa.org/pi/women/programs/girls/report.aspx (accessed August 2011).

Angelides, S. (2004) 'Feminism, child sexual abuse, and the erasure of children's sexuality'. *GLQ*, 10(2): 141–77.

Apple, M. (1999) *Power, Meaning and Identity: Essays in critical educational studies.* New York: Peter Lang.

Apple, M. (2001) *Educating the 'Right' Way: Markets, standards, God, and inequality.* New York: RoutledgeFalmer.

Arendt, H. (1961) *Between Past and Future: Six exercises in political thought.* New York: Viking Press.

Aries, P. (1962) *Centuries of Childhood: A social history of family life*, trans. R. Baldick. New York: Vintage Books/Random House.

Arlington, K. and Stevenson, A. (2012) 'Police threat to parents on children walking alone'. *Sydney Morning Herald*, 9 February. Online. Available at: www.smh.com.au/ nsw/police-threat-to-parents-on-children-walking-alone-20120208-1rezj.html (accessed 19 April 2012).

Austin, J. and Willard, M. (eds) (1997) *Generations of Youth: Youth cultures and history in twentieth century America*. New York: New York University Press.

Australian Associated Press (AAP) (2009) 'Three boys charged with assault of girl', *Sydney Morning Herald*, 30 December. Online. Available at: www.smh.com.au/ breaking-news-national/three-boys-charged-with-assault-of-girl-20091230-ljko. html (accessed 11 January 2010).

Australian Bureau of Statistics (ABS) (2006) *Personal Safety Survey*, cat. no. 4906.0. Canberra: Australian Bureau of Statistics.

Bailey, R. (2011) *Letting Children be Children: Report of an independent review of the commercialisation and sexualisation of childhood*. Department of Education, United Kingdom. Online. Available at: www.education.gov.uk/publications/standard/ publicationDetail/Page1/CM%208078 (accessed 12 December 2011).

Bakhtin, M. (1994) 'Carnival ambivalence', in P. Morris (ed.) (1994) *The Bakhtin Reader*. London: Arnold.

Baldo, M., Aggleton, P. and Slutkin, G. (1993) 'Does sex education lead to earlier or increased sexual activity in youth?'. Ninth International Conference on AIDS, Berlin.

Ball, S. (1990) *Foucault and Education: Disciplines and knowledge*. London: Taylor & Francis.

Beatty, B. and Grant, J. (2010) 'Entering into the fray: Historians of childhood and public policy'. *The Journal of the History of Childhood and Youth*, 3(1): 107–26.

Becker, H. (1963) *Outsiders*. New York: Free Press.

Bell, D. and Binnie, J. (2000) *The Sexual Citizen: Queer politics and beyond*. Cambridge: Polity Press.

Benedict, R. (1938) 'Continuities and discontinuities in cultural conditioning'. *Psychiatry*, 1: 161–7.

Ben-Yahuda, N. (2009) 'Moral panics – 36 years on'. *British Journal of Criminology*, 49: 1–3.

Berlant, L. (1997) *The Queen of America Goes to Washington City: Essays on sex and citizenship*. Durham: Duke University Press.

Berlant, L. (2004) 'Live sex acts (Parental advisory: Explicit material)', in S. Bruhm and N. Hurley, *Curiouser: On the Queerness of Children*. Minneapolis: University of Minneapolis Press.

Berlant, L. and Warner, M. (1998) 'Sex in public'. *Critical Inquiry*, 24(2): 547–66.

Bhana, D. (2008) 'Discourses of childhood innocence in primary school HIV/AIDS education in South Africa'. *African Journal of AIDS Research*, 7(1): 149–58.

Bhana, D. (2009) '"They've got all the knowledge": HIV education, gender and sexuality in South African primary schools'. *British Journal of Sociology of Education*, 30(2): 165–77.

Bhana, D. (2010) 'How much do children know about HIV/AIDS?'. *Early Childhood Development and Care*, 180(8): 1079–92.

Bickmore, K. (1999) 'Why discuss sexuality in elementary schools?' Paper presented at the Annual Meeting of the American Educational Research Association, Montreal, 19–23 April.

Blaise, M. (2005) *Playing it Straight: Uncovering gender discourses in the early child-hood classroom*. New York: Routledge.

Blaise, M. (2009) '"What a girl wants, what a girl needs": Responding to sex, gender, and sexuality in the early childhood classroom'. *Journal of Research in Childhood Education*, 23(4): 450–60.

Blaise, M. (2010) 'Kiss and Tell: Gendered narratives and childhood sexuality'. Special Sexualities Issue: *Australasian Journal of Early Childhood*, 35(1): 1–9.

Board of Studies, New South Wales (1992) *Personal Development, Health and Physical Education, K-6 Syllabus and Support Document*. Sydney: Board of Studies, New South Wales.

Board of Studies, New South Wales (1999a) *Personal Development, Health and Physical Education K–6 Syllabus*. Sydney: Board of Studies, New South Wales.

Board of Studies, New South Wales (1999b) *Personal Development, Health and Physical Education: My growing self, stage 2 – Growth and development K–6 teaching kit*. Sydney: Board of Studies, New South Wales.

Boldt, G. (1997) 'Sexist and heterosexist responses to gender bending', in J. Tobin (ed.) *Making Place for Pleasure in Early Childhood Education*. New Haven and London: Yale University Press.

Bond Stockton, K. (2009) *The Queer Child, or Growing Sideways in the Twentieth Century*. Durham: Duke University Press.

Bourdieu, P. (1991) *Outline of a Theory of Practice*, trans. R. Nice. Cambridge: Polity Press.

Braithwaite, D. (2006) 'Police transfers over "sexual harassment"'. *Sydney Morning Herald*, 24 July. Online. Available at: http://www.smh.com.au/news/national/police-transfers-over-sex-harassment/2006/07/24/1153593241825.html (accessed 4th August 2012).

Bray, A. (2009) 'Governing the gaze: Child sexual abuse moral panic and the post-feminist blindspot'. *Feminist Media Studies*, 19(2): 173–91.

Breckenridge, J. and Carmody, M. (eds) (1992) *Crimes of Violence: Australian responses to rape and child sexual assault*. Sydney: Allen & Unwin.

Brennan, H. and Graham, J. (2012) *Is this Normal? Understanding your child's sexual behaviour*. Fortitude Valley: Family Planning Queensland.

Britzman, D. P. (1997) 'What is this thing called love? New discourses for under-standing gay and lesbian youth', in S. de Castell and M. Bryson (eds) *Radical In<ter>ventions: Identity, politics, and difference/s in educational praxis*. Albany: State University of New York Press.

Britzman, D. P. (1998) *Lost Subjects, Contested Objects: Toward a psychoanalytic inquiry of learning*. Albany: State University New York Press.

Britzman, D. P. (2000) 'Precocious education', in S. Talbut and S. R. Steinberg (eds) *Thinking Queer: Sexuality, culture, and education*. New York: Peter Lang Publishing.

Brody, P. (1984) 'A research-based guide to using pictures effectively'. *Instructional Innovator*, 29(2): 21–2.

Bruhm, S. and Hurley, N. (2004) 'Curiouser: On the queerness of children', in S. Bruhm and N. Hurley (eds) *Curiouser: On the queerness of children*. Minneapolis: University of Minneapolis Press.

Buckingham, D. (2000) *After the Death of Childhood: Growing up in the age of electronic media*. Malden, MA: Polity Press.

Buckingham, D. and Bragg, S. (2004) *Young People, Sex, and the Media: The facts of life?* Basingstoke: Palgrave Macmillan.

Burr, V. (1995) *An Introduction to Social Constructionism.* London: Routledge.

Burrows, L. (2000) 'Fictions, factions, frictions: Constructing the "child" in school physical education'. *Journal of Physical Education New Zealand*, 33(3): 22–36.

Butler, J. (1989) 'Gendering the body: Beauvoir's philosophical contribution', in A. Garry and M. Pearsall (eds) *Women, Knowledge and Reality: Explorations in feminist philosophy.* Boston: Unwin Hyman.

Butler, J. (1990) *Gender Trouble: Feminism and the subversion of identity.* New York: Routledge.

Butler, J. (2004) *Undoing Gender.* New York: Routledge.

Cahill, B. and Theilheimer, R. (1999) 'Stonewall in the housekeeping area: Gay and lesbian issues in the early childhood classroom', in W. J. Letts IV and J. T. Sears (eds) *Queering Elementary Education: Advancing the dialogue about sexualities and schooling.* Lanham: Rowman & Littlefield Publishers.

Calvert, G., Ford, A. and Parkinson, P. (eds) (1992) *The Practice of Child Protection: Australian approaches.* Sydney: Hale and Iremonger.

Canaday, M. (2009) *The Straight State: Sexuality and citizenship in twentieth-century America.* Princeton: Princeton University Press.

Cannella, G. S. and Viruru, R. (2004) *Childhood and Postcolonization: Power, education and contemporary practice.* New York: RoutledgeFalmer.

Carmody, M. (2009) *Sex and Ethics: Young people and ethical sex.* Melbourne: Palgrave Macmillan.

Casper, V., Cuffaro, H. K., Schultz, S., Silin, J. and Wickens, E. (1998) 'Towards a most thorough understanding of the world: Sexual orientation and early childhood education', in N. Yelland (ed.) *Gender in Early Childhood.* London: Routledge.

Chasnoff, D. and Cohen, H. (1997) *It's Elementary: talking about gay issues in schools.* San Francisco: Women's Educational Media.

Chong, D. (2012) 'Home Ministry shelves children's book on sex education'. *The Malaysian Insider*, 21 February. Online. Available at: www.themalaysianinsider.com/malaysia/article/home-ministry-shelves-childrens-book-on-sex-education (accessed 20 April 2012).

Chrisman, K. and Couchenour, D. (2002) *Healthy Sexual Development: A guide for early childhood educators and families.* Washington DC: National Association for the Education of Young Children.

Clark, M. (1989) *The Great Divide: The Construction of Gender in the Primary School.* Canberra: Curriculum Development Centre.

Cohen, S. (1972) *Folk Devils and Moral Panics.* London: MacGibbon and Kee.

Cole, B. (1997) *Princess Smarty Pants.* New York: Putnam.

Connell, C. and Elliott, S. (2009) 'Beyond the birds and the bees: Learning inequality through sexuality education'. *American Journal of Sexuality Education*, 4: 83–102.

Connell, R. W. (1995) *Masculinities.* Sydney: Allen & Unwin.

Cooper, D. (1993) 'An engaged state: Sexuality, governance and the potential for change'. *Journal of Law and Society*, 20: 257–75.

Cooper, D. (1995) *Power in Struggle: Feminism, sexuality and the state.* Buckingham: Open University Press.

Corteen, K. M. (2006) 'Schools' fulfilment of sex and relationship education documentation: Three school-based case studies'. *Sex Education*, 6(1): 77–99.

Corteen, K. and Scraton, P. (1997) 'Prolonging "childhood", manufacturing "innocence" and regulating sexuality', in P. Scraton (ed.) *'Childhood' in 'Crisis'*. London: University College London Press.

Cossman, B. (2007) *Sexual Citizens: The legal and cultural regulation of sex and belonging*. Stanford: Stanford University Press.

Cunningham, H. (1991) *The Children of the Poor: Representations of Childhood Since the Seventeenth Century*. Oxford: Blackwell.

Cunningham, H. (1995) *Children and Childhood in Western Society since 1500*. London: Longman.

Curren, G., Chiarolli, S. and Pollotta-Chiarolli, M. (2009) 'The c words: Clitorises, childhood and challenging compulsory heterosexuality discourses with pre-service primary teachers'. *Sex Education*, 9(2): 155–68.

Currie, D. H., Kelly, D. M. and Pomerantz, S. (2009) *Girl Power: Girls reinventing girlhood*. New York: Peter Lang.

Dahlberg, G. and Moss, P. (2005) *Ethics and Politics in Early Childhood Education*. London: RoutledgeFalmer.

Dahlberg, G., Moss, P. and Pence, A. (1999) *Beyond Quality in Early Childhood Education and Care: Postmodern perspectives*. London: Falmer Press.

Darwin, C. (1859) *The Origin of the Species*. London: John Murray.

Darwin, C. (1871) *The Descent of Man and Selection in Relation to Sex*. London: John Murray.

Dauda, C. (2010) 'Childhood, age of consent and moral regulation in Canada and the UK'. *Contemporary Politics*, 16(3): 227–47.

Davies, B. (1989) *Frogs and Snails and Feminist Tales: Preschool children and gender*. Sydney: Allen & Unwin.

Davies, B. (1993) *Shards of Glass: children reading and writing beyond gendered identities*. Sydney: Allen & Unwin.

Davies, B. (1994) *Poststructuralist Theory and Classroom Practice*. Geelong: Deakin University Press.

Davies, C. (2008a) 'Becoming sissy', in B. Davies (ed.) *Judith Butler in Conversation: Analysing the texts and talk of everyday life*. New York: Routledge.

Davies, C. (2008b) 'Proliferating panic: Regulating representations of sex and gender during the culture wars'. *Cultural Studies Review*, 14(2): 83–102.

Davies, C. (2012) '"It's not at all chic to be denied your civil rights": performing sexual and gendered citizenship in Holly Hughes'. Preaching to the perverted. *Sexualities*, 15(3): 277–96.

Davies, C. and McInnes, D. (in press 2012) 'Speaking violence: Homophobia and the production of injurious speech in schooling cultures', in S. Saltmarsh, K. H. Robinson, and C. Davies (eds) *Rethinking School Violence: Theory, gender, context*. London: Palgrave Macmillan.

Davies, C. and Robinson, K. H. (2010) 'Hatching babies and stork deliveries: Constructing sexual knowledge and taking risks in early childhood education'. Special Issue, Risky Childhoods. *Contemporary Issues in Early Childhood*, 11(3): 249–60.

Davies, C. and Robinson, K. H. (2012) *Reflective Practice with Early and Middle Childhood Education and Child Care Professionals*. Report commissioned by Child Australia, Western Australia, Australia.

Davies, C. and Robinson, K. H (in press 2013) 'Reconceptualising family: Negotiating sexuality in a governmental climate of neoliberalism'. *Contemporary Issues in Early Childhood*.

Denborough, D. (1996) 'Power and partnership? Challenging the sexual construction of schooling', in L. Laskey and C. Beavis (eds) *Schooling and Sexualities*. Deakin, Victoria: Deakin Centre for Education and Change, Deakin University.

Department of Education and Training, Office of Schools, New South Wales (2007) *Controversial Issues in Schools Policy*, no. PD20020045. New South Wales: Director, School and Regional Policy, Department of Education and Training.

Department of Education, New South Wales (1952) *Curriculum for primary schools*. Sydney: A. H. Pettifer, Government Printer.

Donaghy, B. (1997) *Leaving Early: Youth suicide – the horror, the heartbreak, the hope*. Sydney: Harper Collins.

Duggan, L. (1994) 'Queering the state'. *Social Text*, 39: 1–14.

Dunn, J. (1995) 'Connections between emotion and understanding in development'. *Cognition and Emotion*, 9(2–3): 113–285.

Durkheim, E. (1956) *Education and Sociology*, trans. S. Fox. New York: The Free Press.

Durkheim, E. (1982) 'Education', in W. S. F. Pickering (ed.) (2006) *Emile Durkheim: Selected Writings on Education, Vol. 1 – Durkheim: Essays on Morals and Education*. Abingdon: Routledge.

Dyson, S. and Smith L. (2011) '"There are lots of different kinds of normal": Families and sex education – styles, approaches and concerns'. *Sex Education* 12(12): 219–30.

Easteal, P. (1994) *Voices of the survivors*. Melbourne: Spinifex.

Edelman, L. (2004) *No Future: Queer theory and the death drive*. Durham, NC: Duke University Press.

Egan, D. R. and Hawkes, G. (2007) 'Producing the prurient through the pedagogy of purity: Childhood sexuality and the Social Purity Movement'. *Journal of Historical Sociology*, 20(4): 443–61.

Egan, D. R. and Hawkes G. (2008) 'Endangered girls and incendiary objects: Unpacking the discourse on sexualization'. *Sexuality & Culture*, 12: 291–311.

Egan, D. R. and Hawkes, G. (2009) 'The problem with protection: Or why we need to move towards recognition and the sexual agency of children'. *Continuum*, 23(3): 389–400.

Egan, D. R. and Hawkes, G. (2010) *Theorizing the sexual child in modernity*. New York: Palgrave Macmillan.

Ellen (2011) *Nicki Minaj Sings 'Super Bass' with Sophia Grace (Full Version)*. YouTube video clip. Online. Available at www.youtube.com/watch?v=f9573kGBtuE (accessed 26 March 2012).

Elliott, S. (2010) 'Parents' constructions of teen sexuality: Sex panics, contradictory discourses and social inequality'. *Symbolic Interaction*, 33(2): 191–212.

Epstein, D. (1995) 'Girls don't do bricks': Gender and sexuality in the primary classroom', in I. Siraj-Blatchford and J. Siraj-Blatchford (eds) *Educating the Whole Child*. Buckingham: Open University Press.

Epstein, D. and Johnson, R. (1994) 'On the straight and narrow: The heterosexual presumption, homophobias and schools', in D. Epstein (ed.) *Challenging Lesbian and Gay Inequalities in Education*. Philadelphia: Open University Press.

Epstein, D. and Johnson, R. (1998) *Schooling Sexualities*. Buckingham: Open University Press.

Erickson, P. A. and Murphy, L. D. (2003) *A History of Anthropological Theory*, 2nd edn. Peterborough: Broadview Press.

Evans, D. (1993) *Sexual Citizenship: The material construction of sexualities*. London: Routledge.

Fabian, H. (1996) 'Photo-talk: Interviewing young children' Paper presented at the 6th Annual Research Conference of the European Early Childhood Education Association, Lisbon, 1–4 September.

Family Planning Association (2011) *Factsheet: Sex and relationships education*. London: Family Planning Association.

Farrelly, E. (2011) 'Let's shoot straight on gay marriage'. *Sydney Morning Herald*, 25 August. Online. Available at: www.smh.com.au/opinion/politics/lets-shoot-straight-on-gay-marriage-20110824-1ja54.html (accessed 2 February 2012).

Faulkner, J. (2010) 'The innocence fetish: The commodification and sexualisation of children in the media and popular culture'. Special Issue: Children, young people, sexuality and the media. *Media International Australia*, 35: 106–17.

Faulkner, J. (2011) *The Importance of Being Innocent: Why we worry about children*. Melbourne: Cambridge University Press.

Ferfolja, T. (2009) 'State of the field review: Stories so far. An overview of the research on lesbian teachers'. *Sexualities*, 12(3): 378–96.

Fergus, L. and Keel. M. (2005) *Adult Victim/Survivors of Child Sexual Assault*. Australian Centre for the Study of Sexual Assault, Australian Institute of Family Studies. ACSSA No. 1, November. Online. Available at: www.aifs.gov.au/acssa/pubs/wrap/w1.html (accessed 15 April 2012).

Fields, J. (2005) '"Children having children": Race, innocence, and sexuality education'. *Social Problems*, 52(4): 549–71.

Fine, M. (1988) 'Sexuality, schooling and adolescent females: The missing discourse of desire'. *Harvard Educational Review*, 58(1): 29–53.

Fine, M. and McClelland, S. I. (2006) 'Sexuality education and desire: Still missing discourse of desire'. *Harvard Educational Review*, 76: 297–337.

Fishman, S. (1982) 'The history of childhood sexuality'. *Journal of Contemporary History*, 17(2): 269–83.

Fleming, J. M. (1997) 'Prevalence of childhood sexual abuse in a community sample of Australian women'. *Medical Journal of Australia*, 166(2): 65–8.

Foucault, M. (1974) *The Archaeology of Knowledge*. London: Tavistock.

Foucault, M. (1977) *Discipline and Punish: The birth of the prison*, trans. A. Sheridan. New York: Vintage.

Foucault, M. (1978) *The History of Sexuality: Vol. 1, an introduction*, trans. R. Hurley. Harmondsworth: Penguin.

Foucault, M. (1980) *Power/Knowledge: Selected interviews and other writings 1972–1977*. New York: Pantheon Books.

Foucault, M. (1985) *The Use of Pleasure*, trans. R. Hurley. New York: Vintage.

Foucault, M. (1997) '"Society Must be Defended": Lectures at the College De France 1975–76', in M. Bertaini and A. Fontana (eds) trans. D. Macey, pp. 239–64. New York: Picador.

Franklin, C., Grant, D., Corcoran, J., Miller, P. O. and Bultman, L. (1997) 'Effectiveness of prevention programs for adolescent pregnancy: A meta-analysis'. *Journal of Marriage and the Family*, 59: 551–67.

Fraser, N. (1992) 'Rethinking the public sphere: A contribution to the critique of actually existing democracy', in C. Calhoun (ed.) *Habermas and the public sphere*. Cambridge, MA: MIT press.

Freud, S. (1976 [1905]) 'Infantile sexuality', in *Three Essays on the Theory of Sexuality*, trans. J. Strachey. New York: Basic Books.

Gerouki, M. (2010) 'The boy who was drawing princesses: Primary teachers' accounts of children's non-conforming behaviours'. *Sex Education*, 10(4): 335–48.

Giddens, A. (1999) 'Taking Risk'. *Far Eastern Economic Review*, 162(14): 31–2.

Giroux, H. A. (2000) *Stealing Innocence: youth, corporate power and the politics of culture*. New York: St. Martins Press.

Gittins, D. (1998) *The Child in Question*. London: Macmillan.

GLSEN (Gay, Lesbian & Straight Education Network) (2009) '11-year-old hangs himself after enduring anti-gay bullying', 9 April. Online. Available at: www.glsen.org/walker.html (accessed 4 April 2012).

GLSEN (Gay, Lesbian & Straight Education Network) and Harris Interactive (2012) 'Playgrounds and prejudice: Elementary school climate in the United States, a survey of students and teachers'. New York: GLSEN.

Goldman, J. D. G. (2010) 'The new sexuality education curriculum for Queensland primary school', *Sex Education*, 10(1): 47–66.

Goldman, R. and Goldman, J. (1982) *Children's Sexual Thinking: A comparative study of children aged 5 to 15 years in Australia, North America, Britain and Sweden*. London: Routledge & Kegan Paul.

Goldson, B. (1997) '"Childhood": An introduction to historical and theoretical analyses', in P. Scraton (ed.) *'Childhood' in 'crisis'?* London: UCL Press.

Government of Western Australia: Department of Child Protection (n.d.) 'Indicators of Child Sexual Abuse'. Online. Available at: http://mandatoryreporting.dcp.wa.gov.au/Pages/FAQ-Indicatorsofchildsexualabuse.aspx (accessed 12 February 2012).

Greishaber, S. J. (2008) 'Interrupting stereotypes: Teaching and the education of young children'. *Early Education and Development*, 19(3): 505–18.

Groce, N. E. and Trasi, R. (2004) 'Rape of individuals with disability: AIDS and the folk belief of virgin cleansing'. *Lancet*, 363(9422): 1663–4.

Halberstam, J. (1998) *Female masculinity*. Durham, NC: Duke University Press.

Halberstam, J. (2005) *In a queer time and place: Transgendered bodies, subcultural lives*. New York: New York University Press.

Hall, S. (2004) 'Foucault: Power, knowledge and discourse', in M. Wetherell, S. Taylor and S. J. Yates (eds) *Discourse Theory and Practice*. London: Sage.

Harding, V. (ed.) (2006) *Learn to Include*. Dulwich Hill: Learn to Include.

Harris, D. (1987) *Justifying the Welfare State*. Oxford: Blackwell.

Hart, R. A. (1992) *Children's Participation: From tokenism to citizenship*. Florence: United Nations Children Fund, UNICEF.

Hartley, J. and Lumby, C. (2003) 'Working girls or drop-dead gorgeous? Young girls in fashion and news', in K. Mallan and S. Pearce (eds) *Youth cultures: Texts, images, and identities*. Westport and London: Praeger.

Hawkes, G. and Egan, R. D. (2008) 'Developing the sexual child'. Special issue on the history of sexuality of childhood and youth, *Historical Sociology*, 22(2): 443–66.

Haydon, D. (2002) 'Children's rights to sex and sexuality education', in B. Franklin (ed.) *The New Handbook of Children's Rights: Comparative Policy and Practice*. London: Routledge.

Hendrick, H. (1990) 'Constructions and reconstructions of British childhood', in A. James and A. Prout (eds) *Constructing and Reconstructing Childhood: Contemporary issues in the sociological study of childhood*. London: The Falmer Press.

Hier, S. (2003) 'Risk and panic in late modernity: Implications of the converging sites of social anxiety'. *British Journal of Sociology*, 54(1): 3–20.

Hillier, L. and Walsh, A. (1999) 'Abused, silenced and ignored: creating more supportive environments for same sex attracted young people'. *Youth Suicide Prevention Bulletin*, 3: 23–7.

Hillier, L. and Mitchell, A. (2008) '"It was as useful as a chocolate kettle": Sex education in the lives of young same sex attracted people in Australia'. *Sex Education: sexuality, society and learning*, 8(2): 211–24.

Hillier, L., Turner, A. and Mitchell, A. (2005) *Writing Themselves In Again: Six years on. The 2nd national report on the sexuality, health and well-being of same sex attracted young people in Australia*. Melbourne: Australian Research Centre in Sex, Health & Society, La Trobe University.

Holland, J., Mauthner, M. and Sharpe, S. (1996) 'Family matters: Communicating health messages in the family', in *Family Health Research Reports*. London: HEA.

Holland, P. (2006) *Picturing Childhood: The myth of the child in popular imagery*. New York: I. B. Tauris.

Hollway, W. (1984) 'Gender difference and the production of subjectivity', in J. Henriques, W. Hollway, C. Urwin, C. Venn and V. Walkerdine (eds) *Changing the Subject: Psychology, social regulation and subjectivity*. London: Methuen.

hooks, b. (1997) 'Whiteness in the black imagination', in R. Frankenberg (ed.) *Displacing Whiteness: Essays in social and cultural criticism*. Durham: Duke University Press.

Hooton, A. (2001) 'The Moment: Photograph by Anthony Browell'. Interview. *Good Weekend*, 14 July.

Howe, B. and Cavell, K. (2005) *Empowering Children: Children's rights as a pathway to citizenship*. Toronto: University of Toronto Press.

Hughes, K., Cragg, A. and Taylor, C. (1999) *Reducing the Rate of Teenage Conceptions: Young people's experiences of relationships, sex, and early parenthood qualitative research*. London: Health Education Authority.

Hultqvist, K. and Dahlberg, G. (eds) (2001) *Governing the Child in the New Millennium*. New York: RoutledgeFalmer.

Hunt, R. and Jensen, J. (2007) *The School Report: The experiences of young gay people in Britain's schools*. London: Stonewall. Online. Available at: www.stonewall.org. uk/documents/school_report.pdf (accessed 4 April 2012).

Impett, E. A., Schooler, D. and Tolman, D. L. (2006) 'To be seen and not heard: Feminist ideology and adolescent girls' sexual health'. *Archives of Sexual Behavior*, 35(2): 131–44.

Ingham, R. and Kirkland, D. (1997) 'Discourses and sexual health: Providing for young people', in L. Yardley (ed.) *Material discourses of health and illness*. London: Routledge.

Intersex Society of North America (ISNA) (2012) 'What is intersex?'. Online. Available at: www.isna.org/faq/what_is_intersex (accessed 2 April 2012).

Irvine, J. (2006) 'Emotional scripts of sex panics'. *Sexuality Research and Social Policy*, 3(3): 82–94.

Jackson, L. (2006) 'Childhood and Youth', in H. G. Cocks and M. Houlbrook (eds) *The Modern History of Sexuality*. Basingstoke: Palgrave Macmillan.

Jackson, S. (1982) *Childhood and Sexuality*. Oxford: Basil Blackwell.

Jackson, S. and Scott, S. (1999) 'Risk anxiety and the social construction of childhood', in D. Lupton (ed.) *Risk and Sociocultural Theory: New theories and perspectives.* Cambridge: Cambridge University Press.

Jackson, S. and Westrupp, E. (2010) 'Sex, popular culture and the pre-teen girl'. *Sexualities,* 13: 357–76.

James, A. and Prout, A. (eds) (1990) *Constructing and Reconstructing Childhood: Contemporary issues in the sociological study of childhood.* London: The Falmer Press.

James, A. and James, A. (2004) *Constructing Childhood: Theory, policy and social practice.* London: Palgrave Macmillan.

James, A., Jenks, C. and Prout, A. (1998) *Theorizing Childhood.* London: Polity Press.

Jasman, A. (1998) 'Using pictures to elicit student viewpoints'. Paper presented at Murdoch University Teaching and Learning Seminar, Perth, 21 April.

Jemmott, J. B. and Jemmott, L. S. (2000) 'HIV behavioral interventions for adolescents in community settings', in J. Peterson and R. Diclemente (eds) *Handbook of HIV prevention.* New York: Plenum Publishers.

Jenkins, H. (1998) 'Introduction: Childhood innocence and other modern myths', in H. Jenkins (ed.) *The Children's Culture Reader.* New York: New York University Press.

Jenks, C. (1996) *Childhood.* London: Routledge.

John, M. (1995) 'Children's rights in a free market culture', in S. Stephens (ed.) *Children and the Politics of Culture.* Princeton: Princeton University Press.

Katz, C. (2004) *Growing Up Global: Economic restructuring and children's every day lives.* Minnesota: University of Minnesota Press.

Keddie, A. (2009) '"Some of those girls can be real drama queens": Issues of gender, sexual harassment and schooling'. *Sex Education: Sexuality, Society and Learning,* 9(1): 1–16.

Kehily, M. J. (2001) 'Understanding heterosexualities: Masculinities, embodiment and schooling'. Special Issue: Disciplining and punishing masculinities. *Men and Masculinities,* 4(2): 1173-85.

Kellet, M. (2009) 'Children and young people's voices', in H. Montgomery and M. Kellett (eds) *Children and Young People's Worlds: Developing frameworks for integrated practice.* Bristol: Policy Press.

Kellet, M. (2010) *Rethinking Children and Research: Attitudes in contemporary society.* Brisbane: Australian Educational Researcher.

Khayatt, M. D. (1992) *Lesbian Teachers: An invisible presence.* Albany: State University of New York Press.

Kilodavis, C. (2010) *My Princess Boy.* USA: KD Talent LLC Principals and Publisher.

Kim, N., Stanton, B., Li, X., Dickersin, K. and Galbraith, J. (1997) 'Effectiveness of the 40 adolescent AIDS-risk reduction interventions: A qualitative review'. *Journal of Adolescent Health,* 20: 204–15.

Kimmel, M. S. (1994) 'Masculinity as homophobia: Fear, shame, and silence in the construction of gender identity', in H. Brod and M. Kaufman (eds) *Theorizing Masculinities.* Thousand Oaks: Sage.

Kincaid, J. (1992) *Child-Loving: The erotic child and Victorian culture.* New York: Routledge.

Kincaid, J. (1998) *Erotic Innocence: The culture of child molesting.* Durham, NC: Duke University Press.

Kincaid, J. (2004) 'Producing erotic children', in S. Bruhm and N. Hurley (eds) *Curiouser: On the queerness of children*. Minneapolis: University of Minneapolis Press.

Kincheloe, J. L. and Steinberg, S. R. (1997) 'Addressing the crisis of whiteness: Reconfiguring white identity in a pedagogy of whiteness', in J. L. Kincheloe, S. R. Steinberg, N. M. Rodriguez and R. E. Chennault (eds) *White Reign: Deploying whiteness in America*. London: Macmillan.

King, J. R. (1997) 'Keeping it quiet: Gay teachers in the primary grades', in Tobin, J. (ed.) *Making a Place for Pleasure in Early Childhood Education*. New Haven: Yale University Press.

Kirby, D. B. (2008) 'The impact of abstinence and comprehensive sex and STD/HIV education programs on adolescent sexual behavior'. *Sexuality Research & Social Policy*, 5(3): 18–27.

Kitzinger, J. (1990) 'Who are you kidding? Children, power and the struggle against sexual abuse', in A. James and A. Prout (eds) *Constructing and Reconstructing Childhood: Contemporary issues in the sociological study of childhood*. London: The Falmer Press.

Knaus, C. (2012) 'ADFA arrest for indecent acts'. *Sydney Morning Herald*, 28 May. Online. Available at http://www.smh.com.au/act-news/adfa-cadet-arrested-for-indecent-acts-20120528-1zdpk.html (accessed 4th August 2012).

Kobayashi, A. and Ray, B. (2000) 'Civil risk and landscapes of marginality in Canada: A pluralist approach to social justice'. *Canadian Geographer*, 44(4): 401–17.

Kociumbas, J. (1997) *Australian Childhood: A history*. Sydney: Allen & Unwin.

Krulik, N. E. (1997) *Anastasia*. Golden Books.

Kulynych, J. (2001) 'No playing in the public sphere: Democratic theory and the exclusion of children'. *Social Theory and Practice*, 27(2): 231–64.

Lansdown, G. (1994) 'Children's Rights', in B. Mayall (ed.) *Children's Childhoods: Observed and experienced*. London: The Falmer Press.

Larsson, I. and Svedin, C. G. (2002) 'Sexual experience in childhood: Young adults' recollections'. *Archives of Sexual Behavior*, 31(3): 263–73.

Leff, L. and AAP (American Associated Press) (2012) 'Prop 8, California's Same-Sex Marriage Ban, Declared Unconstitutional'. *Huffpost Gay Voices*, 7 February. Online. Available at: www.huffingtonpost.com/2012/02/07/proposition-8-california-same-sex-marriage-ban-ruling_n_1260171.html?view=print&comm_ref=false (accessed 14 February 2012).

Levin, D. E. (2009) 'So sexy, so soon: The sexualisation of childhood', in S. Olfman (ed.) *The Sexualization of Childhood*. Westport: Praeger.

Levin, D. E. and Kilbourne, J. (2008) *So Sexy So Soon: The new sexualised childhood and what parents can do to protect their kids*. New York: Ballantine Books.

Levine, J. (2002) *Harmful to Minors: The perils of protecting children from sex*. Minneapolis: University of Minneapolis Press.

Lloyd, M. (2007) *Judith Butler*. Cambridge: Polity Press.

Luke, C. and Luke, A. (1998) 'Interethnic families: Difference within difference'. *Ethnic and Racial Studies*, 21: 728–54.

Lumby, C. (1998) 'No kidding: Paedophilia and popular culture'. *Continuum*, 12(1): 47–55.

Lumby, C. and Albury, K. (2008) 'Homer versus Homer: Digital media, literacy and child protection'. *Media International Australia*, 128: 80–7.

Lumby, C. and Albury, K. (2010) 'Too much? Too young? The sexualisation of children debate in Australia'. *Media International Australia*, 135: 141–52.

Mac An Ghaill, M. (1994) *The Making of Men: Masculinities, sexualities and schooling.* Buckingham: Open University Press.

McClean, C. (1996) 'Men, masculinity and heterosexuality', in L. Laskey and C. Beavis (eds) *Schooling and Sexualities.* Victoria: Deakin Centre for Education and Change, Deakin University.

McGuire, C., Hogg, C. and Barker, R. (eds) (1996) *Health Promotion and the Family: Messages from four research studies.* London: Health Education Authority.

McInnes, D. (2008) 'Sissy boy melancholy and the educational possibilities of incoherence', in B. Davies (ed.) *Judith Butler in Conversation: Analysing the texts and talk of everyday life.* New York: Routledge.

McInnes, D. and C. Davies (2008) 'Articulating sissy boy queerness within and against discourses of tolerance and pride', in S. Driver (ed.) *Queer Youth Cultures.* New York: SUNY.

McKee, A., Albury, K., Dunne, M., Greishaber, S., Hartley, J., Lumby, C. and Mathews, B. (2010) 'Healthy sexual development: A multidisciplinary framework for research'. *International Journal of Sexual Health*, 22(1): 14–19.

MacNaughton, G. (1993) 'Gender, power and racism: A case study of domestic play in early childhood'. *Multicultural Teaching*, 11(3): 12–15.

MacNaughton, G. (2000) *Rethinking Gender in Early Childhood Education.* Sydney: Allen & Unwin.

MacNaughton, G., Hughes, P. and Smith, K. (eds) (2008) *Young Children as Active Citizens: Principles, Policies and Pedagogies.* Cambridge: Cambridge Scholars Publishing.

McRobbie, A. and Thornton, S. (1995) 'Rethinking "moral panic" for multi-mediated social worlds'. *British Journal of Sociology*, 46(4): 559–74.

Marc, J. (2004) 'Children as citizens: Towards a contemporary notion of child participation'. *Childhood*, 11(1): 27–44.

Marr, D. (2008) *The Henson Case.* Melbourne: Text Publishing.

Martin, K. A. and Luke, K. (2010) 'Gender differences in the ABC's of the birds and the bees: What mothers teach young children about sexuality and reproduction'. *Sex Roles*, 62: 278–91.

Martino, W. and Pallotta-Chiarolli, M. (2003) *So What's a Boy? Addressing Issues of Masculinity and Schooling.* Maidenhead: Open University Press.

Martino, W. and Pallotta-Chiarolli, M. (2005) *Being Normal is the Only Way to Be: Adolescent perspectives on gender and school.* Sydney: University of New South Wales Press.

Mason, G. and Tomsen, S. (eds) (1997) *Homophobic Violence.* Sydney: The Hawkins Press.

Mason, J. and Fattore, T. (eds) (2005) *Children Taken Seriously in Theory, Policy and Practice.* London: Jessica Kingsley Publishers.

Mason, S. (2010) 'Braving it out! An illuminative evaluation of the provision of sex and relationships education in two primary schools in England'. *Sex Education: Sexuality, Society and Learning*, 10(2): 157–69.

Masson, H. (1995) 'Children and adolescents who sexually abuse other children: Response to an emerging problem'. *Journal of Social Welfare and Family Law*, 7: 325–36.

Mayall, B. (2000) 'The sociology of childhood in relations to children's rights'. *International Journal of Children's Rights*, 8: 243–59.

Mayall, B. (2006) 'Child-adult relations in social space', in E. Kay, M. Tisdall, J. M. David, A. Prout and M. Hill (eds) *Children, young people and social inclusion: Participation for what?* Bristol: Polity Press.

Mayle, P. (1973) *Where Did I Come From? The facts of life without any nonsense and with illustrations.* Secaucus, N.J.: L. Stuart.

Mayo, C. (2006) 'Pushing the limits of liberalism: Queerness, children and the future'. *Educational Theory*, 56(4): 469–87.

Meel, B. L. (2003) 'The myth of child rape as a cure for HIV/AIDS in Transkei: A case report'. *Medicine, Science and the Law*, 43(1): 85–8.

Meyer, A. (2007) 'The moral rhetoric of childhood'. *Childhood*, 14(1): 85–104.

Meyers, Z. (2007) 'Protecting 'innocence'? Deconstructing legal regulations of child sexuality'. *The Australian Feminist Law Journal*, 27: 51–69.

Mills, M. (1999) 'Homophobia and anti-lesbianism in schools: Challenges and possibilities for social justice'. *Melbourne Studies in Education*, 40(2): 105–25.

Mills, M. (2001) *Challenging Violence in Schools: An issue of masculinities.* Buckingham: Open University Press.

Mitchell, N. (2012) 'Is this normal? Understanding your child's sexual behaviour'. Audio podcast, 22 February. Life Matters Radio National, Australian Broadcasting Corporation (ABC) Radio, Sydney. Online. Available at: www.abc.net.au/radionational/programs/lifematters/wednesday-22-february-2012/3844022 (accessed on 1 March 2012).

Moran, J. (2001) 'Childhood sexuality and education: The case of Section 28'. *Sexualities*, 4(1): 73–89.

Morris, M. (2000) 'Dante's left foot kicks queer theory into gear', in S. Talburt and S. R. Steinberg (eds) *Thinking Queer: Sexuality, Culture, and Education.* New York: Peter Lang.

Mouzos, J. and Makkai, T. (2004) *Women's Experience of Male Violence: Findings from the Australian component of the International Violence Against Women Survey, Research and Public Policy Series no. 56.* Canberra: Australian Institute of Criminology.

Nabokov, V. (1955) *Lolita.* Paris: The Olympia Press.

New South Wales Department of Education and Communities (2012) *Special Ethics Education: Information for Principals.* Sydney: New South Wales Department of Education and Communities. Online. Available at: www.curriculumsupport.education.nsw.gov.au/policies/ethics/index.htm (accessed on 25 April 2012).

Olfman, S. (2009) 'The sexualization of childhood: Growing older younger/growing younger older', in S. Olfman (ed.) *The Sexualization of Childhood.* Westport: Praeger.

Papadopoulos, L. (2011) *The Sexualization of Young People (Review).* The Report of the Home Office, London.

Piaget, J. (1959) *The Language and Thought of the Child*, 3rd revised edn. London: Routledge & Kegan Paul.

Piaget, J. (1964) *The Early Growth of Logic in the Child.* New York: Harper.

Piaget, J. (1968) *The Psychology of Intelligence.* Totowa: Littlefield Adams.

Piaget, J. (1973 [1929]) *The Child's Conception of the World.* St Alban's: Paladin.

Pink, S. (2005) *Doing Visual Ethnography: Images, media and representation in research.* London: Sage.

Plummer, K. (1990) 'Understanding childhood sexualities'. *Journal of Homosexuality*, 20(1–2): 231–49.

Plummer, K. (1995) *Telling Sexual Stories: Power, intimacy and social worlds*. London: Routledge.

Pollard, R. (2009) 'Elite college students proud of "pro-rape" Facebook page'. *The Sydney Morning Herald*, 9 November. Online. Available at: http://www.smh.com.au/technology/elite-college-students-proud-of-prorape-facebook-page-20091108-i3js.html (accessed 14 December 2011).

Postman, N. (1982) *The Disappearance of Childhood*. New York: Delacorte Press.

Qvortrup, J. (2005) *Studies in Modern Childhood: Society agency and change*. London: Palgrave McMillan.

Rademakers, J., Laan, M. and Straver, C. J. (2000) 'Studying children's sexuality from the child's perspective'. *Journal of Psychology & Human Sexuality*, 12(1–2): 49–60.

Rasmussen, M. (2010) 'Revisiting moral panic in sexuality education'. *Media International Australia*, 135: 118–30.

Renold, E. (2005) *Girls, Boys, and Junior Sexualities: Exploring children's gender and sexual relations in the primary school*. London: RoutledgeFalmer.

Renold, E. (2006) '"They won't let us play ... unless you're going out with them": Girls, boys and Butler's "heterosexual matrix" in the primary years'. *British Journal of Sociology of Education*, 27(4): 489–509.

Renold, E. (2008) 'Queering masculinity: Re-theorising contemporary tomboyism in the schizoid space of innocent /heterosexualized young femininities'. *Girlhood Studies*, 1(2): 129–51.

Renold, E. and Ringrose, J. (2011) 'Schizoid subjectivities? Re-theorizing teen girls' sexual cultures in an era of "sexualization"'. *Journal of Sociology*, 47(4): 389–409.

Reuters and Jensen, E. (2007), '"Gay" tubbies face government ban'. *Sydney Morning Herald*, 29 May. Online. Available at: www.smh.com.au/articles/2007/05/29/1180205190981.html (accessed on 30 May 2009).

Richardson, D. (1998) 'Sexuality and citizenship'. *Sociology*, 32(1): 83–100.

Richardson, N. and Bromfield, L. (2005) *Who Abuses Children?* Resource sheet no. 7. Melbourne: National Child Protection Clearinghouse, Australian Institute of Family Studies.

Riggs, D. W. (2011) 'What about the children! Homophobia, accusations of pedophilia, and the construction of childhood', in B. Scherer and M. Ball (eds) *Queering Paradigms II: Interrogating agendas*. Oxford: Peter Lang.

Ringrose, J. (2011) 'Are you sexy, flirty or a slut? Exploring "sexualisation" and how teen girls perform/negotiate digital sexual identity on social networking sites', in R. Gill and C. Scharff (eds) *New Femininities: Postfeminism, neoliberalism and identity*. London: Palgrave.

Rizvi, F. (1991) 'The idea of ethnicity and the politics of multicultural education', in D. Dawkins (ed.) *Power and Politics in Education*. London: Falmer Press.

Robinson, K. H. (1996) 'Sexual harassment in secondary schooling', unpublished doctoral thesis, University of New South Wales.

Robinson, K. H. (2000) '"Great tits miss!" The sexual harassment of female teachers in secondary schools: Issues of gendered authority'. *Discourse: Studies in the Cultural Politics of Education*, 21 (1): 75–90.

Robinson, K. H. (2002) 'Making the invisible visible: Gay and lesbian issues in early childhood education'. *Contemporary Issues in Early Childhood*, 3(3): 415–34.

Robinson, K. H. (2005a) 'Childhood and sexuality: Adult constructions and silenced children', in Mason, J. and Fattore, T. (eds) *Children Taken Seriously in Theory, Policy and Practice*. London: Jessica Kingsley Publishers.

Robinson, K. H. (2005b) 'Doing anti-homophobia and anti-heterosexism in early childhood education. Moving beyond the immobilizing impacts of "risks", "fears" and "silences". Can we afford not to?'. *Contemporary Issues in Early Childhood Education*, 6(2): 175–88.

Robinson, K. H. (2005c) '"Queerying" gender: Heteronormativity in early childhood education'. *Australian Journal of Early Childhood*, 30(2): 19–28.

Robinson, K. H. (2005d) 'Reinforcing hegemonic masculinities through sexual harassment: Issues of identity, power and popularity in secondary schools'. *Gender and Education*, 17(1): 19–38.

Robinson, K. H. (2008) 'In the name of "childhood innocence": A discursive exploration of the moral panic associated with childhood and sexuality'. *Cultural Studies Review*, 14(2): 113–29.

Robinson, K. H. (2012a) '"Difficult citizenship": The precarious relationships between childhood, sexuality and access to knowledge'. *Sexualities*, 15(3–4): 257–76.

Robinson, K. H. (in press 2012b) 'Negotiating everyday 'sexual harassment' at school – Issues of complexity, contextuality and contradiction', in S. Saltmarsh, K. H. Robinson, and C, Davies (eds) *Reconceptualising School Violence: Context, gender and theory*. London: Palgrave.

Robinson, K. H. and Jones Díaz, C. (2000) *Diversity and Difference in Early Childhood: An investigation into centre policies, staff attitudes and practices. A focus on long day care and preschool in the south west and inner west of Sydney*. Published by Roger A. Baxter, OAS Engineering Pty. Ltd. and The University of Newcastle Research Associates – TUNRA Ltd.

Robinson, K. H. and Ferfolja, T. (2001) '"What are we doing this for?" Dealing with lesbian and gay issues in teacher education'. *British Journal of Sociology of Education*, 22(1): 121–33.

Robinson, K. H. and Jones Díaz, C. (2006) *Diversity and Difference in Early Childhood: Issues for theory and practice*. Maidenhead: Open University Press.

Robinson, K. H. and Davies, C. (2007) 'Tomboys and sissy girls: Young girls' negotiations of femininity and masculinity'. *International Journal of Equity and Innovation in Early Childhood*, 5(2): 17–31.

Robinson, K. H. and Davies, C. (2008a) '"She's kickin' ass, that's what she's doing": Deconstructing childhood "innocence" in media representations'. *Australian Feminist Studies*, 23(57): 343–58.

Robinson, K. H. and Davies, C. (2008b) 'Docile bodies and heteronormative moral subjects: Constructing the child and sexual knowledge in schools'. *Sexuality and Culture*, 12(4): 221–39.

Robinson, K. H. and Davies, C. (2010) 'Tomboys and sissy girls: Power, agency and girls' relationships in early childhood'. *Australian Journal of Early Childhood*, 35(1): 24–31.

Roche, J. (1999) 'Children: Rights, participation and citizenship'. *Childhood*, 6: 475–93.

Rose, N. (1999) *Governing the Soul: The reshaping of the private self*, 2nd edn. London: Free Association Books.

Rosenthal, D. A. and Smith, A. M. A. (1995) 'Adolescents and sexually transmissible diseases: information sources, preferences and trust'. *Australian Health Promotion Journal*, 5: 38–44.

Rousseau, J. J. (1992 [1762]) *Emile*, trans. B. Foxley. London: Dent.

Rout, A. (2011t) 'Gay marriage would lead to breakdown of society, American conservative tells rally'. *The Australian*, 16 August. Online. Available at: www.theaustralian.com.au/national-affairs/gay-marriage-would-lead-to-breakdown-of-society-american-conservative-tells-rally/story-fn59niix-1226116018645 (accessed 2 February 2012).

Roy, E. A. (2011) 'Happy Father's Day, Mum – Gender restrictions a challenge for gay families'. *Sydney Morning Herald*, 17 November, p. 3.

Rush, E. and La Nauze, A. (2006) *Corporate Paedophilia: Sexualisation of children in Australia*, discussion paper. Deakin: Australia Institute.

Ryan, G. (2000) 'Childhood sexuality: A decade of study. Part 1 – research and curriculum development'. *Child Abuse and Neglect*, 24(1): 33–48.

St James Ethics Centre (2012) *Primary Ethics*. Online. Available at: www.primary-ethics.com.au/index.html (accessed on 25 April 2012).

Sanderson, C. (2004) *The Seduction of Children: Empowering parents and teachers to protect children from child sexual abuse*. London and Philadelphia: Jessica Kingsley Publishers.

Sawicki, J. (1991) *Disciplining Foucault: Feminism, power, and the body*. New York: Routledge.

Schwartz, P. and Cappello, D. (2001) *Ten Talks Parents Must Have with their Children about Sex and Character*. Rydalmere: Hodder Headline Australia.

Sedgwick, E. K. (1990) *Epistemology of the Closet*. Berkeley: University of California Press.

Sedgwick. E. K. and Frank, A. (eds) (1995) *Shame and its Sisters: A Silvan Tomkins reader*. Durham: Duke University Press.

Shelman, E. A. and Lazoritz, S. (2005) *The Mary Ellen Wilson Child Abuse Case and the Beginning of Children's Rights in Nineteenth Century America*. Jefferson: McFarland & Company Publishers.

Silin, J. G. (1995) *Sex, Death and the Education of Children: Our passions for ignorance in the age of AIDS*. New York: Teachers College Press.

Silin, J. G. (1997) 'The pervert in the classroom', in J. Tobin (ed.) *Making a Place for Pleasure in Early Childhood Education*. New Haven: Yale University Press.

Sinkinson, M. (2009) '"Sexuality isn't just about sex": Pre-service teachers' shifting constructs of sexuality education'. *Sex Education*, 9 (4): 421–36.

Smith, G., Kippax, S. and Aggleton, P. (2000) *HIV and Sexual Health Education in Primary and Secondary Schools: Findings from selected Asia-Pacific countries*. Sydney: National Centre in HIV Social Research, University of New South Wales, Australia.

Sugg, D. K. (2012) 'What to do when your five-year-old announces he's in love'. *Today Moms*. Online. Available at: http://moms.today.msnbc.msn.com/_news/2012/02/07/10343238-what-to-do-when-your-5-year-old-announces-hes-in-love (accessed 22 March 2012).

Surtees, N. (2005) 'Teacher talk about and around sexuality in early childhood education: Deciphering an unwritten code'. *Contemporary Issues in Early Childhood*, 6(1): 19–29.

Surtees, N. (2006) 'Difference and diversity: "Talk the talk", "walking the talk" and the spaces between'. *International Journal of Equity and Innovation in Early Childhood*, 4(2): 49–65.

Surtees, N. and Gunn, A. C. (2010) '(Re)marking heteronormativity: Resisting practices in early childhood education contexts'. *Australasian Journal of Early Childhood*, 35(1): 42–7.

Taylor, A. (2007) 'Innocent children, dangerous families and homophobic panic', in G. Morgan and S. Poynting (eds) *Outrageous: Moral panics in Australia*. Hobart: Australian Clearing House for Youth Studies.

Taylor, A. (2008) 'Taking account of childhood excess: "Bringing the elsewhere home', in B. Davies (ed.) *Judith Butler in Conversation: Analyzing the texts and talk of everyday life*. New York: Routledge.

Taylor, A. (2010) 'Troubling childhood innocence: Reframing the debate over the media sexualisation of children'. *Australian Journal of Early Childhood*, 35(1) 48–57.

The Lesbian Parents' Play Group (2001) *We're Here – A Resource For Child Care Workers*. Darebin: Darebin Community Health Centre.

Thorne, B. (1993) *Gender Play: Boys and girls in school*. Rutgers University Press: New Brunswick.

Thorne, B. (2009) '"Childhood": Changing and dissonant meanings'. *International Journal of Learning and Media*, 1(1): 19–27.

Thorne, B. and Luria, Z. (1986) 'Sexuality and gender in children's daily worlds'. *Social Problems*, 33(3): 176–90.

Tobin, J. (1997) 'Introduction: The missing discourse of pleasure and desire', in J. Tobin (ed.) *Making Place for Pleasure in Early Childhood Education*. New Haven and London: Yale University Press.

Tolman, D. (2002) *Dilemmas of Desire: Teenage girls talk about sexuality*. Cambridge, MA: Harvard University Press.

Tomsen, S. and Mason, G. (2001) 'Engendering homophobia: Violence, sexuality and gender conformity'. *Journal of Sociology*, 37(3): 265–87.

Turner, B. (1993) *Citizenship and Social Theory*. London: Sage.

UK Youth Parliament (2007) *Sex and Relationships Education: Are you getting it?* London: UK Youth Parliament.

UNESCO (2009) *International Guidance on Sexuality Education: An evidence-informed approach for schools, teachers and health educators, vol. 1 – Rationale for Sexuality Education*. Paris: UNESCO.

United Nations General Assembly (1989) *Resolution 25 session 44, Convention of the Rights of the Child*, 20 November. Available at http://www.undemocracy. com/A-RES-44-25 (accessed 15 March 2011).

Vizard, E., Monck, E. and Misch, P. (1995) 'Child and adolescent sex abuse perpetrators: A review of the research literature'. *Journal of Child Psychology and Psychiatry*, 36: 731–56.

Walker, J. (2001) 'A qualitative study of parents' experiences of providing sex education for their children: The implications for health education'. *Health Education Journal*, 60(2): 132–46.

Walker, J. (2004) 'Parents and sex education: Looking beyond "the birds and the bees"'. *Sex Education*, 4(3): 239–54.

Walker, J. and Milton, J. (2006) 'Teachers' and parents' roles in the sexuality education of primary school children: A comparison of experiences from Leeds, UK, and Sydney, Australia'. *Sex Education*, 6(4): 415–28.

Walkerdine, V. (1997) *Daddy's Girl: Young girls and popular culture*. Cambridge: Macmillan.

Walkerdine, V. (1999) 'Violent boys and precocious girls: Regulating childhood at the end of the millennium'. *Contemporary Issues in Early Childhood* 1(1): 3–23.

Walkerdine, V. (2001) 'Safety and danger: Childhood, sexuality, and space at the end of the millennium', in K. Hiltqvist and G. Dahlberg (eds) *Governing the Child in the New Millennium*. New York: RoutledgeFalmer.

Wallis, A. and Van Every, J. (2000) 'Sexuality in the primary school'. *Sexualities*, 3(4): 409–23.

Walls, N. E., Kane, S. and Wisneski, H. (2010) 'Gay–Straight alliances and school experiences of sexual minority youth'. *Youth & Society*, 41(3): 307–32.

Walsh, J. (2011) *Talk Soon, Talk Often: A guide to parents talking with their kids about sex*. Perth: Government of Western Australia, Department of Health.

Warner, M. (1999) *The Trouble with Normal: Sex politics and the ethics of gay life*. Cambridge, MA: Harvard University Press.

Weedon, C. (1997) *Feminist Practice and Poststructuralist Theory*, 2nd edn. Oxford: Blackwell.

Weeks, J. (1986) *Sexuality*. London: Routledge.

Weeks, J. (1998) 'The sexual citizen', *Theory, Culture and Society*. 15(3–4): 35–52.

Wellings, K., Wadsworth, J., Johnson, A.M., Field, J., Whitaker, L. and Field, B. (1995) 'Provision of sex education and early sexual experience: The relation examined'. *British Medical Journal*, 311: 417–20.

Winn, M. (1984) *Children Without Childhood*. New York: Pantheon Books.

Wolfe, D. and Chiodo, D. (2008) 'Sexual harassment and related behaviours reported among youth from grade 9 to grade 11'. Centre for Addiction and Mental Health Centre for Prevention Science, Toronto. Online. Available at: www.camh.net/News_events/Media_centre/CAMH%20harassment%20paper.pdf (accessed 12 April 2012).

Wolfenstein, M. (1998) 'Fun morality: An analysis of recent American child-training literature', in H. Jenkins (ed.) *The Children's Culture Reader*. New York: New York University Press.

Wood, S. E. (2005) *The Freedom of the Streets: Work, citizenship, and sexuality in the gilded age city* (Gender and American Culture). Chapel Hill: University of North Carolina Press.

World Health Organization (WHO) (2002) *World Report on Violence and Health*. Geneva: World Health Organisation.

Zelizer, V. A. (1985) *Pricing the Priceless Child: The changing social value of children*. Princeton: Princeton University Press.

Index